The Social Authority of Reason

SUNY series in Philosophy
George R. Lucas Jr., editor

The Social Authority of Reason

Kant's Critique, Radical Evil, and the Destiny of Humankind

Philip J. Rossi, SJ

State University of New York Press

Published by
State University of New York Press, Albany

For information, address State University of New York Press,
90 State Street, Suite 700, Albany, NY 12207

Production by Diane Ganeles
Marketing by Anne M. Valentine

Library of Congress Cataloging-in-Publication Data

Rossi, Philip J.
    The social authority of reason : Kant's critique, radical evil, and the destiny
of humankind / Philip J. Rossi.
        p. cm. — (SUNY series in philosophy)
    Includes bibliographical references and index.
    ISBN 0-7914-6429-6 (hardcover : alk. paper)
    1. Kant, Immanuel, 1724–1804—Ethics.   2. Social ethics.   3. Good and evil.
I. Title.   II. Series.

B2799.E8R647 2005
170'.92—dc22   2004011172

10 9 8 7 6 5 4 3 2 1

Contents

Acknowledgments

The first elements of the argument that this book frames on behalf of Kant's understanding of the social authority of reason and its value for contemporary discussions in social philosophy emerged during my tenure as a Visiting Research Fellow at the Institute for Advanced Studies in the Humanities at the University of Edinburgh in 1992. The first full draft of the manuscript was completed during a subsequent Visiting Research Fellowship in 1999. So my first and most extensive debt of gratitude is due to Dr. Peter Jones, then Director of the Institute, and Mrs. Anthea Taylor, the Assistant to the Director, who both made the institute such a welcome place in which to pursue scholarship. I am also grateful to the many other fellows who worked at the institute each of those times; while only a few directly shared in my interest in Kant, conversation with all of them was always rich in substance and provided energy for returning to my own work with renewed interest and conviction. I hope that my mention of the names of just a few—Giancarlo Carabelli, Timothy Engström, Martin Fitzpatrick, Ferenc Hörcher, Andrés Lema-Hincapié, Iain McCalman, Robert Morrison, Andrei Pilgoun, Benjamin Vogel, Andrew Ward, Richard Yeo—will serve as a way to thank all. My thanks to those in Edinburgh would not be complete without a special word of gratitude to the members of the Jesuit community at Sacred Heart Parish for their hospitality during my two terms in residence, especially Fr. Damian Jackson SJ, Fr. Jack Mahoney SJ, and the late Fr. Charles Pridgeon SJ, who served as religious superiors of the community during those times. Fittingly enough, this acknowledgment has been drafted during a short stay in Edinburgh.

Acknowledgments

In the interval between my two opportunities to work in Edinburgh, many other colleagues and their institutions in a variety of places—Chicago, Kaliningrad, Jakarta, Marburg, Manila, Memphis, Milwaukee, Moscow, Seoul and South Bend—afforded me opportunities to test one or another fragment of this work in the form of a conference paper or lecture; there were also a number of patient editors who helped shepherd some of these fragments into print as journal articles or chapters in books. Thanks and acknowledgment are thus also due to the following: Dr. Sidney Axinn, Dr. Vladimir Bryushinkin, Fr. Luis David SJ, Dr. Rainer Ibana, Dr. Leonard Kalinnikov, Dr. Jane Kneller, Dr. V. Lektorski, Dr. G. Felicitas Munzel, Dr. Joseph Pickle, Dr. Hoke Robinson, Dr. Hans Schwartz, Dr. Galina Sorina, Fr. Christopher Spalatin SJ, Fr. Justin Sudarminto SJ, Dr. Burkhard Tuschling, and Dr. Robert Wood. Informal conversation with other colleagues provided much that has been useful in clarifying and correcting my thinking as this project moved ahead. Here, too, I mention just a few—Dr. Sharon Anderson-Gold, Dr. Gene Fendt, Dr. Chris Firestone, Dr. Pauline Kleingeld, the late Dr. Pierre Laberge, Dr. Curtis Peters, Dr. Ramon Reyes, Fr. Jack Treloar SJ, Dr. Howard Williams, Dr. Holly Wilson, and Dr. Allen Wood—to thank all. I owe special thanks to the students in the graduate class I taught in 1998 on Kant's moral philosophy at the Ateneo de Manila, Philippines, since discussion in that course led to the idea I propose in Chapter Four that Kant considered war to be the social form of radical evil. I am also deeply in debt to colleagues in Russia—Dr. Leonard Kalinnikov and Dr. Vladimir Bryushinkin, President and Vice President, respectively of the Russian Kant Society, Dr. Boris Goubman, Dr. Irina Griftsova, and Dr. Galina Sorina—who provided warm hospitality and stimulating intellectual company during the meetings of the Russian Kant Society in Kaliningrad (Königsberg) in which I have been privileged to participate in 1993, 1995, and 1999. The home cities both of David Hume and Immanuel Kant thus have been important venues in the development of this work.

My colleagues in the Department of Theology at Marquette University have provided much intellectual encouragement to me during the long incubation period of this project and I am thankful for their support. The department, the College of Arts and Sciences, and the Graduate School each provided some of the funding that made it possible for me to travel to conferences overseas to present portions of this work. My graduate assistants during these years—Dr. Mark

Ginter, Dr. John Meech, Mr. Aaron Smith, Dr. Wolfgang Vondey—performed a variety of tasks that helped in the research for this project and the preparation of the manuscript for publication.

I am grateful to the editors and publishers who have given permission to incorporate revised material that has appeared in the following previously published essays:

"Autonomy: Towards the Social Self-Governance of Reason," *American Catholic Philosophical Quarterly* 75, 2001: 171–177.

"War: The Social Form of Radical Evil," *Kant und die Berliner Aufklärung: Akten des IX. Internationalen Kant-Kongresses*, Band 4, ed. by Volker Gerhardt, Rolf-Peter Horstmann, and Ralph Schumacher. Berlin: Walter de Gruyter, 2001: 248–256.

Общественный авторитет разума. Критика, изначальное зло и предначение человечества (Russian translation of "The Social Authority of Reason: Critique, Radical Evil, and the Destiny of Humankind"), *Voprosi filosofii* [*Problems of Philosophy*] 7 (Moscow), 2000: 43–52.

"Kant's Ethical Commonwealth: Moral Progress and the Human Role in History": Part I: "The Ethical Commonwealth and the Human Place in the Cosmos"; Part II: "Kant's 'Cosmopolitan Perspective': A View from the Sideline of History?" *Budhi: A Journal of Ideas and Culture* 2/2 (Manila), 1998: 1–24.

"Critical Persuasion: Argument and Coercion in Kant's Account of Politics," *Recht, Staat und Völkerrecht bei Immanuel Kant*, ed. Dieter Hüning and Burkhard Tuschling. Berlin: Duncker & Humblot, 1998: 13–33.

"Public Argument and Social Responsibility: The Moral Dimensions of Citizenship in Kant's Ethical Commonwealth," *Autonomy and Community: Readings in Contemporary Kantian Social Philosophy*, ed. Jane Kneller and Sidney Axinn. State University of New York Press, 1998: 63–85.

Общность республик по законам добдетели: гарантия вечнго мира? (Russian translation of "A Commonwealth of Virtue: Guarantee of Perpetual Peace?") *Kantovskij Sbornik* [Journal of the Russian Kant Society] 20 (Kaliningrad), 1997: 55–65.

"The Social Authority of Reason: The 'True Church' as the Locus for Moral Progress," *Proceedings of the Eighth International Kant Congress*, II/2, ed. Hoke Robinson. Milwaukee: Marquette University Press, 1995: 679–685.

"The Final End of All Things: The Highest Good as The Unity of Nature and Freedom," *Kant's Philosophy of Religion Reconsidered*, ed. Philip J. Rossi and Michael Wreen. Bloomington: Indiana University Press, 1991: 132–164.

List of Abbreviations and English Translations

Citations to the *Critique of Pure Reason* follow the standard convention of providing the pagination from the first (A) and second (B) editions in German.

Kant's other works are cited in the text and notes according to the abbreviations below. The citations first provide the pagination from the appropriate volume of Kant's *Gessamelte Schriften* (*GS*) (Ausgabe der Königlichen Preußichen Akademie der Wissenschaften, Berlin 1902–); after the slash, they provide pagination from the corresponding English translation.

A/B   *Kritik der Reinen Vernunft*. English translation: *Critique of Pure Reason*. Trans. Paul Guyer and Allen W. Wood. The Cambridge Edition of the Works of Immanuel Kant. Cambridge: Cambridge University Press, 1996.

AP   *Anthropologie in pragmatischer Hinsicht*. *GS* 7. English translation: *Anthropology from a Pragmatic Point of View*. Trans. Mary J. Gregor. The Hague: Martinus Nijhoff, 1974.

BF   "Beanwortung der Frage: Was ist Aufklärung?" *GS* 8. English translation: "What is Enlightenment?" Trans. Lewis White Beck. *Kant On History*. Ed. Lewis White Beck. New York: Bobbs-Merrill, 1963.

CJ   *Kritik der Urteilskraft*. *GS* 5. English translation: *Critique of the Power of Judgment*. Trans. Paul Guyer and Eric Matthews. The Cambridge Edition of the Works of Immanuel Kant. Ed. Paul Guyer. Cambridge: Cambridge University Press, 2000.

CprR   *Kritik der praktischen Vernunft. GS* 5. English translation: *The Critique of Practical Reason.* Trans. Mary J. Gregor. *Practical Philosophy.* The Cambridge Edition of the Works of Immanuel Kant. Cambridge: Cambridge University Press, 1966.

EF   "Zum ewigen Frieden." *GS* 8. English translation: "Toward Perpetual Peace." Trans. Mary J. Gregor. *Practical Philosophy.* The Cambridge Edition of the Works of Immanuel Kant. Cambridge: Cambridge University Press, 1966.

GMM   *Grundlegung zur Metaphysik der Sitten. GS* 4. English translation: *Groundwork of the Metaphysics of Morals.* Trans. Mary J. Gregor. *Practical Philosophy.* The Cambridge Edition of the Works of Immanuel Kant. Cambridge: Cambridge University Press, 1966.

IAG   "Idee zu einer allgemeinen Geschichte in weltbürgerlicher Absicht." *GS* 8. English translation: "Idea for a Universal History from a Cosmopolitan Point of View." Trans. Lewis White Beck. *Kant On History.* Ed. Lewis White Beck. New York: Bobbs-Merrill, 1963.

MdS   *Die Metaphysik der Sitten. GS* 6. *The Metaphysics of Morals.* Trans. Mary J. Gregor. *Practical Philosophy.* The Cambridge Edition of the Works of Immanuel Kant. Cambridge: Cambridge University Press, 1966.

MMG   "Mutmaßlicher Anfang der Menschen Geschichte." *GS* 8. English translation: "Conjectural Beginning of Human History." Trans. Emil Fackenheim. *Kant On History.* Ed. Lewis White Beck. New York: Bobbs-Merrill, 1963.

Rel   *Religion innerhalb der Grenzen der bloßen Vernunft. GS* 6. English translation: *Religion within the Boundaries of Mere Reason.* Trans. George de Giovanni. *Religion and Rational Theology.* The Cambridge Edition of the Works of Immanuel Kant. Cambridge: Cambridge University Press, 1996.

SF   *Der Streit der Fakultäten. GS* 7. English translation: *The Conflict of the Faculties.* Trans. Mary J. Gregor and Robert Anchor. *Religion and Rational Theology.* The Cambridge Edition of the Works of Immanuel Kant. Cambridge: Cambridge University Press, 1996.

TP   "Über den Gemeinspruch: Das mag in der Theorie richtig sein, taugt aber nicht für die Praxis." *GS* 8. English translation: "On the common saying: That may be correct in theory, but it is of no use in practice." Trans. Mary Gregor. *Practical Philosophy*. The Cambridge Edition of the Works of Immanuel Kant. Cambridge: Cambridge University Press, 1966.

CHAPTER ONE

—————

The Moral and Social Trajectories
of Kant's Critical Project

Kant: Augustinian *Aufklärer*?

During the last twenty-five years, a number of scholars have undertaken significant re-examination of Kant's critical project within its own historical context.[1] There has also been a parallel reevaluation of the import that Kant's critical project has for a range of issues in contemporary discussions of ethics, political philosophy, social philosophy, and philosophy of religion.[2] Each reassessment has involved taking a fresh look at Kant's relationship to the larger intellectual and cultural movement known as "the Enlightenment" and its role in shaping so called "modernity"—and, not surprisingly, this element in the reexamination of Kant's work has itself been affected by a more extensive reconsideration, occurring across a range of disciplines, of the character and continuing impact of the Enlightenment in its various forms and phases.[3] As a result, studying Kant now requires constant recalibration to keep both his work and his context in a steady focus: They each have become shifting targets, not simply in relation to the vantage point of commentators standing at a two-hundred years' distance, but even, it seems, in relation to each other. Though it is still possible to affirm Kant as an *Aufklärer*—and even a paradigmatic one—one must also remember, first, that Enlightenment in Kant's Prussia took its own particular course different from that, for instance, in France or Scotland, and, second, that Kant's work itself contains both articulated positions and implicit presuppositions in tension with what are commonly taken to be "typical" Enlightenment themes and theses.[4]

1

Not the least of these tensions can be found in the views that Kant expresses in the later stages of his career about the capacity that human beings have to wreak evil and about the extent to which and the manner in which that evil and its consequences might eventually be eradicated from the human condition. For Kant, the evil of which human beings are capable is "radical" on two counts: First, it is the source from which all human moral evil stems; second, it is the form that evil takes at the very core and center of human willing. In this latter sense, it is evil that goes "all the way down" through human willing. These views, given their most extensive exposition in *Religion within the Boundaries of Mere Reason*, do express a measured hope that human beings have the capacity to overcome evil eventually; but they also ironically exhibit far less confidence that human beings will themselves actually do so. This affirmation of a "radical evil" that is "inextirpable" within the dynamics of our human moral agency was apparently not well received by Kant's contemporaries since it seemed to rehabilitate a notion that many other Enlightenment thinkers had strenuously sought to discredit: The Christian doctrine of "original sin."[5]

Despite the presence of an almost Augustinian dissonance struck by the notion of radical evil, Kant's *Religion* has most often been taken, by friendly and hostile critics alike, to be quite in harmony with other Enlightenment efforts to account for religion purely and solely in human terms.[6] If one also places this late work within the context of other writings in which Kant treats religion, the dissonant sound of radical evil seems faint. The links that tie radical evil to discussions of human moral failure in Kant's earlier writings are not altogether clear;[7] in addition, he seems neither to develop this concept further in writings subsequent to *Religion* nor even unambiguously to allude to it again. As a result, his affirmation of the presence of radical evil in humanity seems to stand as no more than a passing moment of pessimism for a thinker who reaffirmed, in one of the last works published during his lifetime, his conviction that humanity does indeed morally progress.[8] Kant's apparent eschewal of further exploration of radical evil suggests that it may be of minimal import even for the other writings that he produced during the last active decade of his life—and, *a fortiori,* for his overall critical project as well as for efforts to appropriate the principles of critique for use in other contexts.

The chapters that follow make a two-part argument against such a minimizing interpretation of Kant's account of "radical evil." Chapters 2 through 5 provide an overall interpretive framework for Kant's critical project within which I set forth the claim that the notion of radical evil marks a key development for Kant's own understanding of the scope of his critical project, albeit a development he leaves incomplete. Radical evil plays a significant role in this development in that it lays bare the full social dimensions of the project of a "critique of reason": Critique is the enterprise of completely socializing the exercise of human reason. Although this social dimension of critique had been present from the very beginning of the project, it does not receive its complete articulation until Kant, in response to the social consequences of radical evil, introduces the idea of an "ethical commonwealth" as the social embodiment of critique. Because radical evil consists in the self-corruption of the very social character of human reason as it is exercised in our moral freedom, it can be overcome only through the discipline—critique—that enables us to exhibit our human freedom as fully social. The ethical commonwealth thus signals Kant's most complete articulation of the social character of the exercise of human reason. In this concept he exhibits the recognition made possible by critique that the exercise of our human freedom is fully embedded in the social relationships we constitute with and for one another. We thus owe one another a "social respect" that makes it possible for us to work with one another in constituting a world that can be inclusively shared as a field for the mutual exercise of our freedom. This shared world is the locus in which we act as agents of human destiny for one another. This shared world takes concrete form in the course of history in the actions, practices, and institutions by which we constitute the full range of human society and culture. Kant envisions this world as taking its final and complete form as an ethical commonwealth shaped by the human social relationships that issue from a shared intent to inclusive social union arising from the mutual respect free moral agents accord to one another.

Chapters 6 and 7 will then argue that, in the light of the more explicit social thrust that a resolution of the question of radical evil requires of critique, the principles of Kant's critical project provide the basis for identifying and addressing radical evil in the challenging guise it now takes in the dynamics of an emergent globalized culture. This contemporary form of radical evil brings into question the basis from which Kant envisioned the establishment of an ethical commonwealth. It denies the possibility that human beings can engage one another in ways that enable them to constitute an inclusively shared world for the mutual exercise of their freedom. This form of radical evil allows us to persuade ourselves that a shared world of the kind envisioned by Kant is not possible because of the irreducible heterogeneity, plurality, and particularity of the interests human beings bring to their engagement with one another in freedom. We take the arena of human interaction in freedom to be a field in which partial and particular interests contend with one another for ascendency—a social dynamic that Kant termed "unsociable sociability"—and in which settlement inevitably arises from the exercise of coercive power and always entails that some lose even as others win.

Commentators from a wide range of interpretive and disciplinary perspectives have noted one problem that seems to be a telling symptom that we have let ourselves become enmeshed in this form of radical evil: Public discussion and deliberation about matters of policy that affect a society as a whole no longer seems to carry with it the presumption that genuine and general consensus on societal goals or a fully common good is possible—let alone worth seeking—in a polity that is pluralist, multicultural, and multiethnic. All that we can hope for is a demarcation of procedures in which the rules that determine the winners and the losers are accepted as fair. Compounding this problem, moreover, are patterns of everyday life that are increasingly driven by cultural dynamics of immediacy and of exchange commodification that level our human connectedness and our human differences down to the sheer multiplicity of contingent particularity and make every particularity subject to exchange valuation. The consequence is that the very possibility of forming a shared intent to social union of the kind envisioned by Kant as the basis of an ethical commonwealth is radically put in question, not only by theories that stress a radical plurality in human social interaction, but also, and more powerfully, by practices that allow us to negotiate a path through life by seeking the satisfaction of our particular interests without heed to the engagement of our freedom with one another as part of a shared human enterprise.

Such a questioning, I shall argue, can be countered by an appropriate contemporary retrieval of Kant's insight into the fundamentally social character of reason and its authority. Kant articulates this insight through his notion of critique: Critique is the self-discipline of reason that arises out of a mutual and fully inclusive shared intent among moral agents to persevere with one another in the argumentative inquiry and deliberative exchange through which they shape social practices in and for a common world. What makes possible such a shared intent to persevere with one another in this enterprise is, in Kant's terms, the *hope* that critique establishes as the trajectory for our moral endeavors. The shared intent to social union that brings about an ethical commonwealth is itself possible only to the extent that we first acknowledge it to be an object of hope. It has not yet come to be— yet it can be brought about (and *only* be brought about) by our own common human efforts. If we lose hope that it can ever come to be, then, indeed, it will not. To the extent that certain dynamics of contemporary culture put in question the possibility of a shared intent to social union, they thereby put in question the very hope upon which the ethical commonwealth is founded. As a result, the task facing a contemporary continuation of Kant's project of critique involves showing not only that such hope is still possible, but also that the very circumstances that give rise to such questioning are themselves precisely what require a reaffirmation of that hope.

The two parts of my argument are thus closely connected: It is precisely in passages that deal with the dynamics of human interaction in social and civic contexts—in the text of *Religion* and in other later writings—where Kant, cautiously, even hesitantly, elaborates the notion of radical evil beyond its initial function as a reinterpretation of the doctrine of original sin and makes it a crucial marker of the fundamental moral and social trajectory taken by his critical project. In particular, this development suggests that the introduction of the notion of radical evil poses a major challenge to the completion of the very enterprise of critique—that is, the inculcation of self-discipline upon the exercise of our human reason. It is thus in response to that challenge that Kant begins to elaborate an account of what may appropriately be termed "the social authority of reason"—that is, an account of how the self-discipline of reason extends to its exercise within the dynamics of human social and civic interaction.

Critique: Self-Discipline for Social Transformation

The first part of my argument will be developed in two stages. The first stage situates *Religion within the Boundaries of Mere Reason*, particularly the discussion of radical evil and its overcoming, within the context of key developments that occur within the critical project as Kant elaborates it in the 1780s and 1790s. The central function of this stage will be to elaborate a general interpretive framework for understanding the aim of the enterprise that Kant names critique. I will argue that Kant's critical project has a fundamentally moral trajectory, which has its focus upon the proper manner for humanity both to conceive of and to attain its destiny as the juncture of nature and freedom. At this general level, Kant's critical project can well be read as an Enlightenment transformation of the account of the unique destiny in the cosmic order that Christianity previously affirmed for humanity, with the difference that the accomplishment of this destiny seems no longer to be the work of grace freely offered by a transcendent God but rather the outcome of a human effort, which is entirely immanent.[9] The critical project is thus not merely an effort to provide a description of humanity's destiny. It has itself a key role to play in the attainment of that destiny: Critique provides human reason with the self-discipline that is necessary and proper to its finite character. This self-discipline is crucial because it is only through the exercise of critical discipline on reason that the destiny befitting the human place in the cosmos, as the unique juncture of nature and freedom, can be adequately discerned and properly attained. Nature and freedom are the primary axes of the Kantian world. His critical philosophy is an enterprise that seeks to understand what being placed at the intersection of those axes—as humanity uniquely is—requires of our thought, of our imagination, and of our action. This means, moreover, that the moral trajectory of the critical project has a thrust that is ultimately transformative: Only through the exercise of a reason that has learned to discipline itself by critique will humanity be able to bring about those transformations of the social conditions of its existence that most properly serve the attainment of human destiny.

The second stage of this part of my argument will then examine the impact that Kant's introduction of the notion of radical evil has upon this transformative trajectory of the critical project. I will indicate how this notion functions as part of a sustained effort, which Kant undertakes throughout the critical project, to elaborate an adequate and coherent account of the positive relationship between what he had distinguished, for important systematic reasons, as the sensible and the intelligible aspects of human activity and existence. Although Kant never abandons this distinction (and, in fact, vigorously reaffirms it in

the face of criticism directed against it), he does reexamine, reformulate, and refine it as he executes the various phases of the critical
project. These various reconsiderations have important bearing upon
how both he—and we—understand the critical enterprise. Kant also
elaborates, through a variety of concepts, a positive side to this relationship between the sensible and intelligible. My discussion, however, will focus on the one that becomes most important for the social
dimension of critique: The "highest good."

The various, sometimes quite different, accounts that Kant provides of the highest good serve as particularly illuminating markers of
his efforts to elaborate the relationship (and the distinction) between
the sensible and the intelligible, especially as this affects the practical
(moral) exercise of reason to which critique assigns primacy. This
makes the highest good an apt focus for my discussion since Kant
finally confers on this notion the status of being the supreme *social*
object of practical reason. The highest good is not merely what Kant
had earlier taken it to be, that is, the proper apportionment of happiness to accord with each *individual's* moral virtue.[10] It is also—and
more fundamentally—nothing more nor less than the destiny that befits
humanity as the unique species that stands as the juncture of nature
and freedom. Human beings thus must make themselves worthy of
their destiny as a species—a destiny that consists in the social project
of working toward the establishment of an ethical commonwealth. It
is thus precisely in virtue of its social character that the highest good
bears most directly upon the transformative trajectory of the critical
project, that is, upon the attainment of humanity's unique destiny as a
species. To the extent that the highest good is the supreme social
object of practical reason, critique is that activity that enables humanity reflectively, self-responsibly, and, thus, more adequately, to sustain
its common efforts to attain the destiny that befits it as the juncture of
nature and freedom.

Radical Evil: Consequences for the Dynamics of
Human Social Interaction

In the context of the transformative trajectory that Kant envisions
for the critical project, the introduction of the notion of radical evil has
a number of consequences for the accounts that he gives of the nature

of humanity's final destiny and of the prospects for humanity's actually attaining it. These consequences are far-reaching. They bring Kant himself to see that, in order to deal with the consequences of radical evil, critique must be brought to bear upon the encompassing problem of the relationship between nature and freedom first and foremost in the arena where humanity gives shape to society and culture. This arena is crucial because it forms the context of the unsociable sociability that enables human beings to turn into a concrete actuality the radical evil that stands as abiding possibility within the structure of their willing.

The central aspect of Kant's dealing with these consequences that my argument then explores bears upon his efforts to construe humanity's final destiny in terms of its *concrete social character*. At issue here is the extent to which Kant fully articulates the consequences of radical evil for what he identifies as specific forms that the dynamics of human social interaction in history must aim to embody in order for humanity to attain its final destiny. My discussion of the consequences of radical evil, therefore, will focus upon the forms of human social interaction that, particularly in his writings of the 1790s, Kant proposes as key moral requirements for the attainment of that destiny. The ethical commonwealth is the most encompassing of these forms, while the "public use of reason," a "cosmopolitan perspective" and the conditions that secure "perpetual peace" also play crucial roles in his account of the concrete social character of our human destiny. I will argue that, while Kant is aware that his account of radical evil has important consequences for the dynamics of human social interaction, he does not fully articulate the bearing of these consequences upon the forms of that interaction that he proposes as necessary for the complete concrete social embodiment of the self-discipline of reason and, thus, as morally necessary for the attainment of human destiny.

The first part of my argument thus reaches the conclusion that Kant is only partially successful in resolving the issues that radical evil raises for the critical project itself. He is successful to the extent that he recognizes that radical evil has consequences for the dynamics of human social interaction and that it must be extirpated from those social dynamics before humanity can fully attain its destiny as the juncture of nature and freedom. He is also successful to the extent that he recognizes—though sometimes only implicitly—that the extirpation of radical evil from the dynamics of human social interaction must itself take a social form. The social consequences of radical evil will not be eradicated as the result of a simple addition of the efforts of individual human moral agents to overcome radical evil as it operates within the dynamics of their own moral agency. Kant's account falls short, however, when he seeks to articulate the concrete social forms that would make possible the extirpation of radical evil in its social consequences. In particular, his accounts of the ethical commonwealth and the conditions that secure perpetual peace are incomplete—and incomplete in ways that suggest that, in the form Kant presents them, they may not be adequate to the central function Kant assigns them in the attainment of human destiny, namely, the transformation of human social dynamics through the self-discipline of reason. The most important way in which Kant leaves these accounts incomplete is that he leaves unspecified the concrete means that will bring it about that moral agents will adopt *the shared intent to social union* necessary to the establishment of an ethical commonwealth.

The Unfinished Tasks of Critique: Social Respect and the Social Authority of Reason

Although the first part of my argument concludes that Kant is only partially successful in resolving the issues the introduction of the notion of radical evil raises, I do not take the points at which his account falters to be failures in principle. As the second part of my argument will propose, they are, rather, unfinished tasks that have been left for a further exercise of critical reason to accomplish—and some of these tasks, as I will also argue, remain at least as urgent for us to address today as they were for Kant and his age. The aim of the second part of my argument thus will be to identify this unfinished part of Kant's critical enterprise and to sketch some possibilities for carrying it out at least a bit beyond where he left it for us. I will do so by showing, first of all, how the notion of an ethical commonwealth is only one part (though a quite important one) of a larger, unfinished effort by Kant to articulate what I term the social authority of reason— that is, the proper manner for human reason to exercise its authority in and for the dynamics of human society and culture. Kant saw clearly enough that, in the context of an ethical commonwealth, the only proper way to exercise the social authority of reason is noncoercively;

yet he left unfinished the task of concretely specifying the means of such noncoercive exercise of the social authority of reason. Two centuries later, articulating the social authority of reason and establishing the proper manner of its exercise remains an urgent enterprise for us because the very possibility of reason having "social authority" and, *a fortiori,* of exercising it noncoercively, has been radically put in question by the cultural dynamics of immediacy, commodification, and competition that are present within the contemporary processes of globalization. I would argue—though here is not the place to do so—that even in a post 9/11 world that these dynamics pose a more fundamental threat than does terrorism to the social authority of reason.[11]

Delimiting the social authority of reason was an important task for Kant because he saw it as the only morally adequate basis on which human beings are empowered to construct a principled social ordering of human existence—and without such a principled ordering of its own existence and activity, humanity would fail to attain the destiny unique to it as the juncture of nature and freedom. At this level, the task of delimiting the social authority of reason may seem less important for us who live in a social and cultural context in which questions of a common human destiny apparently have less urgency and force than they had for Kant and his Enlightenment contemporaries. A society that seeks to enshrine the recognition of the diversity and plurality of the groups within it may be properly hesitant to articulate in a substantive form the commonalities that provide the public framework of the recognition of plurality. Behind such hesitation, moreover, may lurk doubts about the very possibility of locating a stable commonality from which to reference what is "human"—doubts that have been given powerful intellectual articulation by many "postmodern" thinkers. In the context of such hesitation and doubt about the articulation of human commonality, a culture increasingly ordered by and to the dynamics of marketplace choice also provides little space for the operation of the social authority of reason. These dynamics do not seem to require that the authority of human reason be rooted in the social matrix of human existence; that is, that it be an authority that is both forged and ratified only in the self-discipline of an ever-widening circle of human dialogical and argumentative exchange. Whatever "social" authority reason may have is not a function of a shared intent, but merely the aggregate sum of choices made in the marketplace of goods and services—and sometimes even in the "marketplace of ideas." This culture of marketplace choice does not seem to require that we engage one another in sustained, reasoned argument about the terms of our living with each other, about the constitutive social ends that make us a polity, and even less about what ends our common humanity might make incumbent on us. As the culture of marketplace choice intersects with the dynamics of informational, economic, and technological "globalization" to form a successor culture to "modernity," the desirability, the necessity, and even the possibility of "an intent to social union" has radically been called in question. In short, these various dynamics seem to function without reference to the shared intent to a social union constitutive of an ethical commonwealth and necessary for the noncoercive exercise of the social authority of reason.

The dynamics of marketplace choice seem to render otiose questions of our common human destiny. The social recognition of the particularities of our human diversity and the power of postmodernist thought to unmask the partiality of what we once unquestioningly thought universal may mute the articulation of a basic human commonality and make us hesitant to press claims in the name of humanity. The globalization that makes it possible for human beings to forge new and more complex links among themselves also allows them to construe even the most basic form of human connections to be constructs increasingly amenable to determination by the exercise of arbitrary human choice. Yet even as these (apparent) "facts" relegate substantive claims made in the name of reason to a (misguided) chapter in the history of Western thinking, these same facts may themselves be indicative of how urgently the dynamics of society and culture in our contemporary world need an appropriate rearticulation of the social authority of reason. They all encourage us to narrow down the imaginative and conceptual possibilities of construing our human connectedness to a field constituted by the transient interplay of contingent particularities. We are to see ourselves as inescapably enmeshed in historical and cultural particularity that allows, at best, for only partial commonalities constructed on the contingent convergence of particular interests. Thus despite the new possibilities that globalization offers for enlarging the scope of our human connectedness, any intent to a social universality founders upon the need to keep clear the space that difference needs in order to affirm the power of its particularity within the interplay of immediacy. These dynamics thus suggest that, in practice, there is no need for reason to claim social authority; or, if it does claim such authority, the form of its exercise will inevitably be coercive and at the service of the particularities that constitute the entire field of human interests.

These dynamics would not be totally unfamiliar to Kant since they exhibit the unsociable sociability that he saw forming the horizon against which human beings engage one another in contention over their partial interests. We remain enclosed within the horizon of unsociable sociability, and thus within an ambit in which every authority, including reason, must ultimately resort to coercive power for enforcement, so long as we refuse to recognize that our freedom provides us with the capacity to constitute a larger and far more appropriate horizon for the exercise of that very freedom as fully mutual. This horizon is made possible in terms of what Kant affirms as the "interest" of reason itself. This interest of reason constitutes a horizon for our engagement with one another that goes beyond that provided by the immediacy of any of our particular interests, as genuine and as demanding as they may be. On Kant's account, over and against the particular interests we bring with us in our engagement with one another, and in virtue of which we seek for ourselves such things as property, power, and recognition, there is an interest we take in constituting a shared world of action for one another through the exercise of our freedom. This is *an inclusive and universal interest in the freedom of each of us and of all of us*, the freedom that most fundamentally constitutes us as members of the human species. The inclusive and universal character of this interest is manifest in the exercise of our human freedom and it forms the basis for the social authority of reason.

This interest enables us to enlarge the horizon within which we engage one another in freedom beyond that of the contention of particular interests. This enlarged horizon enables us to accord one another what I term the social respect that provides the possibility for a noncoercive exercise of the authority of reason. Social respect exhibits an inclusively universal intent to social union that enables us to place the dynamics of our unsociable sociability fully under the self-governance of reason proper to our human vocation to be the juncture of nature and freedom. Kant thus envisioned in his account of the ethical commonwealth a form of social dynamics quite different from those bound within the horizon of unsociable sociability. He saw the social dynamics of an ethical commonwealth arising from a social respect that members of that commonwealth have for one another's freedom: A mutual moral recognition of one another from which we, each and all, can thereby envision the possibility of our constructing, on the basis our freedom, a shared world. From this mutual moral recognition arises the shared intent to social union constitutive of an ethical commonwealth.

He also saw that such social respect requires us to engage one another in what he termed "the public use of reason." This is an inclusive deliberative exchange framed by a horizon of hope for reaching agreement about the terms of our living with each other. Engaging in the public use of reason is a task that as members of an ethical commonwealth we cannot shirk and in which we must persevere. Two "facts" demand it. The first is a "fact of nature": We have no choice but to live as social beings. The second is a "fact of reason": Our freedom as rational agents to set ends for ourselves. The conjunction of these two facts means, for Kant, that free rational beings who, as we do, have no option but to live together, can do so in the manner that befits their freedom only to the extent that they come to uncoerced agreement about the terms of their living with each other. Since we cannot extricate ourselves from the social circumstances of our human existence, we are thus under the exigency of constructing together terms for our living with one another in a shared world. Anything less would be unworthy of who we are, a contradiction of what Kant, rightly in my judgment, sees as our vocation as free beings.

What implications might Kant's understanding of the social dynamics for an ethical commonwealth then have on our own situation early in the twenty-first century? We find ourselves in circumstances of social plurality within the context of a globalized marketplace culture that, for all the potential it has for enlarging and deepening our human connectedness, harbors an inner dynamic by which we further enmesh ourselves in the interminable contention of unsociable sociability. The prevalence of skepticism and even despair about the possibility of our reaching agreement on the social goals that set the terms of our living together is, I believe, a symptom that we still have not fully engaged one another though a commitment to mutual social respect—the fundamental moral recognition we owe one another as human beings bound to one another in freedom as fellow citizens of an ethical commonwealth. We seem to have all too readily put aside the possibility of engaging one another in the public use of reason that is product of social respect, that is, in deliberative exchange premised on mutual communication to attain shared understanding and aimed at reaching agreement on how together to shape a shared world. In its place we seem to have let the dynamics of immediacy, contention, and commodification turn our engagements with one another about the terms of our living together in society into yet one more round of bargaining over loss and gain in which the best result one could hope for is a relatively stable realignment of interests that will position us better in the inevitable next round of contention.

This is nothing other than the self-corruption of radical evil manifest in social form: Resigned acceptance that the horizon for the human social dynamics in which we mutually exercise our freedom can take the form only of contention, struggle, and finally war. Since we are ultimately incapable of constituting a fully shared human world with one another, we must always reserve the right to place our particular interests above that of any one else's. The final form of this self-corruption is the abandonment of hope that transformation of these dynamics lies within human power—an abandonment of hope that then makes it pointless to try to engage with one another in the construction of a shared world. The best we can do is cobble together for our own protection whatever fragments are at hand without illusion that the result will or has to fit into the inclusive patterns of intelligibility and significance that constitute a "world" to share fully with others. There can be no such thing as an interest of reason nor, *a fortiori*, the social authority of reason.

If we are indeed enmeshed in this social form of radical evil, then the shift in horizon required for us to engage one another in the public use of reason can quite rightly be understood as the social counterpart to the moral conversion from radical evil that Kant sees as necessary for individual moral agents. Kant's understanding of the unique status humanity has as the juncture of nature and freedom leads him to affirm that our freedom makes it possible for us to envision and to effect a quite different social dynamic for dealing with one another about the fundamental terms of our living with one another in society. Kant articulates expectations for human beings, both individually and as a species, which are considerably higher than those provided by a horizon of resignation to our unsociable sociability. Our freedom provides a horizon of hope that encourages continuing engagement with one another in reasoned argument about the terms of our living with each other, about the constitutive social ends that make us a polity, and about ends our common humanity makes incumbent on us—not under the dynamic of unsociable sociability, but under that of an ethical commonwealth. Kant takes us to be capable of a mutual moral recognition that requires us, in the concrete circumstances of finite human existence, to engage one another in argument and activity to construct a common world.

Kant is not so naive as to think that the construction of such a common world will be easy, or that it will ever be fully finished. He nonetheless sees it as a task we cannot shirk. As we cannot extricate ourselves from the social circumstances of our human existence, we are under the exigency of constructing together terms for our living with one another in a shared world (*Rel,* 6: 93–100/129–134). Despite what the dynamics of immediacy, contention, and commodification would have us believe about ourselves, there are compelling reasons for taking on the higher expectations Kant has articulated. The circumstances of our human existence as needy, limited beings on a planet of finite resources currently press upon us more and more urgent questions about our willingness and our ability to share this particular world—in the literal sense as a global space for living—with fellow human beings and, indeed, with our fellow living beings. The basis for our sharing of this world merely as a place of survival, let alone as a possible field for human interaction on the basis of freedom, may no longer be sustainable merely on the dynamisms of unsociable sociability by which those currently dominant wittingly or unwittingly force others to share the world on terms dictated by their interests—until, of course, some others gain the ascendency.

As a result, the beginning of the conversion needed to extricate ourselves from the contemporary social form of radical evil in which we have implicated ourselves might properly start by disciplining ourselves to remember the two "facts" from which Kant shaped his notions of the ethical commonwealth and the public use of reason. These facts place us into a relationship of mutual moral responsibility: Our freedom to set ends for ourselves inevitably takes place within the context of our need to live with one another and thus requires us to engage one another in argument and activity to construct a common world for one another. In our current context of globalization, moreover, we need the additional reminder that social respect for one another's freedom consists in more than the ideal of "classical" liberalism, that is, allowing maximum space for all to pursue their own freely set ends with minimal interference from one another and from the state. This context also requires that social respect for one another's freedom enables us to *persevere with one another in deliberative exchange* in the hope of reaching agreement about the terms of our living with one another, a hope that includes within its ambit substantive social ends. In the absence of such hope we diminish our understanding and respect for our potentiality as free moral subjects and fellow human beings to construct a truly common world for us all to share. The presence of such hope, on the other hand, is manifest when we acknowledge our shared public obligation to sustain the social conditions for reasoned public deliberative exchange about the terms of our living with one another. These are the conditions enabling all of us to engage in the sustained argument with one another over our social goals that Kant termed the public use of reason.

Argument, of course, is not action. Providing the conditions for the public use of reason does not automatically guarantee that any agreement reached under its auspices will truly be for the common good of each and all in a particular polity, let alone for the global society of nations. It may be the case that, in our early twenty-first century circumstances of apparent societal fragmentation, providing the conditions for the effective exercise of the social authority of reason requires even more of us than simply sustaining the social conditions for reasoned public discourse. It may require us, as well, to give special attention to the fundamental bases that enable us to establish and sustain what I have termed social respect for one another's freedom: The mutual moral recognition of one another from which we can envision the possibility of our constructing, on the basis of our freedom, a shared world. The bases for social respect most fundamentally lie, I believe, in the practices and institutions that link us together as a public community in which the exercise of our freedom is ordered to the attainment of justice for all.[12] If this is so, then a further implication of the mutual moral responsibility we have to one another as citizens may very well be that we must make our engagement in the public use of reason an effective instrument for securing justice in a free society. Most crucial among the agreements we must persevere in seeking with one another in reasoned public argument are those that bear upon establishing, sustaining, and, when necessary, reforming political, economic, or social institutions and policies so that they most fully secure justice for all.

In the context of a civic culture that seems to make normative the studious avoidance of reasoned public argument about the terms of our human life in common—be it as members of a particular local polity, or globally as a species upon a planet with a finite stock of resources— the second part of my argument will therefore conclude that there is something crucial that we can—indeed even must—learn from Kant's effort to delimit an ethical commonwealth. What Kant can teach us, even over a gap of two centuries, is that members of a democratic polity stand under the clear moral necessity of a commitment to engage other one another in an ever enlarging circle of inquiry, argument and deliberation to find as well as to construct a world of meaning and value to share in common as the enduring, noncoercive basis for living with one another in freedom.

CHAPTER TWO

The Human Place in the Cosmos I:
Critique at the Juncture of Nature and Freedom

The Relation between Nature and Freedom as Focus of the Critical Project

The principal goal of this chapter and chapter 3 will be to present a general interpretive framework for understanding the aim of the enterprise that Kant names "critique." The main thesis for which I will argue is that the critical project has a fundamentally moral trajectory, which is focused upon the proper manner for humanity both to conceive of and to attain its destiny as the juncture of nature and freedom, a destiny that Kant comes to designate as "the highest good." In this formulation, the expressions "to conceive of" and "to attain" are both significant. The critical project is not merely an effort to provide a description of humanity's destiny; it has itself a key role to play in the attainment of that destiny: Critique provides the self-discipline necessary to the exercise of a human reason that has come to the proper recognition of its finite character. This self-discipline, moreover, has a transformative thrust: Only the exercise of a reason self-disciplined by critique will enable humanity to bring about those transformations of the social conditions of its existence that will most properly serve the attainment of human destiny. The work of these two chapters will thus provide the context for then examining, in chapters 4 and 5, Kant's introduction of the notion of radical evil and the impact it has upon the moral trajectory of critique. There I will argue that this notion makes it possible for Kant to articulate more adequately, though still incompletely, how the self-discipline of reason is to function in the social dimensions of human existence.

This way of interpreting Kant's critical project may cut across the grain for readers accustomed to seeing Kant's major philosophical works treated primarily as epistemological and metaphysical treatises. It may also run counter to a fairly common presumption, especially among readers whose interest in Kant focuses principally on his moral philosophy, that the fundamental principles and concepts of his ethics can be readily detached from his epistemological and metaphysical views, or at least from the ones that are more problematic. On this presumption, one can espouse Kantian ethics without having to consider oneself, as Kant himself did, a transcendental idealist.[1] Conversely, one could also propound a Kantian program for epistemology or metaphysics without thereby committing oneself to be a Kantian in ethics. There are important historical, systematic, and interpretive issues that lie beneath the surface of these ways of reading Kant—not the least of which, in my judgment, concern Kant's own oft-repeated insistence on the systematic integrity of his own project. Though some of the more important ones will be addressed in the course of my argument, my main purpose is not to argue against the centrality of epistemological and metaphysical concerns to Kant's critical enterprise, nor to gloss over the genuine difficulties raised by the epistemological and metaphysical claims that he advances. My main purpose, rather, is to argue that these concerns function within what I take to be the larger and more fundamental philosophical focus Kant's critical project has upon the destiny of the human species as a unique yet integral part of a cosmic order. Nature and freedom are the primary axes of the Kantian world; and his critical philosophy is an enterprise that seeks to understand what being placed at the intersection of those axes—as humanity uniquely is—requires of our thought, of our imagination, and of our action.

The Relation of Freedom to Nature: Establishing Transcendental Freedom

Many texts can be cited to support the view that Kant considered freedom and nature to be among the most important concepts treated within his critical philosophy. The presence of these multiple affirmations, however, does not by itself constitute a sufficient basis for grounding the claim that the central focus of the critical project is the relationship between nature and freedom, a fact attested by the large body of often useful and even distinguished Kant commentary that has been written without commitment to the more complex and controversial claim I am advancing. According to this claim, the centrality of the relationship between freedom and nature for Kant's critical project is not simply that this relationship stands as one major focal point for the larger set of concepts and principles that constitute the project; it is first and foremost about the way in which the necessity of critique arises in virtue of what Kant perceives to be the ineluctably problematic character of that relationship. One way to put this claim is to pose it with reference to the very first sentence of the "Preface" to the first edition of the *Critique of Pure Reason*: It is the relationship between freedom and nature that gives rise to ". . . the peculiar fate [of human reason] in one species of its cognition that it is burdened with questions that it cannot dismiss, since they are given to it as problems by the nature of reason itself, but which it also cannot answer, since they transcend every capacity of human reason" (A vii).

Given the scope of this claim, the case for it cannot be made simply by citing or listing Kant's various affirmations of the importance of the concepts of freedom and of nature—or even, for that matter, his affirmations of the importance of the relationship between freedom and nature as a problem *within* the critical project. A more appropriate and illuminating way to do this will be to examine, first, how Kant takes the relationship between freedom and nature to set the very problem that requires the development and application of the reflective procedure he terms critique; and, second, how he understands critique to provide the proper resolution of that problem. In making this examination, it is important to note that Kant's own articulation of each point does not remain fully static as he executes the critical project. Qualifications, expansions, even reversals mark the development of Kant's own understanding both of what gives rise to the need for critique and of how critique addresses the problem that necessitates it. These shifts in Kant's thinking—particularly when they mark a further reflection upon the scope of the task he has set before himself—can thereby prove quite useful for this examination.

Thus the first step in the case in support of the claim that the relationship between nature and freedom is the governing issue that gives rise to the critical project will be to examine a set of texts that mark out a shift in Kant's thinking in the eight-year period that runs from the initial publication of the *Critique of Pure Reason* (1781) to the publication of the *Critique of Practical Reason* (1788). This shift concerns Kant's understanding of freedom not only with respect to its role as a central concept within the critical project, but also—and more germane for my purposes—with respect to its bearing upon the scope and procedure of the enterprise of critique. These texts indicate that, in changing his thinking about the appropriate strategy to employ for establishing "transcendental" (i.e., moral) freedom as a central concept within the critical project, Kant has also shifted his thinking about the systematic import that the changed manner of its showing has for the overall project of critique.

This latter shift provides a significant indication of both how and why the overarching issue for his whole project is the question of how the exercise of human moral freedom stands in relation to the nexus of necessary causal connections that constitute "nature," and vice-versa. This shift, moreover, can be appropriately correlated to three other developments in Kant's thinking during this period, all of which bear upon the question of the central focus of the critical project. The first is the introduction of the notion of autonomy to characterize freedom.[2] The second is Kant's countenancing a significant breach of the firm barrier that the *Critique of Pure Reason* had initially set between the "world" governed by the causal connections of nature and the "world" constituted by the self-governance of reason. The third is the elucidation of a notion of the highest good in which the moral self-governance of reason functions as a necessary condition for the attainment of the historical and social destiny of the human race. These developments are closely related and, as I shall show later in this chapter and chapter 3, they collectively provide the basis from which critique can itself now be seen as an enterprise in which human beings must be engaged in consequence of their unique position as the concrete locus of the relationship between freedom and nature. Critique, as the fundamental form of the self-governance and self-discipline of reason, makes it possible for human beings to comport themselves a manner that befits this unique status; and it is only through such comportment that the destiny befitting the human species can be attained.

Consider of the following three texts, cited in the order of their publication. The first text is from the first section ("The Canon of Pure Reason") of the second chapter of the "Transcendental Doctrine of Method," which is the second, shorter (and too often neglected) of the two major parts into which Kant divides the *Critique of Pure Reason*.[3] The specific section in which this text is located bears the title "On the ultimate end of the pure use of our reason."

> We thus cognize practical freedom through experience, as one of the natural causes, namely a causality of reason in the determination of the will, whereas transcendental freedom requires an independence of this reason itself (with regard to its causality for initiating a series of appearances) from all determining causes of the world of the senses, and to this extent seems to be contrary to the law of nature, thus to all possible experience, and so remains a problem. Yet this problem does not belong to reason in its practical use, so in a canon of pure reason we are concerned with only two questions that pertain to the practical interest of pure reason, and with regard to which a canon of its use must be possible, namely: Is there a God? Is there a future life? The question about transcendental freedom concerns merely speculative knowledge, which we can set aside as quite indifferent if we are concerned with what is practical, and about which there is already sufficient discussion in the Antinomy of Pure Reason. (A 803–804/B 831–832)

The second passage is found in the preface to the *Groundwork of the Metaphysics of Morals*, in the course of Kant's discussion of the function of that work in relation to other writings in ethics that he was planning subsequently to undertake:

> Intending to publish some day a metaphysics of morals, I issue this groundwork in advance. Indeed there is really no other foundation for a metaphysics of morals than the critique of a pure practical reason, just as that of metaphysics is the critique of pure speculative reason, already published. But in the first place the former is not of such utmost necessity as the latter, because in moral matters human reason can easily be brought to a high degree of correctness and accomplishment, even in the most common understanding, whereas in its theoretical but pure use it is wholly dialectical; and in the second place I require that the critique of a pure practical reason, if

it is to be carried through completely, be able at the same time to present the unity of practical with speculative reason in a common principle, which must be distinguished merely in its application. But I could not yet bring it to such completeness here without bringing into it considerations of a wholly different kind and confusing the reader. (*GMM*, 4: 391/47)

The third comes from the preface to the *Critique of Practical Reason*. It is part of a discussion in which Kant explicates the relationship of the first two *Critiques* to one another and to the critical project as a whole.

For, if as pure reason it is really practical, it proves its reality and that of its concepts by what it does, and all subtle reasoning against the possibility of its being practical is futile.

With this faculty transcendental *freedom* is also established, taken indeed in that absolute sense in which speculative reason needed it, in its use of the concept of causality, in order to rescue itself from the antinomy into which it unavoidably falls when it wants to think the *unconditioned* in the series of causal connection; this concept, however, it could put forward only problematically, as not impossible to think, without assuring it objective reality, and only lest the supposed impossibility of what it must at least allow to be thinkable call its being into question and plunge it into an abyss of skepticism.

Now, the concept of freedom, insofar as its reality is proved by an apodictic law of practical reason, constitutes the *keystone* of the whole structure of a system of pure reason, even of speculative reason; and all other concepts (those of God and immortality), which as mere ideas remain without support in the latter, now attach themselves to this concept and with it and by means of it get stability and objective reality, that is, their *possibility* is *proved* by this: that freedom is real, for this idea reveals itself through the moral law. (*CprR,* 5: 3–4/139)

These passages indicate that Kant's understanding about what serves as the appropriate strategy for establishing transcendental freedom had moved through three stages in this eight-year period. In the first stage, Kant considers his discussion of the causality of freedom and the causality of nature in third antinomy adequate for the critical establishment of transcendental freedom, but he does not provide an estimate of the systematic importance of doing so by means of the arguments offered in that particular section of the Transcendental Dialectic. In the second stage, he now takes the establishment of transcendental freedom to be the work of a separate critique—suggesting that the third antinomy no longer solely suffices for that task; the significance of this critical establishment of freedom, moreover, is still not at the level of the "extreme importance" assigned to the critique of theoretical reason. In the third stage, however, Kant now proposes that the elaboration of a separate critique of practical reason is needed to provide not only the adequate critical establishment of freedom but also the "keystone" for the whole critical project; although the argument and commentary on the third antinomy retain the probative significance for Kant's critique of speculative reason, more is needed to establish freedom with respect to critique as a project encompassing the whole range of the uses of reason.

Two questions are pertinent here: What precisely is the nature of this shift in Kant's thinking? What significance does this shift have in relation to the claim that I have made about the central focus of the critical project? An important part of the answer to the first question lies in the fact that despite the monumental intellectual breakthrough that Kant effected in the first *Critique*, for which he had good reason to claim as the philosophical counterpart to Copernicus's revolution in natural science, he did not provide—and, in fact, was not yet in a position to provide—in that initial critical work the full outline of the project to which he would devote the more than two decades remaining to his life. As Paul Guyer has noted ". . . although it is natural for us now to read Kant's three great *Critiques* . . . as if they were conceived as the continuous expression of a single coherent system, in fact, each of the later two works was unplanned at the time of its predecessor and represents some considerable revision of it."[4] To the extent that the critical project was—even after the publication of the third *Critique* as its putative completion—a constant "work in progress," Kant rarely fails to rethink and rearticulate even its most basic concepts and arguments, sometimes in response to criticism but at least equally as often as a result of his own further probing of the issues at hand. In the case of the three passages cited above, Kant's rethinking about the systematic significance of the way in which freedom is established seems shaped in large measure by the need to spell out more fully the notions of the practical interest of reason and the practical use of reason that first *Critique* had initially adumbrated within the "Transcendental Dialectic" (A466/B 494) and the "Transcendental Doctrine of Method" (A 809/B 837).

If this is correct, then this shift here can be considered as one instance in which undertaking the execution of a particular part of the critical project—in this case, a critique of the practical (moral) use of reason—requires Kant to rethink the configuration of the entire project. What had apparently been envisioned as, at most, a supplemental part of the project at the time of the writing of the first *Critique*, starts to loom larger and larger as Kant first more fully outlines that part in the *Groundwork* and then later brings it to completion in the arguments of the second *Critique*. This, however, suggests little that is remarkable in the process through which Kant came to make this shift, since he is a thinker who seems never to tire of reexploring in a more thorough fashion the conceptual territories through which he has often traversed. It does not, however, clarify the import of this particular shift, either for Kant's own execution of the critical project or for the overall interpretive claim I am advancing about that project.

To do this, it will be helpful to recall that the context in which he places the very first of these three passages is a discussion of the "ultimate end" of the pure use of our reason—a topic to which he will return in the two subsequent *Critiques*, most notably in the *Critique of the Power of Judgment*. While the ultimate end of the pure use of reason is the explicit topic of the first two sections of the "Canon of Pure Reason," in the second of these sections, Kant is also directly concerned with the relationship between the theoretical and practical uses of reason and thus, implicitly, with the unity of reason. It is in this second section that he enunciates the famous three questions—What can I know? What ought I do? and, For what may I hope?—that he considers both to articulate and to unify the theoretical and practical "interests" of reason. These same two sections, finally, offer an instructive foreshadowing of the main issues that Kant treats in later ethical writings, such as the *Groundwork of the Metaphysics of Morals*, the *Critique of Practical Reason*, and *Religion within the Boundaries of Mere Reason*. Each one of these elements individually suggests that the issue of the proper manner of establishing the reality of transcendental freedom will be of major import for Kant's critical enterprise. It is, however, the location of this issue within his consideration of the ultimate end of the use of reason that provides the clearest indication that the relationship between freedom and nature is centrally at stake not only in this discussion but also for the whole critical project.

Kant's discussion of the ultimate end of the use of pure reason in this section, as well as in other parts of his critical writings, manifests a teleological dimension to the human use of reason that is deeply embedded throughout the whole of Kant's critical project. Put in its most direct terms, Kant takes it as given that human reason has a final end and that this end, at root, has itself been *given to* human reason: Human reason does not itself determine what constitutes its ultimate end; that end, instead, has been given to it, even though reason, in its practical use, that is, as bearing on "that [which] is possible through freedom" (A 800/B828), is itself the power for setting [its own] ends. This ultimate end of reason, moreover, has been given to it "by nature."

> Thus the entire armament of reason, in the undertaking that one can call pure philosophy, is in fact directed only at the three problems that have been mentioned [the freedom of the will, the immortality of the soul, the existence of God]. These themselves, however, have in turn their remote aim, namely, **what is to be done** if the will is free, if there is a God, and if there is a future world. Now since these concern our conduct in relation to the highest end, the ultimate aim of nature which provides for us wisely in the disposition of reason is properly directed only to what is moral. (A800–801/B 828–829)

There is a fundamental tension here and it is precisely this tension that fuels the engine of the entire critical project. Human reason's own inner dynamic is ordered to setting its own ends, but this is an ordering that *has been set for* human reason. Human reason is embedded in and functions within an order that is not fully of its own making; yet the function of human reason within that order is itself to set forth ends that will constitute the ordering of human activity.

In this context, the shift in what Kant considers to be the proper manner of establishing the reality of transcendental freedom and in his assessment of the systemic importance of so establishing it provides an important indication that he has brought the critical project into a sharper and closer focus upon the relationship between nature and freedom as its central concern. The "questions that reason cannot dismiss" surely and necessarily arise from reason's own activity—but they just as surely and just as inevitably arise because reason is itself situated in a context not of its own making. Whatever human reason makes—and, more centrally for Kant's project—whatever it makes of itself, it makes as part of a "cosmos" that is ineliminably "given." The work, as well as the play, of reason takes place at the intersection of what is of reason's own making and what is not of its own making— even when the exercise of reason enables humanity to raise itself "above" the workings of its own "givenness." Kant elegantly expresses this point at the conclusion of the second *Critique* when he singles out "the starry skies above" and "the moral law within" as the fundamental reference points from which all the enterprises of human reason take their bearings.

How, then, does this shift in Kant's thinking, which now leads him to propose an explicit critique of practical reason as the proper manner of establishing the reality of transcendental freedom, provide support for the claim that the critical project has its fundamental focus upon the relationship between nature and freedom? It does so, I believe, because it marks a more explicit and fundamental recognition on Kant's part that the work of the first *Critique* was only the necessary first step in a project that he can now more adequately articulate as encompassing the full range of the relationship to the cosmos that humanity establishes through the exercise of reason. The first *Critique* provided only the first lesson in the self-discipline in which human reason must instruct itself. By curbing the ambition that reason has in its theoretical use—the ambition of providing an account of the workings of the world of nature articulated in terms of a set of unconditioned principles—the first *Critique* deals with only one of the activities through which reason stands in relation to a cosmos that is not of its own making. This activity, though fundamental to reason and expressive in its own proper way of the inner dynamic of reason, is not the central locus of that dynamic, which Kant locates as properly in the practical interest of reason. It is in and through the practical interest of reason, an interest that finds its proper expression in freedom, that the fundamental dynamic of reason in relation to the cosmos finds expression.

Yet, as Kant now comes to recognize, this dynamic also stands in need of self-discipline—that is, in need of critique. Kant's proposal for a critique of practical reason and his recognition of its central importance to his project thus represents an explicit acknowledgment that the relationship of reason in its practical employment (i.e., freedom) to nature is at the heart of the enterprise of critique. Once reason has learned the first lesson of self-discipline of reason—to curb the ambitions of its theoretical use—it is now ready for the far more central lesson of critique: It is now ready to learn the self-discipline that is proper to its practical use. It is ready to learn that self-governance of freedom that Kant terms "autonomy."

The Relation of Freedom to Nature: From Spontaneity to Autonomy

Against the background provided by this shift in Kant's thinking about the need for a critique of practical reason, it should not be surprising that during the same period his articulation of the dynamic of transcendental freedom moves from a concept suited to the work of the first *Critique*, "spontaneity," to a concept suited to the now more fully envisioned task of a critique of practical reason, "autonomy." The introduction of the concept of autonomy, I shall argue in this section, enables Kant to present the dynamic of practical reason as a discipline proper to the self-governance of reason in its practical use and expression as freedom.

It is not merely an accident of terminology in the *Critique of Pure Reason* that Kant does not yet identify the exercise of freedom as "autonomy." The discussion of freedom in the first *Critique* is cast, instead, in terms of the notion of "spontaneity" (A 444–451/B 472–479; A 533/ B 561). This is quite in keeping with the general role that the notion of spontaneity plays in Kant's characterization of the function of reason as the synthesizing power operative in human consciousness's cognizing of objects; in this context it serves well as an appropriate term to characterize initially the function of reason, as transcendental causality, in human consciousness's determining of action. Thus, to the extent that Kant understands the notion of spontaneity to be a fundamental characteristic of reason, it allows him to identify human willing, insofar as it can be a spontaneously determining source of action, as an exercise of reason. As long as this simple identification of willing with the practical exercise of the spontaneity of reason suffices, Kant is able consistently to maintain that there is no need for a separate critique of practical reason. The more focused analysis of willing that Kant proposes in the *Groundwork*, however, indicates that he eventually found this identification of freedom with spontaneity inadequate, by virtue of its generality, for specifying the properly practical character that pure reason exhibits in determining the will as a source of human action. The practical character of pure reason is more properly expressed as its capacity for self-governance, and autonomy will prove to be more apt term than spontaneity for marking this out.

Kant's introduction of the notion of autonomy to characterize the function of reason in the human determination of action is nonetheless by no means intended to deny his previous characterization of willing as an exercise of reason in virtue of its spontaneity. It serves, rather, to mark out more clearly a characteristic of the spontaneity of reason that, even though it is proper to the entire exercise of reason, is exhibited most clearly in the practical use of reason: The spontaneity of reason in *all* its uses has an ordering principle—and that ordering principle is its own self-governance. Autonomy, as Onora O'Neill has argued, is central not just to that part of the critical project explicitly concerned with the practical exercise of reason; it is central to the whole enterprise.[5] The need for reason to exercise governance of its own spontaneity lies at the very root of critique: It is not a project to place *external* constraints upon claims that have been made on behalf of reason but to place human reason under *its own internal self-discipline* by which it acknowledges the limits that its finitude within the cosmos places on its use. In consequence, Kant's formulation of the notion of autonomy to characterize the manner in which reason exercises self-governance in its practical use will prove important not only for the critical examination of the practical use of reason but also for the final systematic shape of the entire critical project.

There are two closely related aspects of the interpretation that I will be proposing for Kant's notion of autonomy here and throughout the course of this work that may sound unfamiliar, if not downright odd, to readers accustomed to what has claim to being the main English language interpretive perspective on Kant's (or perhaps more precisely, Kantian) ethics for much of the twentieth century. One aspect, which will be treated in detail in a number of later sections, is the close correlation that I will claim Kant's understanding of autonomy has with both the social character of human moral agency and the social character of reason itself. Until recently, this is a correlation that has generally been overlooked, in large measure, it seems, because the term "autonomy" has taken on a highly individualist cast in the context of the political, economic, and popular culture that has emerged in the democratic societies of the North Atlantic during the past two centuries.[6] Some recent work in Kant's ethics has suggested that such an individualist reading of autonomy does not accurately represent his own thinking: The prevailing cultural reading of autonomy places such stress on the first element of this Greek-derived compound—on the *auto*, the self—that it overlooks that fact the other part of the compound—the *nomos*, the law—is a concept whose fundamental intelligibility is embedded in ordered human social relationships. An understanding of autonomy that places equal stress on each of its roots will thus construe the morally legislative self, not as an individual isolated from social relations, but as one whose morally legislative capacity bears fundamental reference to the [universally] legislative community of which she is a part by virtue of her rationality. It is this connection between one's rationally legislative power and other rationally legislative agents that Kant seeks to capture in his image of "a kingdom of ends."

Related to this aspect of autonomy is a second that also may sound unfamiliar to those accustomed to treatments of autonomy that take it primarily to be the self's power to *choose*. Without denying that Kant takes the exercise of autonomy to involve a moral agent's capacity to make choices, the interpretation offered here sees as more fundamental to Kant's use of this notion the agent's capacity for *self-governance in accordance with principles*. On this interpretation, it is not the case—as interpretations that see autonomy as fundamentally the self's power to choose often hold—that *any* choice that a moral agent makes is an autonomous one. Only some exercises of an agent's choice (or, in keeping with Kant's terminology, only some maxims) are successful as exercises as autonomy as well. The successful ones are those in which the agent's choice is made in accord with a principle for action that the universal community of legislative agents could and would also adopt. Choices made on bases other than this— that is, choices made from maxims that would not gain the assent of agents who are members of a kingdom of ends—are what Kant would call heteronomous. Though these maxims and the actions that follow from them surely issue from an agent's power of choice, they fail to be autonomous precisely because they do not meet the most exhaustive of tests that Kant proposes for their adequacy to serve as a principle of action for an autonomous agent: The test of being appropriate for the self-governance of a legislative member of a kingdom of ends.

The third section of the *Groundwork of the Metaphysics of Morals* is a particularly important text for indicating the systematic importance for critique of Kant's introduction of the terminology of autonomy to characterize freedom in its character as the exercise of practical reason.[7] Kant's discussion in this section is significant for a number of the elements that I am proposing in the interpretation of autonomy as the self-governance of reason. First, this section links the analysis of moral agency that Kant presented in the second section of the *Groundwork* back to discussions of self-awareness and self-knowledge presented in the first *Critique*. These links and the issues that remain unresolved in Kant's treatment of them bear upon a question that is never far from the surface throughout the critical project: What precisely constitutes the unity of reason? Second, and directly relevant to the present discussion, this section indicates how Kant's previous characterization of the activity of reason as spontaneity stands in relation to this new characterization as autonomy: As the *active* principle in cognizing, reason is spontaneous, a self-active source in contrast to the receptivity of sensibility; but, it is also an ordered and ordering activity, giving rise, as understanding, to the rules (i.e., categories) that are necessary to constitute "experience." All of this Kant had spelled out in the first *Critique*. The more refined analysis of the practical use of reason that he starts to develop in the *Groundwork* now requires him to characterize more precisely the way in which reason, as a self-active source with respect to the ordering of (moral) action functions: Here it functions as *auto*-nomy, for the moral ordering of action, for it to be moral, must be self-imposed. Finally, this section also begins to elaborate major issues about the relationship between the sensible and intelligible "worlds" that face the project of critique and about which more will be said in the next section.

The Relation of Freedom to Nature: Breaching the Barrier between the Sensible and the Intelligible "Worlds"

I have already suggested that the introduction of autonomy has a significant consequence for the critical project in that it leads Kant to recast the distinction between the sensible "world" and the intelligible "world." This consequence is important in its own right, because Kant considers this distinction, which he variously expresses in a set of contrasting concepts—"sensible"/"intelligible" (or "supersensible"), "phenomenon"/"noumenon," "appearance"/'thing-in-itself'—to be central to the critical project.

> On the contrary, there is now disclosed a very satisfying confirmation of the speculative *Critique's consistent way of thinking*—one which was hardly to be expected before—inasmuch as it insisted on letting objects of experience as such, including even our own subject, hold only as *appearances* but at the same time on putting things in themselves at their basis and hence on not taking everything supersensible as a fiction and its concept as empty of content; now practical reason of itself, without any collusion with speculative reason, furnishes reality to a supersensible object of the category of causality, namely to *freedom* (although, as a practical concept, only for practical use), and hence establishes by means of a fact what could there only be *thought*. (*CprR*, 5: 6/141)

Although Kant never abandons this distinction (and, in fact, vigorously reaffirms it in the face of criticism directed against it), he does reexamine, reformulate, and refine it as he executes the various phases of the critical project. These various reconsiderations have important bearing upon how both he (and we) understand his critical enterprise. As I shall argue below, the specific way he reconsiders this distinction in parallel to the two shifts we have been discussing—to a separate critique to establish transcendental freedom and to the notion of autonomy to characterize freedom—adds one more link in the case for taking the critical project to be centrally concerned with the relationship between nature and freedom.

In this section, therefore, I will first show that Kant's recasting of the distinction between the sensible world and the intelligible world occurs here in function of his turning of the critical project to an explicit examination of the practical use of reason. I will then argue that in recasting this distinction Kant breaches the apparently impenetrable barrier set between them in the first *Critique* under the heading of the distinction between phenomena and noumena (A 254–256/B

310–312). As chapter 3 will show, Kant's reconsideration of this distinction—which extends beyond the period we have so far examined—has major consequences for the articulation of the critical project: It will make possible a more wide-ranging articulation of the social dimensions of the critical project, particularly in terms of the development of the notion of "the highest good."

Before proceeding further with the main discussion of this section, however, an important clarification is in order regarding the way I will be interpreting this much controverted distinction. Although I use the terminology of "world" here and in other instances in connection with the distinction between the intelligible and the sensible, this is not intended to indicate support for interpretations of the distinction that make it an ontological dualism. The distinction that Kant makes between "the intelligible" and "the sensible" is not between two distinct "kinds" of reality—let alone a distinction between "appearance" and "reality." It is a distinction between two distinguishable ways—irreducible to one another—that human beings deal with the single "world" or "reality" of which they find themselves inextricably a part. Put a bit over-simply, this is an epistemic, though not only an epistemic, distinction, but it is not a metaphysical one.[8] In consequence, the problem of the relationship between the intelligible and the sensible is not a problem of accounting for "interaction" between them—in the manner of the problem that arises for a Cartesian dualism of extended matter and thinking self. It is a problem of the range of the claims that we can validly make about the relation between these two ways of our dealing with the world, given the fact that they are irreducible to one another. The "barrier" that Kant thus erects between the sensible and the intelligible is thus principally a prohibition against reductionism: A restriction on assimilating one way of speaking to another, particularly with respect to those matters (God, freedom, and immortality) in which we are almost inevitably tempted to do so. The "breaches" that he eventually allows in this "barrier," such as identifying "respect" as a sensible effect of intelligible causality, thus signal his identification of a small range of matters that he eventually recognizes as presenting little risk of such reductive assimilation of our two necessary ways of speaking about them.

Kant initially posed the distinction between the sensible and the intelligible in its critical form for the purpose of establishing limits to the speculative use of "transcendent ideas"—that is, God, freedom, and immortality—by reason.[9] This initial critical use, it should be noted, already has embedded in it the principle that the limitation of the use of reason is legitimate only in the form of appropriate self-limitation: Reason has responsibility for its own self-governance. When Kant then turns to an explicit critical examination of the practical use of reason, it soon becomes evident that this distinction cannot be posed in precisely the same manner for a different purpose: Exhibiting the immanent, yet nonetheless objective, practical reality of one of those "transcendent" ideas, freedom. This development involves, minimally, a shift in the function of that set of related contrasts—sensible-intelligible, phenomenon-noumenon, appearance-thing-in-itself—from principally a negative one of marking a limit to the theoretical use of reason to a positive one of marking out the proper character of the practical use of the self-same reason.

For instance, Kant proposes the notion of noumenon in the first *Critique* primarily as a reminder that human reason, properly aware of its own limitations in its theoretical use, has no right in this use to make a positive characterization of its own power as "intelligible causality;" that is, its power to be "an originating source of action," which is the meaning of "freedom" for reason in its theoretical use. Yet even in the first edition of the first *Critique*, Kant gives indications that the notion of the noumenon and its parallel concepts have a function that foreshadows the positive use to which they will need to be put in a critique of the practical use of reason. These indications, not surprisingly, arise within discussions of the practical employment of reason in that first major critical work (A 542–557/B 570–585). Reason, with reference to its governance of human willing, represents itself as the source of intelligible causality:

> However many natural grounds or sensible stimuli there may be that impel me to **will**, they cannot produce the **ought** but only a willing that is yet far from necessary but rather always conditioned, over against which the ought that reason pronounces sets a measure and goal, indeed, a prohibition and an authorization. Whether it is an object of mere sensibility (the agreeable) or even of pure reason (the good), reason does not give into those grounds which are empirically given, and it does not follow the order of things as they are presented in intuition, but with complete spontaneity it makes its own order

according to ideas, to which it fits the empirical conditions and according to which it even declares actions to be necessary that yet **have not occurred** and perhaps will not occur, nevertheless presupposing of all such actions that reason could have causality in relation to them; for without that, it would not expect its ideas to have effects in experience. (A 548/B 576)

Kant's discussion here of the (intelligible) causality of reason, though cast in terms of spontaneity, clearly understands the spontaneity to function in some way as an ordering principle with relation to action. What is not yet clear from this passage, however, is the relationship that the ordering activity that issues from "the ought that reason pronounces [to] set a measure and goal" bears to the ordering that is proper to what Kant here terms "natural grounds." This is significant in that it indicates that even in the first stages of Kant's efforts to present a critical account of the practical use of reason, the relationship between the ordering that issues from human freedom (reason in its practical use) and the causal ordering of nature already looms large.

As Kant develops, in the *Groundwork* and in the second *Critique*, a more complete elucidation of freedom as the self-governance of reason in human moral agency, the issue of the relationship between freedom and nature takes a more specific form. Kant must now specify the concrete role such agency can—and, indeed, must—play in shaping the sensible "world" into the configuration called for by the intelligible, that is, moral "world." Such concrete specification, however, presents particularly a major difficulty because the way in which Kant presented the distinction between the sensible and the intelligible in the first *Critique* seems to preclude the possibility of providing any account that could specify concrete effects of the intelligible upon the sensible:

> Thus in our judgment of free actions in regard to their causality, we can get only as far as the intelligible cause, but we cannot get **beyond** it; we can know that actions could be free, i. e., that they could be determined independently of sensibility, and in that way that they could be the sensibly unconditioned condition of appearances. But why the intelligible character gives us exactly these appearances and this empirical character under the circumstances before us, to answer this surpasses every faculty of our reason, indeed it surpasses the authority of our reason even to ask it. . . . (A 557/B 585)

Kant regularly affirms throughout the critical project that the establishment of the possibility of there being such effects of intelligible causality is important, particularly for a critical vindication of the practical
use of reason. One affirmation is found in a passage from first *Critique*
cited previously: (reason) "makes its own order according to ideas . . .
nevertheless presupposing of all such actions that reason could have
causality in relation to them; for without that it would not expect its
ideas to have effects in experience" (A 548/B 576). One of his clearest
affirmation of this possibility comes from the third *Critique*, a work
that lies beyond the time frame we have so far considered. It is useful
to cite it here, however, in that it shows the place to which Kant's
thinking will shortly lead:

> Now although there is an incalculable gulf fixed between the
> domain of the concept of nature, as the sensible, and the do-
> main of the concept of freedom, as the supersensible, so that
> from the former to the latter (thus by means of the theoretical
> use of reason) no transition is possible, just as if there were so
> many different worlds, the first of which can have no influence
> on the second: yet the latter **should** have an influence on the
> former, namely the concept of freedom should make the end
> that is imposed by its laws real in the sensible world; and
> nature must consequently also be able to be conceived in such
> a way that the lawfulness of its form is at least in agreement
> with the possibility of the ends that are to be realized in it in
> accordance with the laws of freedom. (*CJ*, 5: 175–176/63)

Once he sets to the work of executing a critique of practical
reason, however, Kant must do more than simply affirm the general
possibility that an intelligible cause can have an sensible effect; he
must now identify concretely what such an effect might be. Kant provides an initial identification of a such a concrete sensible effect that
arises from intelligible causality in the *Critique of Practical Reason*:
The feeling of respect, he affirms, has its origin precisely in the intelligible causality of reason that he identifies with autonomy (*CprR*, 5:
75–79/200–204). This affirmation in the second *Critique* is especially
notable on at least two counts. First, it vividly contrasts with Kant's
previously stated reluctance, in the *Groundwork*, to make such a concrete identification, despite the fact that in this earlier work he had
already singled out respect as an important element with regard to

exercise of autonomy (*GMM*, 4: 459–461/105–106).[10] Second, Kant specifically notes the singular status of the claim he is making with regard to what he previously affirmed about the possibility of making such a concrete identification.[11]

Although Kant's identification of respect as a sensible effect of intelligible causality marks an important development in his rethinking of this basic distinction, it does not by itself resolve the larger problem that still faces his more general account of the relationship between the two "worlds" or "standpoints" demarcated by this distinction. Kant's discussion of respect, as well as his related discussion of "the fact of reason," seem to be singular, perhaps even *ad hoc*, responses to an issue that requires a more systematic resolution. Kant's variously expressed claims that the "world" that is ordered in accord with the autonomous exercise of practical reason must have effects upon the sensible "world" that is ordered in terms of causal interaction seems to need more than the single point of contact provided by the feeling of respect.

Although it does not anticipate all of the developments in Kant's subsequent dealings with this issue, there is a passage in the first *Critique* that anticipates one important direction he eventually will pursue in an effort to resolve this larger issue. This passage suggests the ordering that issues from the spontaneous, self-governing activity of reason in its practical use bears upon the activity by which human agents mutually constitute the totality of connections that make them, each and all, members of that intelligible realm that Kant calls a "*corpus mysticum* of . . . rational beings," or, following Leibniz, "the realm of grace" (A 808/B 836; A 812/B 840).

> I call the world as it would be if it were in conformity with all moral laws (as it **can** be in accordance with the **freedom** of rational beings and **should** be in accordance with the necessary laws of **morality**) a **moral world**. This is conceived thus far merely as an intelligible world, since abstraction is made therein from all conditions (ends) and even from all hindrances to morality in it (weakness or impurity of human nature). Thus far it is therefore a mere, yet practical, idea, which really can and should have its influence on the sensible world, in order to make it agree as far as possible with this idea. The idea of a moral world thus has objective reality, not

as if it pertained to an object of intelligible intuition (for we cannot even think of such a thing), but as pertaining to the sensible world, although as an object of pure reason in its practical use and a *corpus mysticum* of the rational beings in it, insofar as their free choice under moral laws has thoroughgoing systematic unity in itself as well as with the freedom of everyone else. (A 808/B 836)

Put in other words, I believe that in this passage Kant opens up a further possibility for identifying the effects of the intelligible causality that is exercised in the practical use of reason. The exercise of freedom brings a "moral world" into being by giving shape and order to the concrete social relationships of human beings and to the dynamics that govern human social action. Kant, however, does not immediately attend to the development of this possibility. There are a variety of reasons for this, including the fact that other issues, which emerge as Kant moves forward on the critical project in the 1780s occupy his efforts. But one of the main reasons has to do with the fact that further exploration of this possibility must wait until Kant has more fully articulated his account of the highest good as the object of practical reason—and has articulated it in such a way that its character as fundamentally social has clearly emerged. Although hints of the social character of the highest good can be discerned as early as the first *Critique* and in other writings of the 1780s, it is only with the publication of *Religion with the Boundaries of Mere Reason* that Kant seems fully to affirm the social character of the highest good. In consequence, he is also able in the same work to propose the notion of an ethical commonwealth as a fundamental way in which the causality of freedom can bring into being the concrete social relationships among human beings that will fully constitute a moral world. Chapter 3 will examine Kant's account of these two concepts for the bearing they have on the primary focus of the critical project on the relationship between nature and freedom.

CHAPTER THREE

The Human Place in the Cosmos II:
Critique as the Social Self-Governance of Reason

Chapter 2 presented three main considerations in favor of taking Kant's critical project to have its fundamental focus on the relationship between nature and freedom. The first was the shift in Kant's thinking about the manner in which the reality of transcendental freedom could be established; this shift led him to undertake a task he had not previously fully envisioned as a necessary part of the critical project, namely, a critique of the practical use of reason. The second was his introduction of the concept of autonomy as an appropriate characterization of freedom; this represents an important development over his previous characterization of freedom as an aspect of the spontaneity of reason. The significance of this development is that autonomy highlights the self-governance of the spontaneity of reason, which Kant considers fundamental to the practical use of reason. The third consideration focused on yet another shift in Kant's thinking, this one involving the set of coordinate concepts—the sensible and the intelligible and their related variants such as phenomenon and noumenon—that he consistently maintained articulated a distinction that served as the very nerve of the critical project. Taken separately, each consideration bears upon one or more aspects of the relationship between nature and freedom as a major problem internal to the critical project. Taken in coordination with one another, as aspects of Kant's developing articulation of the full scope of the critical project, these considerations suggest that the relationship between nature and freedom is not merely a problem internal to the critical project. It is, rather, the encompassing problem that gives rise to the need for the self-discipline of reason that Kant calls critique.

41

In this chapter, I propose to track further dimensions of the way
in which Kant's critical enterprise engages the relationship between
freedom and nature. These dimensions—the notion of the highest good
as the object of the practical use of reason and the notion of the ethical
commonwealth as the form of human social relationship necessary for
the attainment of the highest good—emerge more fully in Kant's thinking at least partly in consequence of the developments charted in chapter
2. A central link that ties these further dimensions to the developments
presented in chapter 2 is the notion of autonomy as the self-governance
of reason. Thus my procedure in this chapter will be, first, to sketch
out an understanding of autonomy as the self-governance of reason
and, second, to show how the highest good and the ethical commonwealth each take shape in Kant's thinking as elements that bear upon
the *social* self-governance of reason. This will then prepare the way
for chapter 4, which will explore the consequences that Kant's introduction of the notion of radical evil has for the social self-governance
of reason. These consequences, as the remaining chapters will then
argue, are far-reaching. They bring Kant himself to see that, in order
to deal with the consequences of radical evil, critique must be brought
to bear upon the encompassing problem of the relationship between
nature and freedom first and foremost in the arena where humanity
gives shape to society and culture. Of greater moment, however, is the
fact that Kant's insights into critique as an enterprise for dealing with
the social consequences of radical evil retain—and seem even to have
increased—their pertinence for humanity at the start of the twenty-first
century: If we engage one another as members of an ethical commonwealth, that is, in the forms of social relationship called for by the
social self-governance of reason, we have reason to hope that, despite
the enormous range of particularities and differences that mark our
human condition and have compelling power to set us at odds with
one another, we can still together shape our lives as individuals, as
communities, and as societies, so as to constitute a world that serves
the good of each and all. If, however, we remain unwilling to engage
one another as members of an ethical commonwealth—in Kant's words,
if we remain in the "ethical state of nature"—then we all eventually
will be both perpetrators and victims on what Hegel called the "slaughter
bench of history" by letting our particularities and differences so set
us at odds that the only common ground we are willing to provide one
another is that of the graveyard.[1]

Autonomy: Toward the Social Self-Governance of Reason

Interpretations of Kant's notion of autonomy that are relational—that is, that locate its fundamental context in terms of an individual moral agent's relationship to others in society—are no longer as problematic as they once seemed (see chapter 2). Still, the strength and persistence of a view that sees Kantian autonomy as individualist—that is, as standing in fundamental tension with the roles and relationships that are constitutive of an agent's membership in a community—requires that an account be given of why a relational rather than an individualist reading more adequately represent's Kant's own view of autonomy.[2] What I shall therefore do in this section is provide a brief though, I hope, adequate account of the considerations that lie within Kant's own texts that argue that his own understanding of autonomy sees it as fundamentally—and appropriately—embedded within the context of the full range of human relationality. In terms of the larger argument of this chapter, this section will make the case that in proposing autonomy as the proper characterization of freedom, Kant at least implicitly affirms the social character of the self-governance of reason that he later articulates more explicitly in the concepts of the highest good and the ethical commonwealth.

Before arguing in behalf of a relational understanding of autonomy, it will be useful to consider some of the factors that lie behind the strength and persistence of an individualist reading of this concept. While it may be the case that some of these factors have their origin in the cultural dynamics of individualism generated in the interplay of a democratic polity with a market economy, the ones most pertinent to my argument are those that can be located within Kant's own texts. The strength and persistence of this reading as Kant's own has its origin in the fact that he does treat the notion of autonomy in ways that do provide a basis for what I have termed an individualist reading. There is no doubt, for instance, that Kant takes *autonomy* to be crucial to the full integrity of the individual choices that one makes as a moral agent. There is also little doubt that in the texts that have become standard reading for courses in ethics—most notably the second part of *The Groundwork of the Metaphysics of Morals*—Kant does not make it all that evident—save in the image of the kingdom of ends—that autonomy can be, let alone should be, appropriately rendered as an account of the *social* self-governance of reason. He offers what has often been taken to be a picture of moral decision making in which an individual (and apparently abstract) moral agent makes choices that seem not to be at all affected by the concrete features of our human condition, such as one's relation to other human beings in the specific society of which one is a member. One makes one's decisions as an abstract member of a timeless "intelligible world" standing, at best, in an abstract, formal relation with an equally abstract set of fellow members of that world.

The strength of this individualist reading of Kant's notion of autonomy, however, rests to a large degree, first, on detaching the arguments of the *Groundwork* from the larger conceptual structure of Kant's critical project and, second, on taking this text as Kant's definitive statement on moral philosophy rather than an intermediate, albeit quite significant, exposition of a still developing account of moral life that undergoes further refinement and even significant revision for more than another decade. One consequence of this isolation of the concepts and arguments of the *Groundwork* from both their systematic context in the critical project and their place in the historical development of Kant's thinking is that this text is read without reference to his first efforts to envision the form and function of a critical exposition of morality in the first *Critique* or to his later treatments, sometimes strikingly different, of the same central issues in other texts from the late 1780s and throughout the 1790s. When read in the wider context provided by other major texts from different stages of Kant's exposition of the critical project, however, one begins to see the lineaments of a more complex account of moral agency and autonomy than that provided by individualist readings focused principally on this one text. One striking way in which the picture becomes more complex is that reference to this larger array of texts brings into higher relief the social embeddedness of moral agency and autonomy that Kant only hints at in the text of the *Groundwork* with the image of a kingdom of ends.

A key initial point of reference is the passage from the "Canon of Pure Reason" cited toward the end chapter 2 (A 808/B 836) in which Kant defines a "moral world" as "the world as it would be if it were in conformity with all moral laws (as it **can** be in accordance with the **freedom** of rational beings and **should** be in accordance with the necessary laws of **morality**)" and in which he then refers to the "objective reality" of this world as an "object of reason in its practical use" and "a *corpus mysticum* of the rational beings in it, insofar as their free choice under moral laws has thoroughgoing systematic unity in itself as well as with the freedom of everyone else." A few pages later he further explicates the interconnectedness of the agents in this "moral world" by reference to Leibniz's concept of a "realm of grace":

> Leibniz called the world, insofar as in it one attends only to rational beings and their interconnection in accordance with moral laws under the rule of the highest good, the **realm of grace**, and distinguished it from the **realm of nature**, where, to be sure, rational beings stand under moral laws but cannot expect any successes for their conduct except in accordance with the course of nature in our sensible world. Thus to regard ourselves as in the realm of grace, where every happiness awaits us as long as we ourselves do not limit our share of it through the unworthiness to be happy, is a practically necessary idea of reason. (A 812/B 840)

This passage presages elements that eventually will enter into Kant's account of critique as the social self-governance of reason; for example, the kingdom of ends, the object of practical reason, radical evil, the universal principle of justice. It also suggests, as well, some problems that recur in his later development of that account; for example, the moral function of the ends of action, moral "weakness" and "impurity" in relation to radical evil, and, most notably, the relation between nature and freedom in terms of what he calls here the "realm of nature" and the "realm of grace," not all of which he is able to bring to a satisfactory resolution. Of these elements, the ones that I believe bear most directly upon the social character of autonomy are those that express Kant's understanding both of the unity of reason and of comprehensive unifying dynamic of reason, an understanding that he images and conceptualizes in terms such as world, realm, or kingdom.

To understand how Kant's use of this terminology bears on the notion of autonomy as the social self-governance of reason, it is crucial to recall that Kant takes reason itself to be a mark of the interrelatedness of the beings who exercise it. Kant gives clear affirmation of this in the first *Critique*, in the second section of the first chapter of the "Transcendental Doctrine of Method," a discussion that bears the title "The discipline of pure reason with regard to its polemical use." Two passages are of particular relevance, since they each use the establishment and operation of civic order in society as an extended image for the critical use of reason. The first is the opening paragraph of the section:

> Reason must subject itself to critique in all its undertakings, and cannot restrict the freedom of critique through any prohibition without damaging itself and drawing upon itself a disadvantageous suspicion. Now there is nothing so important because of its utility, nothing so holy, that it may be exempted from this searching review and inspection, which knows no respect for persons. The very existence of reason depends upon this freedom, which has no dictatorial authority, but whose claim is never anything more than the agreement of free citizens, each of whom must be able to express his reservations, indeed even his *veto*, without holding back. (A738–739/B 766–767)

The second passage is part of a later discussion in the same section in which Kant offers a defense of what he will later term the public use of reason:

> Without this [the critique of reason as the true court of justice], reason is as it were in the state of nature, and it cannot make its assertions and claims valid or secure them except though **war**. The critique, on the contrary, which derives all decisions from the ground-rules of its own constitution, whose authority no one can doubt, grants us the peace of a state of law, in which we should not conduct our controversy except by **due process**. What brings the quarrel in the state of nature to an end is a **victory**, of which both sides boast, although for the most part there follows only an uncertain peace, arranged by an authority in the middle; but in the state of law it is the **verdict**, which, since it goes to the origin of the controversies themselves, must secure a perpetual peace. (A751–752/B 779–780)

As Onora O'Neill ably argued, the juridical and political imagery that runs deeply throughout Kant's writings needs to be taken as a particularly revealing clue to his thinking about the nature and function of human reason.[3] These passages indicate that we would not be far off the mark in taking Kant to understand critique as the very process by which reason (freely) brings itself to be exercised socially—and to understand autonomy as the freedom by which reason acknowledges and takes upon itself the task of being governed socially. If this is so, there is all the more reason to agree with O'Neill's assessment that autonomy is at the very heart of critique and to urge, perhaps even more strongly than she does, that critique is itself a social task.[4]

A similar strong and explicit stress on the social character of reason, however, is not immediately evident in the *Groundwork*, though I believe one could argue that it is implicit in the confidence that Kant exhibits throughout that work in the reliability of ordinary moral judgment.[5] In the development of his arguments in the *Groundwork*, Kant's explicit focus simply is on matters other than the way in which the newly introduced concept of autonomy expresses the fundamentally social character of reason. Yet it is not difficult to find key elements in his arguments that at least presuppose, if not explicitly confirm, the social character of the exercise of (moral) reason. A particularly clear statement of this is in the affirmation of morality as "the lawgiving by which alone a kingdom of ends is possible" (4: 434/84), a description that, in slightly different terminology, echoes what he had written in the "Canon of Pure Reason" about the social character of the world that is to be effected by the moral exercise of reason. In characterizing the moral exercise of reason as autonomy, Kant quite evidently highlights the fact that responsibility for the appropriate moral exercise of reason rests squarely in the hands of individual moral agents, and this is the aspect of his discussion that gives much of the persuasive power to what I have termed individualist understandings of autonomy. By affirming, in the concept of autonomy, each individual agent's responsibility for the exercise of reason, Kant neither denies nor weakens his prior claims about the social character of reason—yet his strong affirmation of individual responsibility here does bring to light an issue that plays a role in the development of the notion of the highest good: The precise character of the bearing that an individual's appropriate exercise of moral reason has upon effecting the highest good in its social form. As the next two sections will show, the articulation of this issue and the (partial) resolution of it that Kant provides in the concept of an ethical commonwealth allow him to provide a more complete account of how critique concretely functions as the social self-governance of reason.

The Highest Good: From Purity of the Will to Social Goal

As the previous section indicated, claims that attribute an intrinsically social character to Kant's notion of autonomy have to be vindicated over against interpretive traditions that downplay, overlook, or even deny this possibility. The situation is a different with respect to claims about the social character of Kant's notion of the highest good. Although much of the commentary on this idea has focused on issues arising from Kant's use of it in connection with the question of the relation of virtue to happiness for individual moral agents, there seems to be general recognition that there is a social dimension to Kant's treatment of the highest good and that this dimension more visibly emerges during the later stages of his work on the critical project.[6] There has been, however, little analysis of the relationship between these two aspects of Kant's understanding of the highest good.

One reason for this lack of analysis, it seems, is that the main consensus among commentators is that Kant's various articulations of the notion of the highest good are, at best, incomplete and, at worst, incoherent with respect to one another. There is, in fact, an important body of commentary that generally configures his discussions of the highest good—at least as it pertains to the final outcome of the moral efforts of individual agents—along two divergent lines manifesting an internal inconsistency that Kant never satisfactorily resolves.[7] Along one of these lines, the attainment of the highest good is construed as a ideal feature of an atemporal, intelligible world and functions as an element in practical reason's postulation of personal immortality; this line is particularly prominent in the second *Critique*. Along the other one of these lines, the focus of the highest good shifts from the promise it holds forth for atemporal attainment of happiness in due proportion to virtue to the role it plays in sustaining an agent's moral effort in this life; this line emerges in the third *Critique* and in *Religion within the Boundaries of Mere Reason*. The social dimension of the highest good seems to have little bearing upon the resolution of these divergences, however, even for those commentators who try to find consistency in Kant's thought as it moves along both lines.

A further—and perhaps more fundamental—reason for a lack of attention to the relationship between the individual and the social aspects of Kant's treatment of the highest good is that the very notion of the highest good is often taken to have little systematic import for the critical project as a whole. This estimation of the irrelevance of the highest good, not surprisingly, comports well with a reading of the critical project that places its center of gravity on the metaphysical and epistemological issues, even when those issues are taken to bear upon the relationship between nature and freedom. Such a reading recognizes the highest good as a concept that Kant uses in his efforts to articulate the unity of the theoretical use of reason dealing with the workings of nature with the practical use of reason governing the exercise of freedom. Yet the highest good appears to be one of Kant's "softer" concepts with respect to this issue, something of an afterthought with respect to other more crisply reasoned efforts to grapple with the question of the unity of reason. In addition to this, some of Kant's more extensive treatments of the social dimensions of the highest good appear in works such as *Religion within the Boundaries of Mere Reason* and the occasional essays of the 1780s and 1790s, works that are often considered not to be among the central texts of the critical project.

In contrast to these negative assessments of the systematic importance of the highest good, the interpretation I am proposing here considers the highest good, particularly in its function as the social goal of the exercise of (practical) reason, to be of major systematic importance for Kant's project of critique. At the same time, this interpretation also acknowledges that recognition of its importance is significantly hampered by the slow and halting manner in which the social dimensions of the highest good emerge in the course of the critical project. In fact, as the second main part of this work will argue, to the extent that Kant did not himself complete a full articulation of the social dimensions of the highest good and its consequences, that task—which, arguably, is now even more important than it was in Kant's own day— has now become incumbent upon us.

In order to make the case for the systematic importance of the highest good as a social goal, it will first be necessary to sketch briefly the main stages by which Kant's treatment of this notion comes to an explicit recognition of the social dimension of the highest good and begins to explore its consequences. Once this is done, it will then be possible to assess the significance of this development. This assessment will be made in the light of, first, the larger claim for which I have been arguing from the outset of this work, that is, that the fundamental focus of the critical project is on the relationship between nature and freedom and, second, the specific claim advanced in the previous section about the social character of reason, particularly in the form of its practical exercise, autonomy.

It is possible to make an argument that Kant's earliest critical treatment of the highest good is located in the discussion of a "moral world" in the "Canon of Pure Reason" in the first *Critique*. As the passages previously cited from that section indicate, that discussion acknowledges a fundamental social relatedness in the moral use of reason and construes the outcome of that moral use in terms of a systematic connectedness that is properly termed a "world." Yet, as Kant begins an explicit examination of reason in its practical use, the focus of his discussions of the highest good, both in the *Groundwork of the Metaphysics of Morals* and the *Critique of Practical Reason*, seems to shift. In those texts, this notion stands for the outcome that an individual can hope for in consequence of conscientious adherence to the moral law. An intriguing exception to this—and one that makes the highest good represent the moral purity of an individual in a most austere guise—is a passage in the *Groundwork* in which a good will, or perhaps the *formation* of a good will, is identified as the highest good. In the various arguments Kant advances in the *Groundwork*, however, the highest good plays, at most, a subordinate role. This is not surprising in that this text also contains little detailed discussion of the immortality of the soul or the existence of God—the two claims which, when later advanced as the postulates of pure practical reason in the second *Critique*, will require an appeal to the notion of the highest good in the arguments that Kant proposes on their behalf.

It is undeniable that in these arguments the highest good is construed in terms that refer unambiguously to the ultimate moral destiny of individuals and that such destiny is articulated in ways that do not explicitly involve an agent's relationship to fellow members of a kingdom of ends. Much the same can be said for the way Kant treats this notion two years later in the *Critique of the Power of Judgment*, with the proviso that this discussion is set against the background of another major effort on his part to reformulate the bearing that each element of the critical project has upon the resolution of the issue of the relationship between nature and freedom. This is important in that it suggests that an account of the highest good will be incomplete unless it explicitly locates the systematic role this notion plays within the overall critical project. As Kant's still later discussions of the highest good will indicate, this part of the task was not fully accomplished in either the second or the third *Critique*.

The case, then, for relegating the highest good to the periphery of the critical project is a strong one so long as Kant's extensive discussions in the second and third *Critiques* are taken as his most definitive exposition of this concept. There is good reason, however, to think that it is not so. A number of key passages in the works that Kant produced in the 1790s indicate that the social character of the highest good noted at the start of the critical project has now become an explicit focus for further exploration on Kant's part. The most significant, though not the only, texts that support the case for this development in Kant's thinking about the highest good come from *Religion within the Boundaries of Mere Reason*; others are found in the essays "Theory and Practice" and "Toward Perpetual Peace," the *Rechtslehre*, and the concluding essay in the *Conflict of the Faculties*. Of all these, one of the most important is found in Book Three of *Religion*:

> Now, here we have a duty *sui generis*, not of human beings toward human beings but of the human race toward itself. For every species of rational beings is objectively—in the idea of reason—destined to a common end, namely the promotion of the highest good as a common good to all. But, since this highest moral good will not be brought about solely through the striving of one individual person for his own moral perfection but requires rather a union of such persons into a whole toward that very end, [i.e.] toward a system of well-disposed human beings in which, and through the unity of which alone, the highest moral good can come to pass, yet the idea of such a whole, as a universal republic based on the laws of virtue, differs entirely from all moral laws (which concern what we know to reside within our power), for it is the idea of working toward a whole of which we cannot know whether as a whole it is also in our power. (*Rel*, 6: 97–98/132–133)

This claim stands in contrast—though hardly in contradiction—to what Kant had affirmed in the first *Critique* (A 809–810/B 837–839) and even more strongly stressed from the *Groundwork* through the *Critique of the Power of Judgment*, namely, that the highest good is the moral destiny of which human beings, as *individuals*, must make themselves worthy and that it consists in the proper *individual* apportionment of happiness to virtue (*CprR*, 5: 130/245; *CJ* 5: 450/315). Here, however, Kant claims that human beings must also make themselves worthy of a destiny that pertains to them as *species* and that this moral destiny consists in the *social* project of working toward the establishment of an ethical commonwealth.

At one level this text can be seen as a return to the more social understanding of the highest good that was present in the discussion of the moral world in the "Canon of Pure Reason." This explicit reaffirmation of the social character of the highest good, however, is not the only reason for calling attention to this passage. Of greater importance is the context in which Kant makes this affirmation. Book Three begins with a particularly powerful description of what Kant had in earlier writings termed "unsociable sociability": the human "propensity to enter into society, bound together with a mutual opposition which constantly threatens to break up the society" (*IAG*, 8: 20/ 15). Within the larger argument of *Religion*, Kant introduces unsociable sociability as the condition for the actualization of the human propensity to choose to do evil that he had analyzed in Books One and Two. While that analysis showed what it is in the make-up of our human wills that makes it possible for each of us to choose to do evil, it did not account for human beings *actually* doing so. To account for that, Kant points us to our unsociable sociability: the social interaction that is a necessary feature of our human existence gives rise to the emulation, comparison, and competition with others from which arises the abiding temptation to the Kantian form of "original sin." This is the temptation to make an exception in one's own favor in the face of the universal demand of a moral law that bears the stamp of one's own self-governing reason. Put in terms of the interpretation of critique that I have been proposing, unsociable sociability provides the occasion for the self-corruption of the self-governance of reason that Kant will eventually designate as radical evil.

Within this context, Kant's affirmation of the highest good as a social goal represents a major advance beyond the social dimension he had claimed for it in previous stages of the critical project. The analysis of radical evil that Kant provides in *Religion* uncovers a further dimension to the workings of human finite reason upon which the self-discipline of critique must be exercised. The evil that takes root from the dynamics of unsociable sociability is radical in that it is the corruption of the very social character of reason. Critique, therefore, must now be applied to reason as it functions in the ordering of human social dynamics and relationships. In order to counter this radical social self-corruption of reason, Kant proposes a notion of the highest good that explicitly makes it a social goal and that must itself be rooted in a form of social dynamics that appropriately exhibits the self-governance of reason. Fundamental to the advance that this marks in Kant's account of social character of the highest good is that he now coordinates the highest good with an account of the social dynamic that will enable humanity to attain this goal destined for it as the species in which nature and freedom converge: The ethical commonwealth. It is to that account that we will now turn to complete the discussion of critique as the social self-governance of reason.

The Ethical Commonwealth: The Self-Governance of Reason for a Moral World

As the passage quoted from Book Three of *Religion within the Boundaries of Mere Reason* indicates, Kant introduces the notion of an ethical commonwealth within a discussion that affirms the fundamentally social character of the end for which the human species is destined (*Rel*, 6: 97–98/132–133). In this context, the ethical commonwealth can be construed as Kant's attempt to articulate the form by which reason will govern the social relationships and processes through which humanity attains this goal. Kant notes that the establishment of an ethical commonwealth involves human beings in a unique task: It is a duty "not of human beings toward human beings but of the human race toward itself" (*Rel*, 6: 97/132). As Kant further explicates this duty in Book Three of *Religion*, its uniqueness consists *in the intention to social and moral unity*, which it enjoins as an overarching focus for the whole range of our human activity (*Rel*, 6: 97–98/133): Human beings must *work together* to establish the *social* conditions that enable each and every member of the ethical commonwealth to develop and sustain the disposition to work for this common destiny for the human species.

My discussion of the ethical commonwealth in this section will focus on two aspects of Kant's presentation in *Religion*. First, I will show how this notion requires Kant to offer an account of the moral world that promises specification of the concrete historical and social dynamics that exhibit the social self-governance of reason. Kant had not offered in any systematic manner this kind of specification in his prior characterizations of the social dimension of the moral world; that is, in terms of notions such as the kingdom of ends. Second, I will show how his specification of the concrete historical and social dynamics of the social self-governance of reason remains incomplete. This part of my discussion will indicate that behind this incompleteness lies an issue far more fundamental for his project of critique, and for ours as well: The social consequences of radical evil. Chapter 4 will then consider the range and the outcome of Kant's efforts to deal with these consequences.

The earlier Kantian image of the moral world as a kingdom of ends made the point that freedom, understood as the self-governing power of reason, requires that we think of ourselves, not as isolated individuals, but as members of an intelligible world of equal, self-legislative agents (*GMM*, 4: 433–434/83–84).[8] Although his image places Kant's account of moral life within a social context, the destiny which, under this image, appropriately crowns human moral existence is simply the integrity of an individual life lived in accord with a good conscience. The inner conformity of individuals as moral agents to their membership in a kingdom of ends (or an intelligible world of freedom) serves as both a necessary and a sufficient condition for the attainment of human destiny, but this destiny is understood as bearing singly on individuals, in the apportionment of happiness to individual moral agents in proper accord with the moral quality of the life each one has led (*CprR*, 5: 129–132/136–138).

This earlier account framed in terms of the separate destiny of individual moral agents, however, no longer seems to provide a complete answer to the question that Kant now enunciates as central to his inquiry in *Religion*: "What is then the result from this right conduct of ours?" (*Rel*, 6: 5/58). Because Kant now conceives the answer to this question as more explicitly social, each individual's inner conformity to membership in this realm, though it remains a necessary condition for the attainment of human destiny, can no longer serve as a sufficient one, at least for the destiny of the human species. What is now required is a social form that exhibits the outcome of human moral conduct. It is this social form that Kant names an ethical commonwealth, which he describes as a "society in accordance with, and for the sake of, the laws of virtue—a society which reason makes it a task and duty of the entire human race to establish in its full scope" (*Rel*, 6: 94/130).

Kant's affirmation of the explicitly social character of the highest good and of the ethical commonwealth as the social form through which it is to be attained are not the only elements of Book Three of *Religion* that enlarge his previous account of the moral world. Of equal importance is attention that Kant now pays to the concrete historical character of the process through which the human species works toward the destiny proper to it as the juncture of nature and freedom. This—like the other two elements—is not a totally new development for the critical project. From the very beginning, Kant had seen the critical project to be at the service of the "vocation" properly incumbent upon humanity as the sole species known to be possessed of finite reason: To serve as the unifying juncture between the fully determined causal workings of nature and the self-governed spontaneity of freedom (A 815–819/B 843–847; *CprR*, 5: 146–148/257–258; 161–162/ 269–270; *CJ*, 5: 403–404/273–274). Kant clearly articulates the general outline of this vocation at least as early as the *Critique of Pure Reason*; yet the identification of the concrete locus in which human beings can and must effect the juncture between the two realms of nature and of freedom only emerges slowly, and with some struggle, in the course of his actual execution of the project. As Kant continues to probe the issues of the uses and the limits of human finite reason, the possibility begins to emerge more clearly that *the exercise of this specific human vocation takes place most properly in the workings of human society, culture, and history*. Human society, culture, and history hold a unique place within the sensible order of nature: Their workings can make manifest, in the development of human social institutions and moral practices, certain "outer" effects in the sensible order of nature, which issue from, and are indicative of, human agents' "inner" intelligible conformity to their membership in the moral world constituted by freedom as the self-governance of reason (*AP*, 7: 327– 330/188–190).

Until the publication of *Religion within the Boundaries of Mere Reason*, Kant's occasional writings on history, politics, and culture seem to have articulated this possibility with more force and clarity than had the writings presenting the critical project in a more systematic way (e.g., *IAG*, 8: 20–23/15–18; 27–28/22–23; *EF*, 8: 365–367/ 334–336; *MMG*, 8: 114–115/58–59; see, however, *CJ*, 5: 429–434/ 297–301). The significance of Kant's discussion of this possibility in

Religion—which shares characteristics both with the occasional writings and with the *Critiques*—is thus not that it introduces something brand new to the scope of the critical project, but that he now attempts a systematic specification of this possibility. Kant presents fulfillment of this vocation as taking place through the establishment and development of a concrete human institution—which he identifies as "the church"—that serves to establish and foster the concrete social practices that will bring about the attainment of the ethical commonwealth. These discussions—in *Religion* and elsewhere—of the possibility that the specific human vocation as the juncture of nature and freedom is most properly exercised in the workings of human society, culture, and history are thus directly relevant to the general interpretive claim I have advanced about the focus of the critical project on the relationship between nature and freedom. These discussions indicate that the critical project can and should be embodied in concrete forms of social practice if human beings are effectively to fulfill their vocation as the juncture of nature and freedom.

In order to see how this possibility systematically bears upon the overall scope of the critical project it will be helpful to see it as the articulation of a set of claims about the way in which human society and culture are themselves implicated in the realms of both nature and freedom. They are so implicated because they stand as both the material for, and the outcome of, the human efforts to live out that vocation by effecting (even unwittingly) the juncture of both realms. These claims are fourfold. On the one hand, society and culture are implicated in the order of nature inasmuch as

1. human beings, as embodied organisms, are part and product of the order of nature (*IAG*, 8: 19-20/13-14); and
2. the natural world provides material necessary for shaping society and culture into concrete practices and institutions (*IAG*, 8: 22/16–17).

On the other hand, they are also implicated in the working of freedom inasmuch as

1. the concrete practices and institutions of society and culture can also be shaped in accord with the motives and intentions we have as moral agents (*TP*, 8: 308–312/305–309); and

2. these practices and institutions provide the specific conditions
   under which human agents shape their motives and exercise
   their intentions (*Rel*, 5: 95–96/130–132; *EF*, 8: 365–367/
   334–336).

As we shall shortly see, Kant's efforts to specify these claims in terms
of the concrete workings of the social dynamics of the ethical commonwealth require another reconsideration on his part of the fundamental critical distinction between the sensible and the intelligible.
Similar to the reconsiderations of this distinction that Kant made in
connection with the introduction of the notion of autonomy and with
his rethinking of the proper manner of establishing the reality of transcendental freedom, this reconsideration arises from a deepening of
Kant's articulation of the self-governance of reason. Like them, it will
then have an important bearing on the overall shape and scope that
Kant gives to the critical project itself. In this instance, reconsideration
is required because Kant has again enlarged the scope of the self-
governance of reason. He has done so by proposing the ethical commonwealth as the social form through which the human species is to
attain the highest good as its moral destiny and the fulfilment of its
vocation as the juncture of nature and freedom. In virtue of this concept, the critical project is now committed to undertake the task of
specifying the concrete character of the moral world that is to issue in
human history, society, and culture as the historical outcome of the
social self-governance of reason.

   Yet a specification of the concrete character of the moral world to
be brought into being by the social dynamics of the ethical commonwealth requires a further enlargement of what can be recognized as
effects, within the sensible workings of nature, of the operation of the
intelligible causality of reason in its practical use. Chapter 2 noted the
earlier enlargement Kant made in the *Critique of Practical Reason*
where he identified the feeling of respect as the singular instance in
which the intelligible origin of a sensible effect can be recognized.
The notion of an ethical commonwealth, however, opens the prospect
that there is a larger field of effects in the sensible order that we should
be able to recognize as having their origin in the intelligible ordering
that reason governs in its practical use. This enlargement is needed
because, on Kant's account, there is no guarantee that the workings of
nature—including, of course, those elements of our human make-up

which, as sensible, are part of nature—will or even can, of themselves, sustain us in *the inner* (i.e., "intelligible") *disposition* of self-governance of reason that is necessary to our vocation as the juncture of nature and freedom, let alone bring about the attainment of the moral destiny to which that vocation is ordered. We do have legitimate reason to hope that nature will, at the least, not be intractable in the face of our efforts to live in accord with our unique human status. Yet even if nature fully cooperates with these efforts, it is, first and foremost, the responsibility of our human agency, as the locus of freedom, *to give shape to elements of nature*—again, including those elements of nature in ourselves—in order to provide proper conditions for our living in accord with our human vocation (*AP*, 7: 327–330/188–190). These conditions are to be found principally in the forms, practices, and institutions of human society and culture. Shaped from elements of nature by human agency, these stand as particular instantiations of the unique human place in the cosmos as the juncture of nature and freedom and thus make it possible for each and all to acknowledge and to live in accord with their status as members of the intelligible order of freedom.

Two related problems, however, face Kant in the execution of the program of specifying the concrete social forms of the self-governance of reason announced by the concept of the ethical commonwealth. They are difficult problems to resolve, because the first arises from claims that he had previously made in connection with the distinction between the sensible and the intelligible and the second arises in connection with the very condition that the ethical commonwealth is constructed to counter: Radical evil. Chapter 4 will point out that there may be a connection between these two issues that can be located at the most basic level of Kant's thinking and that accounts for his inability to construct a fully satisfactory response to them.

The first problem concerns the fact that one of the functions of the distinction between the sensible and the intelligible is to preserve what Kant considers to be a morally necessary cognitive opacity in the relationship between an agent's inner moral disposition and that agent's concrete outer conduct. Kant seems well aware both that good may sometimes result even from morally flawed intentions and dispositions and that even morally correct intentions and dispositions do not automatically insure that the actions issuing from them will unerringly effect good. This places limits on what we can reliably say about the relationship between an agent's intentions and dispositions (in his terminology, "maxims") and that agent's conduct. As a result, he holds that between the maxims for action an agent forms and the action the agent does there is no simple correlation that allows an observer, or indeed, even the agent herself, to read off the intelligible (i.e., moral) character of agent's maxim from the performance of a particular action. In addition, a maxim for action that an agent forms even on the basis of a constant disposition to adhere to the principle of the self-governance of reason does not guarantee successful execution of the action for which the maxim calls.[9] A similar cognitive opacity also holds for the larger field of outer activity in which the practices of society and culture run their course. However well such practices apparently conform to an external moral norm for action—which, for Kant, is justice—this does not provide a reliable index of the intelligible moral character of the maxim by which they were determined. Conversely, there also seems to be no guarantee that, for any particular set of agents, their inner conformity to their status as members of an intelligible kingdom of ends can, with any reliability, be recognized as bringing about in the sensible world of society and culture those effects that lead to the attainment of the moral destiny of the human species (A 809–810/B 837–838; *Rel*, 6: 139/165). Whether it be personal conduct or social practice, Kant is reluctant to sanction the general cognitive reliability of judgments that link the working of nature with the exercise of freedom.

Despite this affirmation of a cognitive opacity with respect to interrelation of the intelligible and the sensible, Kant does not thereby affirm that they simply run their course as orders independent of each other. Not does he hold that they concur with each other in terms of mechanistic necessity, or of preestablished harmony, or of arbitrary divine decree. There are some general claims about them that can be reliably made, though they function principally to exclude certain mistaken ways that we are inevitably tempted, according to Kant's reckoning, by the exercise of the theoretical use of our reason to characterize their relationship. What Kant thus holds with regard to what can be affirmed about their relationship can be formulated in the following three claims. First, human beings, as the only (known) participants in *both* the sensible and the intelligible orders, must acknowledge that, as finite rational beings, they are unable to discover (or construct) a *theoretically* sound, adequate and comprehensive principle that governs these two orders and accounts for their relationship (*CprR*, 5: 132–136/247–250; *CJ*, 5: 403–404/273–274). Second, despite this limitation, human beings can nonetheless affirm, on critically valid practical (i.e., moral) grounds, the priority of the intelligible order as the proper source of the principle for determining the moral ordering of their own action: They must dispose themselves to act (freely) in conformity with the governing norm of the intelligible order (*CJ*, 5: 453–458/318–322). This norm is autonomy, the self-governance of reason. Third, and most important, human beings may legitimately *hope* that, in sustaining the disposition to act autonomously, the conduct consequent upon that disposition has power to give to the sensible order a shape that more adequately expresses and represents the governing norm of the intelligible order (*Rel*, 6: 121–124/151–153). These principles, even as they make it possible for him to affirm the ethical commonwealth as the locus from which the intelligible self-governance of reason can have concrete effect on the sensible workings of human society, culture, and history, also require him to make the procedure for the concrete identification of such effects not a matter of *cognition* but a matter of *hope*.

In consequence, we cannot state what such concrete effects will be as a matter of predictive knowledge; we can, however, state what we hope they will be, not as an empty velleity, but as what can appropriately be envisioned as issuing from conduct governed by the exercise of reason in its practical use. In Kant's usage, they are matters of hope validated by reason. They are not mere imaginings of what might somehow be possible; they are rather what our practical use of reason exhibits to us as *possibilities that are to come to be* in virtue of *what ought to be*. A key function of hope, further, is its role in sustaining perseverance in one's moral effort. Hope that is validated by the practical use of reason is what enables human beings to persevere in pursuit of the proper vocation of the human species to be the juncture of nature and freedom.

Even though a hope validated in terms of the practical use of reason makes it possible to envision consequences that follow from what ought to be, Kant still leaves unspecified what he envisions to be the final concrete form that the ethical commonwealth will take, with the notable exception that it will assure perpetual peace:

Such is therefore the work of the good principle—unnoticed to human eye yet constantly advancing—in erecting a power and a kingdom for itself within the human race, in the form of a community according to the laws of virtue that proclaims the victory over evil and, under its dominion, assures the world of an eternal peace. (*Rel*, 6: 124/153)

The lack of further specification is not mere unwillingness on Kant's part to sketch some kind of utopian or eschatological possibility. In fact, with regard to the perpetual peace that he does specify, he makes it quite clear in later writings (most firmly in "Toward Perpetual Peace" and *The Metaphysics of Morals*) that this is neither utopian nor eschatological. It is a possibility that both can and must be made actual by the exercise of practical reason. Further specification, however, seems to be something that he cannot give, inasmuch as the final form of the human moral world can emerge only as the consequence of the totality of particular human conduct, of which only that of the past has taken definite shape.

This, however, seems to relegate the notion of an ethical commonwealth to the status of being an almost-empty abstraction or just a different image under which Kant represents an atemporal realm of moral relations. Yet Kant's intent in using this image seems to be to characterize the concrete task that the duty to promote the highest good places upon all human persons in their own particular circumstances. He affirms, moreover, that the task is precisely to make the invisible and atemporal moral world a public and visible one. The actual shape such public and visible exhibition of the moral world takes in the course of history is concretely determined by human activity (*Rel*, 6: 105–106/ 138–139). Yet a close reading of Book Three of *Religion* yields little in the way of a detailed picture of the concrete forms that human social relationships would take in an ethical commonwealth.

A clear illustration of the problem of making such matters of hope concrete and particular occurs at the very beginning of Kant's discussion of "the church" as the visible form that the ethical commonwealth takes in human history. In his account of the church Kant affirms that the power proper to the authority of the church ought to be noncoercive. This noncoercive power distinguishes the church's moral role in human culture and society from those played by other institutions, most notably the state. As Kant conceives of the church, it is an institution—perhaps the only institution—whose authority rests solely upon the power most proper to reason, viz., the noncoercive power to convince (*Rel*, 6: 98–100/133–134). The church makes the ethical commonwealth possible by establishing *a set of ordered social relationships and practices based on a noncoercive authoritative principle*. Although Kant is very clear about what the ordered social relationships and practices based on such a principle would *not* be like ("it has nothing in its principles that resembles a political constitution" [*Rel*, 6: 102/136]), he is less definite about what they would and should be like. His account resorts to an image of a household or family (*Hausgenossenschaft, Familie*) conceived according to an ideal principle of entirely voluntary association. How this principle functions to shape concrete forms of social practice and organization that make possible the ethical commonwealth, however, is far from clear. Kant's formal treatments of familial and household relationships (*MdS*, 6: 277–284/426–432; *AP*, 7: 303–311/166–173) seem to be of little help on this point. They certainly acknowledge that the voluntary character of the marriage contract forms the basis of familial and household relationships; yet their subsequent discussions of the internal dynamics of the relationships consequent upon that voluntary contract focus upon considerations of possession, right, and power. These are considerations that presuppose the possibility of the exercise of coercive power.

This particular discussion of the concrete form to be taken by the church in virtue of the noncoercive character of its social authority is important not only for its bearing upon the first problem facing Kant's efforts to specify the concrete effects that arise from the intelligible ordering that an ethical commonwealth is to give to human social relationships. It also has a bearing upon the problem that arises from Kant's analysis of radical evil. Kant's analysis first traces the root of evil back to a corruption of the self-governance of reason that has its origin in the exercise of our human freedom. While this shows how the structure of our human willing makes evil possible, it does not, as noted at the end of the preceding section, account for why human beings actually do evil. To account for this, Kant must locate the exercise of human willing *precisely in the context of our (necessary) human participation in society* (*Rel*, 6: 93–94/129–130; cf. *IAG*, 8: 20–22/15–16). As noted earlier, Kant sees evil taking root in us from the dynamics of unsociable sociability and this evil is radical because it enables us to corrupt the very social character of reason.

For Kant the problem of evil—both its origin and its overcoming—thus is one in which individual and social processes are inextricably linked. They are linked in such a way, moreover, that even if individuals one by one could successfully extirpate the evil by which they have disordered (and continue to disorder) their wills, this does not guarantee the extirpation of evil from the social dynamics of human life. The moral salvation of individual human beings, by itself, neither ensures nor constitutes the moral destiny of the human species. A merely additive combination of individuals—that is, one that lacks the form and dynamics of social relationship—who have the proper inner disposition to conform to the self-governance of reason would not be sufficient to attain the highest good in its social form. The inner effort of morally well-disposed individuals, no matter how many of them there may be, will not bring about the highest good in the absence of the forms of social relationship that exhibit the self-governance of reason.

Yet it is not any form of social relationship subject to the self-governance of reason that is called for. Those forms of social relationship that require that self-governance of reason be exercised in an *external* manner—that is, ones that allow coercive enforcement of such governance—will not be sufficient for the attainment of the highest good. Civil society, which, for Kant, is the prime instance of a social relationship subject to the self-governance of reason exercised externally, establishes only a juridical, not an ethical commonwealth. Even when this form of ordering social relationships is fully in accord with the external requirements of the self-governance of reason, it will not bring about the highest good in the absence of the form of social relationship that Kant called a *corpus mysticum* in the first *Critique* and describes in *Religion* as "a union of such [well disposed] persons into a whole toward that very end . . . in which and through the unity of which alone, the highest moral good can come to pass" (6: 97–98/133).

Kant thus maintains that even though progress toward the moral destiny of the human species might be signaled by the establishment of a just (even a fully just) political order, such external order in society does not by itself provide a guarantee that the ethical commonwealth has been, or will be, secured. The establishment of an external order of justice stands as a necessary element of the social dynamics that lead to an ethical commonwealth, but by itself is not and cannot be sufficient to bring it about definitively. This is so because the power and authority that the order of justice exercises over human conduct is coercive—a form of power and authority by which the self-governance of reason properly limits the external exercise of freedom, but which finally stands impotent in the face of radical evil. The exercise of coercive power cannot provide the most fundamental condition for the establishment of an ethical commonwealth. This condition is the extirpation the evil which is radical because it issues from the uncoerced depths of human freedom. Coercion stands impotent before these depths.

All this, I believe, suggests an important point about the way in which radical evil enables us to corrupt the self-governance of reason. The core of radical evil for Kant consists in our seeking to exempt ourselves, in the name of reason, from the self-governance of reason: We seek a special place for ourselves in the kingdom of ends, a realm in which by definition there are no special places. Radical evil enables us—ironically, through an exercise of our freedom—to believe that we can place ourselves beyond the self-governance of reason as it is exercised in its most fundamental social form. This is the self-governance of reason that arises from an uncoerced, mutual acknowledgment of the unique status and vocation we share with one another as fellow human beings—a recognition that frees us from self-induced illusions that we need a "special place." Because radical evil strikes at the very social form of the self-governance of reason it can be fully extirpated only through the establishment of an ethical commonwealth; that is, a social relationship in which the acknowledgment of our common humanity and common human vocation arises as a conviction to which we mutually and freely assent.

In the earlier phases of the critical project, and even before, Kant had certainly given consideration to the sources of human moral failure and misconduct. It is even possible to see, in the light of his extensive discussion in *Religion*, some places in which these earlier treatments anticipate features of his account of radical evil. Yet the full dimensions of radical evil and the consequences it has for Kant's critical enterprise do not emerge until most of the major elements of the critical project have been set forth. Kant himself does not provide any clear indication of what occasioned his turning to an explicit and extended discussion of evil at this point; one plausible suggestion is that the course of events taken by the French Revolution may lie behind this reconsideration of the possibilities for evil present in human wills. Whatever the reasons may be, the introduction of the notion of radical evil brings into bolder relief the social dimension of the project of critique precisely by the fundamental challenge it presents to the social character of reason. As I have suggested earlier, Kant's response to this challenge is only partly successful. It is to a closer examination of the social consequences of radical evil and Kant's response to the challenge these present to the very enterprise of critique that we now will turn.

CHAPTER FOUR

The Social Consequences of "Radical Evil"

In order to see the full dimensions of Kant's account of the social consequences of radical evil, it will be particularly useful to consider the way in which *Religion within the Boundaries of Mere Reason*, the text in which Kant introduces this concept, functions against the background of other philosophical and theological efforts to delimit the contours of human destiny. My reason for doing so, in the context of the larger interpretive framework that I have proposed for the critical project, is to provide at least a sketch of the position this work has frequently been taken to hold within the overall critical project and which my interpretation seeks to revise. According to this more or less standard interpretation, even though *Religion* represents Kant's mature systematic treatment of religion in accord with the principles of his critical project, it is a work that simply applies those principles to a particular form of human activity. It thus does not contain any significant advance in Kant's thinking on the matters that are central to the critical project.[1]

In contrast to that assessment, this chapter will present a case for taking *Religion* to mark a major development in Kant's thinking about the scope and function of the critical project. In particular, *Religion* provides an extensive and, on many counts, Kant's most explicit account of the social dimensions of the critical project. It does so precisely because it recognizes the radical evil of which human beings are capable as the most fundamental threat to that project in its social character. So the first section of this chapter will look at this text in its guise as a study of religion that has been taken to enshrine the reduction of religion to morality. In contrast to this still widely prevalent interpretation of Kant's text, I will indicate in the second section

67

how Kant's study of religion shows it to be, nonreductively, the human activity that serves as the principal locus for the exercise of the social self-governance of reason. I will next consider, in the third section, Kant's understanding of the threat that radical evil poses to the social self-governance of reason: Radical evil arises from reason so at war with itself that the attainment of human destiny is put at constant risk of foundering on the shoals of human social antagonism and division. This threat can be countered, in Kant's view, only by a moral commitment to work for perpetual peace—the project that, as chapter 5 will show, carries Kant's hope for the full embodiment of the social self-governance of reason.

Morality and Human Destiny: Against the Enlightenment Stream?

Concern for the final destiny of the human individual—or what a long-standing tradition has termed the "salvation" (or "damnation") of the "soul"—has frequently been understood as a central feature of Christian theology and practice. This effort to discern the possibilities that shape the final and definitive outcome of one's life has often, though not always, intersected with a concern about the moral quality of the life that each person lives and with the extent to which that moral quality has a bearing upon such destiny: Is the weal or the woe of that final state contingent upon the good or the ill that one has done in the life that precedes it?

Kant was thus by no means the first philosopher or religious thinker to insist that an adequate account of our final destiny as human beings requires that such destiny stand in close dependence upon the moral quality of our lives. Kant's insistence in this regard, moreover, is quite in keeping with a broad current of the criticism of religion to which many streams of Enlightenment thought contributed: To the extent that a body of religious belief and practice systematically fails to promote a good moral life among its adherents, this provides a good reason for doubting its claim to be a true religion worthy of acceptance by rational human beings. Conversely, to the extent that a body of religious belief and practice systematically promotes a good moral life among its adherents, this provides a good reason for at least seriously considering its claim to be a true religion.[2] In short, the capacity that the beliefs and practices of a particular religion have for the promotion of a good moral life provides at least a necessary condition for acceptance of that religion's claim to truth. On this point Kant's critical project is clearly consonant with the moral concerns that constituted one important current of the intellectual culture of the Enlightenment. The requirement that our human destiny stand in close dependence on the moral quality of our lives thus represents, for a thinker such as Kant, the stringency and the nobility of the moral standards to which humankind should hold itself bound: The only destiny worthy of an enlightened humanity is the one that emerges in consequence of lives lived in full accord with the demands of morality.

Considered as part of this larger stream of Enlightenment criticism of religion, Kant's principal contribution in *Religion* then seems to lie not in the originality of the basic connection he makes between morality and human destiny nor even in his strong insistence that morality serve as the fundament upon which such destiny rests. Kant's contribution lies, instead, in the way his thought crystallizes a characteristically "enlightened" perspective on the proper relation between religion and morality. Kant expresses this perspective most succinctly in the very first paragraph of the preface: "Hence on its own behalf morality in no way needs religion" (*Rel*, 6: 3/57). From this perspective, the moral—the good or the evil that we may do—is, in some important sense, more fundamental than the religious—the relation in which we may stand to that transcendent reality and source of being that bears, in Christian tradition, the name "God."[3] To the extent that morality could (and should) be conceived as autonomous from (revealed) religion, its relation to religion could (and should) also be conceived in terms that reverse what previously had been assumed as the proper order of priority, in which religion served as the (secure) foundation for morality. From this "enlightened" perspective morality now could be assigned a fundamental normative priority over religion in matters of everyday conduct as well as in the matter of human destiny. The moral is so fundamental that it determines the function of religion in the attainment of humanity's final destiny. Religion has a role in such attainment just to the extent that it actively serves to encourage human moral progress. From the assignment of normative priority to morality over religion, it is only a short step to religion's marginalization and eventual reductive elimination: As humanity moves closer to the destiny for which sound moral practice prepares it, religion will become increasingly peripheral as a distinctive human practice and will, instead, find itself being reductively purified or transformed into (a form of) morality.

The fact that Kant's perspective on the matter of human destiny emerges out of a pervasive moral concern that was shared by many Enlightenment thinkers makes it tempting to read the text of Kant's *Religion* as no more than a brief for the eventual reductive transformation of religion into morality: This reduction is the desirable, even necessary, outcome of a progressively deeper rooting of morality into the practices of human life.[4] My suspicion, however, is that such a reading is a bit *too* easy, even on its own terms, let alone in terms of the systematic function this text has in the larger critical enterprise. This reductive reading of *Religion* skims too lightly over some turbulent cross currents that occasionally eddy up to the surface of Kant's discussion.[5] These eddies indicate elements of Kant's thought that run counter to such a reductive program for religion. They carry his account of human moral destiny in directions that lead to conclusions that, in important respects, are by no means typical of what is often represented—particularly for purposes of polemics against modernity— as Enlightenment thought. There are crucial points at which Kant stands at a distance—and perhaps even at odds with—views and perspectives, especially on religion, which have often been considered an intrinsic part of those currents.

So even as I admit that much in the text of Kant's earlier writings, as well as in *Religion*, rides easily upon a current flowing toward a reductive elimination of religion in favor of morality, I would also argue that in *Religion* there are counter currents challenging such a reductive program on what have often been two of its basic presuppositions. One presupposition is that the matter of our human final destiny, just as the matter of our human moral life, has to do principally (or even solely) with the individual. The second is that the growth of human knowledge and of human control over the environing world of nature has moral progress as its inevitable concomitant or outcome.[6] In addition to having reservations about these presupposition, Kant is also alert to the drift that such a reductive current has toward eventual moral shipwreck. This drift, in fact, is a consequence of human over-reaching and overconfidence in the struggle against the evil that, in Kant's view, is inextirpably rooted in the human will in its exercise of that self-governance of reason we call freedom.

The Extirpation of Evil: A Social Task?

What is certainly correct in the standard reading of *Religion*, even in its more reductive forms, is that it manifests Kant's deep concern with the integrity and responsibility of the structure of individual moral agency. The irony of Kant's treatment of this in *Religion*, however, is that, as Gordon E. Michalson Jr.'s *Fallen Freedom* has argued, the analysis he offers when he pays explicit attention to the possibilities of human moral failure then creates problems for his earlier accounts of human moral agency. Michalson argues that Kant's account embeds the source of evil so deeply in the human will that it renders problematic the possibility that individual moral agents can, by dint of their own efforts, actually extricate themselves from it.[7] By so strongly stressing the extent to which the very exercise of freedom makes it possible for human agents to order their fundamental maxim for action to evil, Kant seems to leave little room for then reordering that maxim back to the good, even though such reordering is incumbent upon them. Put in the terminology of the *Groundwork*, radical evil seems to render it impossible for individuals to succeed in forming a good will by their own best efforts, despite the fact that this is the fundamental moral task our reason enjoins upon us.

The issues with which Kant struggles here bear strong affinity—and not accidentally—to those that were at stake in the classical disputes in Christian theology that arose in consequence of the Pelagian view that grace is not necessary either to enable persons to move out of sin or to lead a moral life: Human effort, unaided by divine or supernatural help, is sufficient in each case. Kant's earlier writings show Pelagian tendencies inasmuch as his stringent view of individual moral accountability leads him to deny the need for any kind of external help, such as "grace," to enable human beings to orient their wills toward good, a view rendered rather flatly in twentieth-century moral philosophy as the dictum "ought implies can." Yet the notion of radical evil goes against the grain of this Pelagian tendency in his earlier writings, perhaps because he had not previously seen the formation of a good will requiring, as its necessary first step, a *reorientation*, that is, a turn *away* from evil, as well as a turn *toward* good.[8] Within the context of an analysis of moral agency that has been altered by the introduction of the concept of radical evil, the formation of a good will now requires something more than individual human effort, perhaps even the operation of an analogue to grace, to make it possible for human beings to reorient their wills away from evil and toward good. As we shall see below, the need for such an analogue seems even more urgent once we articulate—perhaps more fully than Kant himself did—the social consequences of the notion of radical evil. Consideration of these consequences will lead Kant to articulate an understanding of religion as that which makes possible the social relationships necessary for human beings to exercise in full the social self-governance of reason. The appropriate way to see the emergence of this development is to follow the steps Kant takes in tracing the struggle between radical evil and the self-governance of reason.

In Books One and Two of *Religion*, Kant's treatment of radical evil had an almost exclusive focus upon the conflict between good and evil that takes place within the willing of individual human moral agents. He locates the ground of this conflict in the possibility that faces human moral agents with respect to the fundamental maxim informing each of their moral choices. Even as the very condition of possibility for moral choice is the recognition that one's willing stands under the unconditional imperative of universal law—and that this alone can serve as sufficient incentive in forming the maxim for one's choice—moral agents nonetheless remain free to form a maxim exempting themselves from the universal demands of that law. This freedom to exempt oneself is thus the "inextirpable" root of moral evil. As a further part of his account in these two books, Kant also argues that the very freedom of moral agents, which is the ground for radical evil, also provides them with the capacity to overcome it: "The human being must make or have made *himself* into whatever he is or should become in a moral sense, good or evil" (*Rel*, 6: 44/89). To the extent that both the ground of radical evil and the capacity to overcome it lies within the exercise of each moral agent's freedom, the controlling question of Kant's inquiry in *Religion*: "What then is the result of this right conduct of ours?" (*Rel*, 6: 5/58) seems answered. The moral destiny of each one of us lies within our own individual hands: No one but I can make me good or evil. As a result, establishing the claim that each human being has this inner capacity for overcoming radical evil, might seem sufficient to complete the task Kant set forth for himself in this work. It would leave little apparent room for arguing against a Pelagian reading. Yet Kant does not end his inquiry here—and the reasons for continuing the inquiry bear directly upon the threat that radical evil presents to the social self-governance of reason.

At the outset of Book Three, Kant indicates the conceivability of ending his account of radical evil at this point—were it not for the fact that, by virtue of their social relationships to one another, human beings must continually struggle to remain constant in their adherence to the universal demands of the moral law. In isolation from one another, human beings would be in circumstances that offer no occasion for the inner division of their wills to become manifest; in the absence of others, one is in no position to make an exception in one's own favor. All that changes *"as soon as he is among human beings . . . it suffices that they are there, that they surround him, and that they are human beings, and they will mutually corrupt each other's moral disposition and make one another evil"* (*Rel*, 6: 94/129). While Kant's observation here certainly deserves attention as an astute piece of moral psychology, it is more than that. Within Kant's overall argument in *Religion*, *it marks the point at which the struggle to overcome radical evil takes, of necessity, a public and social form.* The division interior to human willing cannot be fully overcome merely by the separate inner efforts of each moral agent: Unless a way can be found to establish "an enduring and ever expanding society, solely designed for the preservation of morality by counteracting evil with united forces—however much the individual human being might do to escape from the dominion of this evil, he would still be held in incessant danger of relapsing into it" (*Rel*, 6: 94/130).

The claims Kant makes here with respect to the social contexts that occasion the actualization of radical evil are open to a variety of interpretations. Although it is possible to take Kant's claims as affirming the pristine innocence—and, presumably, the (moral) preferability—of an asocial human condition, there are a variety of considerations, both internal and external to the text of *Religion*, which decisively count against this. The most crucial one internal to the text of *Religion* is Kant's quite clear insistence on the *sui generis* character of the "duty . . . of the human race toward itself"—a duty that concerns the "promotion of the highest good as a good common to all" and requires "a union of such [morally well disposed] persons into a whole toward that very end" (*Rel*, 6: 97/132–133). The good Kant identifies here is particularly significant for determining the extent to which the social context of human existence is an integral feature of Kant's accounts of radical evil and the highest good in relation to the project of critique. This is so because the social union that Kant describes here as constitutive of the ethical commonwealth is precisely that which fully and finally overcomes the social dividedness constitutive of the ethical state of nature in which human beings make actual their propensity to evil. The endpoint of the moral journey of humanity—which starts in the social dividedness that enables evil—is thus the moral union of persons in an ethical commonwealth constituted to overcome that dividedness.

Kant's coordination of the ethical commonwealth to the attainment of the highest good as a social goal pushes the boundaries of the religious question of salvation and damnation beyond a concern with the destiny of the individual.[9] It also pushes the boundaries of the moral question of individual responsibility that had been such a focus of his previous discussions. As we have already noted, Kant's accounts of moral life prior to *Religion* can be read with a Pelagian eye. Each of us must—and so each of us can—overcome evil entirely by individual effort, unaided by the "outside" assistance theology calls grace. In *Religion*, however, Kant's clear-eyed recognition of the limitations that our freely self-incurred evil subsequently places upon our power to escape its grasp tests such a Pelagian reading to its utmost. Although Kant does not unambiguously argue in a way that definitively fails this test, he does seem to open room for the operation of an analogue to grace to effect the "revolution in one's cast in mind" that the conversion from evil to good requires.[10]

With regard to the moral destiny of the human species, however, Kant's account is less amenable to a Pelagian reading. Far from forbidding recourse to outside help in order to overcome evil, it seems, instead, to require it. While Kant makes it clear that such destiny is in our own hands—for otherwise it would not be a destiny worthy of our freedom—he also does not believe that its attainment is possible without the assistance of what he variously terms God, nature, providence, or history. There are, to be sure, elements of Kant's discussion of the establishment of the ethical commonwealth in *Religion* that seem to affirm that full attainment of the human destiny requires only the unanimous inner conformity by all moral agents to the dictates of the moral law—an additive or collective Pelagianism, if you will. Yet these are interwoven with other elements which affirm that even such unanimity of inner conformity to the moral law by individuals taken singly cannot be relied upon to bring about the full attainment of an ethical commonwealth precisely as a social goal; this requires as well some form of "outside" assistance in the form of providence or God's moral governance (*Rel*, 6: 97–98/132–133; 100–101/135; 121–124/ 151–153). This may strike us as surprising. In view of Kant's apparent reluctance to abandon a Pelagian account of the overcoming of evil on the part of individuals, we should plausibly expect him to hold that the definitive and final overcoming of evil in human society and culture, represented in the image of an ethical commonwealth, comes about simply in consequence of everyone's successfully forming and sustaining a good will individually.

It is not mere happenstance that Kant makes this acknowledgment of an apparent need for some form of grace in connection with his affirmation that final success in the struggle with radical evil requires an explicit intent to social union on the part of moral agents. The conjunction of these two elements indicates that, in pursuing the question of radical evil into its social roots and social form, Kant has had to reconceptualize both the religious question of salvation and the moral question of responsibility in the light of the social form of the highest good. This reconceptualization gives reason enough to think that Kant is not simply proposing in *Religion* the reductive elimination of religion in favor of morality. If *Religion* is not a brief for the transformation of religion into morality without remainder, what then is it? How would a nonreductive reading of this text then illuminate its position with respect to Kant's larger critical project? To answer these questions, we need to place the reconceptualization of both religion and morality that Kant proposes in the context of his effort to bring the project of critique to bear upon the issue of the relationship between nature and freedom. In particular, we need to ask what bearing the answer that Kant gives—the ethical commonwealth—to the principal question addressed in *Religion*—"What is to result from this right conduct of ours?"—has upon the relationship between nature and freedom. How does a social union of the kind envisioned in the ethical commonwealth—a social union so constituted to overcome definitively the social dividedness of the ethical state of nature and thus to vanquish radical evil—function in the fulfilment of the human vocation to be the unique juncture of nature and freedom?

Part of the answer to this lies in the way that Kant now construes religion as having a social task that is distinct from, even while being complementary to, that of morality. Book Three of *Religion* is not only a locus for a reconsideration of grace and for an affirmation of the need for an explicit intent for social union, it is the locus in which Kant identifies the concrete historical form of the ethical commonwealth with the church, which he describes as a "free, universal and enduring union of hearts" (*Rel* 6: 102/136). In so doing, Kant thus presents religion—or more accurately, the community that authentic religion forms—as the locus in which human agents are enabled to give concrete form to the unitive intent that the social self-governance of reason needs in order to function publicly in the manner most fitting to humanity's unique vocation, that is, noncoercively. In Kant's account of the church, the *manner* in which the self-governance of reason is exercised is crucial. It constitutes the central point of his "ecclesiology": The human social union that alone has the power to extirpate radical evil can be brought into being by the self-governance of reason only if it is done so noncoercively. Kant conceives of the church as an institution—the only institution—whose authority rests solely upon the power proper to the full social self-governance of reason, that is, the noncoercive power of free and open argumentative exchange among persons who hold one another in full mutual respect.

Kant's depiction of the church as the locus of the social self-governance of reason could quite understandably be taken to be so far removed from orthodox Christian ecclesiology that it lends further credence to the view that *Religion* is nothing more than a reductionist treatise to promote a religion of reason that is, simply and without remainder, morality. Yet, as the next two sections will indicate, a closer examination of Kant's account of the ethical commonwealth's role in the attainment of human destiny suggests otherwise. The image of the ethical commonwealth has more than accidental affinity with a long-standing stream of Christian thinking about the social character of the church. This way of thinking arises from the Hebrew prophetic vision of a restored and renewed community expressed in the latter portions of the book of Isaiah and then flows through Christian theologians such as Augustine. It is a tradition that envisions the community constituted as a people of God to be the locus for a new form of human social relationship. Between this earlier theological vision and Kant's account of the church as the ethical commonwealth there is a crucial point of connection that exhibits the radically transformative power of the new social relationships each envisions. In the case of the prophetic vision, the exhibition of this power gives witness to the salvific action and providence of God; in the case of the ethical commonwealth, the exhibition of this power manifests the full reach of the social self-governance of reason. In both cases, however, what is exhibited as the concrete manifestation of this transformative power is the same: The establishment of enduring peace amid the vast diversity and seemingly intractable contention of humankind.

War: The Social Form of Radical Evil

In this section I offer a further explication and justification of the claim just enunciated. These are needed to complete that case proposed in this chapter about the significant role that *Religion within the Boundaries of Mere Reason* plays in the development of Kant's critical project. It is my contention that Kant's presentation of the ethical commonwealth in Book Three of *Religion* shows the church to be the human community that most fully exhibits the social self-governance of reason. It does so in virtue of the form of social relationship in which its members stand to one another, a form of social relationship that is brought about noncoercively through a common and explicit intent to social union. This form of social relationship—without which there can be no definitive establishment of lasting peace among the various peoples that constitute humanity—is itself what I will call, in parallel to the social consequences of radical evil that it seeks to counter, the "social consequence" of critique. The ethical commonwealth, which brings the self-governance of reason to bear upon the formation and operation of human social practices, is thus itself an outcome of the critical project. Though one can in retrospect see preliminary adumbrations of this in certain passages of the first *Critique*, an explicit and more fully detailed articulation of it does not emerge until *Religion* and, somewhat later, "Toward Perpetual Peace."

Put in terms of Kant's writings in the 1790s, this claim proposes a close conceptual link between Book Three of *Religion* and the 1795 essay "Toward Perpetual Peace" and argues for the importance of that link within Kant's critical project. The basis for this claim rests upon a number of key similarities between Kant's account, in Book Three of *Religion*, of the role of an ethical commonwealth in overcoming radical evil and his proposal in "Toward Perpetual Peace" (reiterated in *The Metaphysics of Morals*) for an international order to secure an enduring peace among nations. Put in terms of Kant's earlier writings and the larger interpretive framework I have been elaborating for the nature and scope the critical project, this claim focuses upon his most fully articulated account of the principal role that human beings are morally bound to take in fulfilling humanity's vocation to be the juncture of nature and freedom. Through the social dynamics of the ethical commonwealth, human beings bring about the possibility for the definitive establishment of peace. In doing this, they exhibit the social self-governance of reason in which the causal workings of nature and the exercise of human freedom are effectively brought into juncture.

In order to show how this claim is articulated within Kant's texts, we have to return to a consideration of his account of how radical evil arises out of the necessary social conditions of human existence. The central focus of this consideration will be on how the radical evil that arises from reason at war with itself puts the attainment of human destiny at risk of foundering on the shoals of human social antagonism. Even though Kant had previously pointed out this social antagonism within the dynamics of human moral life as an unsociable sociability, his treatment of it in *Religion* in connection with the origin of radical evil makes it more evident than before that the threat posed by radical evil is to the very self-governance of reason.

In the essay "Idea for a Universal History with a Cosmopolitan Intent" Kant had described humanity's unsociable sociability as follows:

> *The means employed by nature to bring about the development of all the capacities of men is their antagonism in society, so far as this is, in the end, the cause of a lawful order among men.*
>
> By "antagonism" I mean the *unsocial sociability* of men, i.e., their propensity to enter into society, bound together with a mutual opposition which constantly threatens to break up the society. (*IAG*, 8: 20/15)

Unsociable sociability can rightly be considered Kant's way of indicating the deeply ambivalent moral function of human social relationships. This ambiguity affects the human moral situation with respect to the conflicts that both individual human moral agents and human social institutions face in their efforts to follow the internal and external demands of the moral law in an appropriate manner. Unsociable sociability expresses Kant's quite shrewd insight into an aspect of the human psyche that manifests itself in the dynamics both of personal conduct and of social relationships: Even as we take one another as potential friends, we also measure one another as potential rivals. As a result we need to organize the structures of personal and social life to enable us both to cooperate and to compete with one another. As nicely put as Kant's expression of this insight may be, unsociable sociability—understood principally as an aspect of human moral psychology—may not immediately seem to carry major conceptual weight in the development of the project of critique and its function with respect to the relationship between nature and freedom.

When Kant depicts unsociable sociability at the beginning of Book Three in *Religion*, however, it is more than just a way to characterize the moral ambivalence of human social relationships. In this context, unsociable sociability is an integral element in the completion of his account of radical evil in human life. It functions as the condition for actualizing the human propensity to evil (*Rel*, 6: 93–95/129–130). The social interaction that is a necessary feature of human existence gives rise to the emulation, comparison and competition with others from which arises the abiding temptation to the Kantian form of original sin: to make an exception for oneself in the face of the universal demand of the moral law.[11] Just as a fundamental tension within the rational willing of individual human beings lies at the root of each agent's capacity for evil—the claim Kant makes in Books One and Two—so also does a fundamental tension within our relationship to one another as human beings lie at the root of our capacity to thwart one another's rational willing within the context of our social interaction—a key claim that I take Kant to make in Book Three. Both tensions, so Kant's argument runs, have their sources in the way in which we each use our freedom as finite rational agents on our own individual behalf. In consequence, both tensions manifest that fundamental inversion of incentives to act that Kant terms radical evil.

Human social dividedness thus plays a key role in Kant's account of the origin of radical evil. The exigence of the social conditions in which human beings must live and act triggers the comparisons with others on which we then seek to justify maxims that would exempt us from the universal requirements of the moral law. It is of no little importance, in my judgment, that Kant finds it appropriate to portray the radical evil that manifests itself even in the inner division of human willing under images of conflict, combat, and warfare. The opening words of Book Three, which summarize the claims for which Kant had argued in Book One and Two, offer just one sample: "The battle that every morally well-disposed human being must withstand in this life, under the leadership of the good principle, against the attacks of the evil principle, can procure him, however hard he tries, no greater advantage than freedom from the *dominion* of evil" (*Rel*, 6: 93/129). Kant continues to use similar images in Book Three's presentation of the establishment of an ethical commonwealth as the social form through which victory in the struggle with radical evil will finally be attained.

What is notable about his presentation here, however, is not just his continued employment of the images of struggle and combat. Nor is it even the quite important fact that these images echo aspects of his discussions of an international political order both prior to (e.g., "Idea for a Universal History with a Cosmopolitan Intent") and after *Religion* (e.g., "Toward Perpetual Peace"). What is most notable for our discussion of the social self-governance of reason is that these images clearly echo those used in the first *Critique*—for example, in the section "The discipline of pure reason with regard to its polemical use" and, with more obvious irony, in the "Preface" to the second edition—*to describe the inner conflict within reason itself* that gives rise to the necessity of the project of critique. Though Kant does not explicitly make the identification, the repeated use of these images suggests not only that war is the fundamental way in which radical evil manifests itself in the social dynamics of human life but that even within reason itself radical evil exhibits itself as a conflict over the social form of our human existence: How are we to deal with our likeness and our difference with one another? Radical evil, in all its forms arises in response to a condition of social dividedness. This dividedness, however, is not merely the separation of mutual isolation but the conflict that arises from comparison, emulation, and competition. This conflict is made possible precisely by the recognition both of likeness and difference in our fellow human beings, either of which can serve as a basis either for associative bonds or for mutual antagonism: Though like is drawn to like, our *Doppelgänger* is our most feared rival; though the otherness of the other is a threat, we find ourselves unerringly drawn to the otherness of what we are not. Our unsociable sociability runs deep, deep enough to lie at the heart of the dynamics not only of our human moral, social, cultural, and political life, but at the heart of reason itself.

The resonances among these texts are not accidental. The ethical commonwealth of *Religion* and the federation of nations of "Toward Perpetual Peace"—and behind them both, the project of critique—all have the same aim: To put a final end to human warfare in all its forms, internal and external. The ethical commonwealth is to provide the conditions under which the relations that human beings have to one another may no longer serve as a basis on which one might claim an exemption for oneself from the requirements of moral law—and thus set one self, at least internally, at war with one's fellow moral agents. The federation of nations is to provide the conditions under which the relations of nations to one another may no longer serve as a basis on which one nation may claim an exemption for itself from the principles of international law that Kant articulates as the articles—both "preliminary" and "definitive"—for perpetual peace.[12] The project of critique is to put an end to reason's own inner war with itself. In Kant's estimation, moreover, this conflict of reason within itself is the most fundamental of all inasmuch as it propels and sustains the other two.

Kant's account of the "war" in all three cases contains what I consider to be a clear marker of the fact that the inner war of reason with itself is the most fundamental one. In all of these wars freedom, that is, reason in its practical use, plays an absolutely indispensable role for ending hostilities and bringing about peace. Freedom can play this role, moreover, only if it functions in the manner proper to the human vocation as the juncture of nature and freedom: As the noncoerced and noncoercive social exercise of reason's own self-governance. Kant thus indicates that human freedom will play a definitive role in bringing about both the ethical commonwealth and the international federation for perpetual peace only to the extent that it is exercised in the form of *noncoercive* action with respect to the freedom of other moral agents. Even though human beings can, indeed must, be compelled to leave the juridical state of nature to enter into civil society, they cannot be similarly compelled to leave the ethical state of nature to enter the ethical commonwealth; they can do so only as an uncoerced exercise of their own freedom (*Rel*, 6: 96/131). In the same way, nations cannot be compelled into the international federation for perpetual peace; even though "the great artist Nature" provides the conditions for the formation of such a federation—most notably through a war-weariness from which nations and their citizens finally perceive the economic ruin that war eventually brings even to the victors (*EF*, 8: 350/323–324)—the definitive step into such a federation must ultimately be uncoerced (*EF*, 8: 355–357/327–328). In this latter discussion, moreover, Kant makes clear allusion to his depiction in *Religion* of the human struggle to overcome radical evil: "This homage that every state pays the concept of right (at least verbally) nevertheless proves that there is to be found in the human being a still greater, though at present dormant, moral predisposition to eventually become master of the evil principle within him (which he cannot deny) and also to hope for this from others" (*EF*, 8: 355/326–327).

Although this remark indicates that Kant sees a close connection between the conditions for attaining peace among nations and the overcoming of radical evil on the part of agents in an ethical commonwealth, it does not fully adumbrate a connection back to the internal conflict within reason that gives rise to the project of critique. To see this, we must first go back to Kant's discussion of "The discipline of pure reason in its polemical use" in the first *Critique* and then assess its bearing upon his later treatments of unsociable sociability, radical evil, and international conflict. Though tucked away within the undeservedly neglected second part of the *Critique of Pure Reason*,[13] Kant's discussion of what he terms the "polemical use" of reason anticipates a number of the points he will finally and more fully elaborate in *Religion* and the essays on politics and culture. When read in the light of these later discussions, this section of the first *Critique* suggests that behind both the inner moral conflict over radical evil and the wars that arise among nations is a conflict deeply rooted within the dynamics of human reason itself. This conflict arises when reason overreaches itself; it is the failure of reason to govern itself. As in his later discussions in the works explicitly focused on moral reason, this failure originates in the self-deception of making an exception in one's own favor. In this case, reason seeks to exempt its speculative ambitions from the social dynamics appropriate to the assessment of such theoretical claims.

Kant first enunciates a principle with regard to the patterns of deceit and self-deceit in human conduct generally:

> There is a certain dishonesty in human nature, which yet in the end, like everything else that comes from nature, must contain a tendency to good purposes, namely an inclination to

hide its true dispositions and to make a show of certain assumed ones that are held to be good and creditable. . . . (A 747–778/B 775–776)

He then proceeds to note the presence of this pattern within the operation of human reason:

I am sorry to perceive the very same dishonesty, misrepresentation and hypocrisy even in the utterances of the speculative way of thinking, where human beings have far fewer hindrances to and no advantage at all in forthrightly confessing their thoughts openly and unreservedly. For what can be more disadvantageous to insight than falsely communicating even mere thoughts, than concealing doubts which we feel about our own assertions, or giving a semblance of self-evidence to grounds of proof which do not satisfy ourselves? (A 748–749/B 776–777)

This discussion almost immediately precedes the previously noted analogies in which Kant likens critique to a court of justice and to the establishment of civil society from out of a "state of nature." It offers a brief glimpse of his views about the morally educative role of nature and culture that Kant more fully elaborates in his writings on history and lectures on anthropology—views that are not irrelevant to the larger question of the moral and transformative trajectory of critique. However, what makes this discussion of the conflict of reason within itself specifically pertinent to Kant's treatment of radical evil and perpetual peace is that he here casts the resolution of this conflict within reason itself as one that issues from a social process:

To this freedom, then, there also belongs the freedom to exhibit the thoughts and doubts which one cannot resolve oneself for public judgment without thereupon being decried as a malcontent and a dangerous citizen. This lies already in the original right of human reason, which recognizes no other judge than universal human reason itself, in which everyone has a voice; and since all improvement of which our condition is capable must come from this, such a right is holy, and must not be curtailed. (A 752/B 780)

Reason can thus discipline itself to proper self-governance only through free, uncoerced submission to open and public testing, the process that Kant later calls the public use of reason. In the absence of such a free and uncoerced exchange, however, there is the risk that a dynamic of violent combat will be taken to be the appropriate process for resolving the inner conflict that sets reason at odds with itself.

Just as it is possible to read the account of the ethical commonwealth in *Religion* in terms of the cultivation of a purely inner moral disposition, this discussion from the first *Critque* could be read as pertaining merely to a form of intellectual "combat" that has little or no bearing on the external order of human society. Such a reading might be supported by the fact that even as this passage adumbrates notions that Kant later articulates as radical evil, the public use of reason, and unsociable sociability, he does not himself fully and explicitly connect these later notions back to this earlier treatment of the inner conflict within reason. In fact, a notable mark of this earlier discussion is that Kant, in addition to the analogies that liken critique to a court of justice and to the dynamic that brings about the establishment of civil order within reason, also likens critique to the perspective of the spectator at a gladiatorial combat—though a combat that the perspective of critique allows one to watch with equanimity because it is ultimately a play of shadows:

> Thus instead of charging in with a sword, you should instead watch this conflict peaceably from the safe seat of critique, a conflict which must be exhausting for the combatants but entertaining for you, with an outcome that will certainly be bloodless and advantageous for your insight. (A 747/B 775)

Kant's use of this image suggests a tension within his own account with respect to precise character of the role that critique will play in social dynamics that lead to the resolution of these various conflicts. Even as the development we have been tracing moves in the direction of giving critique an active role in forming the dynamics of the social relationships that are appropriate to humanity's vocation, Kant will also present critique, as he does here and, even more notably, in the final essay in *The Conflict of the Faculties*, as a view from the sideline of history.[14]

Over against this view in which critique sits detached from engagement in human history, however, stand the parallels that Kant explicitly makes between the conditions that require human beings to work for the establishment of a federation of nations and the conditions that require them to work as well for the establishment of an ethical commonwealth. These parallels argue against a reading that keeps the discipline of critique aloof from engagement with the concrete dynamics of human history.[15] In both cases the radical evil of exempting ourselves from the requirements of universal moral law puts us in nothing less than a state of war. In the case of the inner conflict that arises in the speculative use of reason, humanity also runs at least the risk of civil strife—Kant's images here suggest this is more than a conflict between nations—even though it ultimately proves to be, under the clear-sighted judgment of critique, a mere sham combat, an illusion induced by the pretensions reason has about the scope of its speculative use. In all these cases, however, the image of armed combat, real or symbolic, clearly captures the kind of risk that Kant thinks humanity runs when it refuses to discipline reason to its own proper self-governance. War thus may be not only radical evil in its social form, it may very well be the core of the moral corruption that Kant sees human beings ever prone to inflict upon one another. Thus, before passing final judgment on the extent to which the opposition that critique presents to radical evil is that of a purely inner discipline of human dispositions or one that also requires concrete embodiment in a public, social form, it will be important to examine one proposal that Kant makes that clearly is directed to the external ordering of human social dynamics through the exercise of the self-governance of reason: His proposal for the elimination of war among nations and the moral commitment to work for perpetual peace that it entails on the part of all human persons.

CHAPTER FIVE

The Social Authority of Reason:
The Ethical Commonwealth
and the Project of Perpetual Peace

> Such is therefore the work of the good principle—unnoticed to human
> eye yet constantly advancing—in erecting a power and a kingdom for
> itself within the human race, in the form of a community according to
> the laws of virtue that proclaims the victory over evil and, under its
> dominion, assures the world of an eternal peace (*Rel*, 6: 124/153).

A Commonwealth of Virtue: Guarantee of Perpetual Peace?

The preceding chapter presented a case for taking Kant's treatment of the ethical commonwealth in *Religion within the Boundaries
of Mere Reason* to be an explicit effort to show how the social self-
governance of reason is to be brought to bear upon human social
relationships. A key part of that case was built upon the role that Kant
gives the ethical commonwealth in the human species' struggle with
radical evil: Radical evil will be fully extirpated only by the definitive
establishment of the form of social relationship among moral agents
that Kant names the ethical commonwealth. Kant assigns this role to
the ethical commonwealth because he holds that the simple addition
of the sum total of the efforts of individual moral agents to banish
radical evil from the inner working of their wills is not sufficient for
the task. Even though radical evil consists in an inversion of the maxims
of individual agents, such that one's supreme maxim allows one to
exempt oneself from the universal requirement of moral law, a reversal

of each individual's maxims back to a proper order of adherence to moral law is a necessary, but not a uniquely sufficient condition for the elimination of radical evil. To overcome radical evil fully moral agents must do so in terms of an explicit intent of social union. This intent consists in the willingness to enter into relations with one another that stand under the social self-governance of reason.

There is need for this social intent in the extirpation of radical evil because, even though the structure of each individual's human willing makes it possible, radical evil becomes actual only in virtue of the human social dynamic that Kant terms unsociable sociability. This indicates that radical evil itself is, in a fundamental sense, social. It arises as a corruption of the social self-governance of reason wherein one makes an exception in one's own favor from what the governance of reason requires of all. As a corruption of the social self-governance of reason, radical evil can then only be overcome socially. This will be accomplished through an effective intent to the form of social union—an ethical commonwealth—that will enable human beings to exercise with one another the full social self-governance of reason. In so doing, the human species is thereby enabled to attain the highest good, which, according to Kant, is the hoped for answer to the main question posed in *Religion*: What is to result from our right conduct? Kant depicts the securing of this intent to social union in his exposition of the ethical commonwealth as the church—the commonwealth of virtue that, as I shall argue in this chapter, has a major role to play in bringing about perpetual peace.

Chapter 4 also claimed that this aspect of *Religion* provides an important further elaboration on Kant's part of the scope of the critical project. In particular, the ethical commonwealth represents an effort to specify the bearing the critical project has upon the concrete shape of human life in society. This case, however, cannot be made by reference only to the text of *Religion*. It requires us to place Kant's treatment of the ethical commonwealth in a context provided by a range of his other discussions of the dynamics of human social existence, most notably those that treat unsociable sociability and the public use of reason, the latter a topic that Kant discusses as early as the first *Critique* as part of his treatment of "the polemical use of reason."

Among these treatments, his 1795 essay "Toward Perpetual Peace" provides a particularly significant point of reference; first of all, by key parallels it exhibits to the discussion of the ethical com-

monwealth in Book Three of *Religion* and, second, by the problems
that it raises with respect to the adequacy of the account that Kant
now seems to be proposing for the function of the critical project in
the attainment of human destiny. Kant's proposal for perpetual peace
brings to the fore questions about the extent to which it is possible
to specifically identify, from the discipline that critique requires of
human reason for its inner self-governance, the concrete forms of
social relationship and practice that will be most effective in securing the human destiny to which we are called by our vocation as the
unique juncture of nature and freedom. These questions arise because Kant seems to provide two conflicting scenarios for the emergence of perpetual peace. He affirms, in Book Three of *Religion*, that
the establishment of the social self-governance of reason in the form
of a commonwealth of virtue is necessary for securing perpetual
peace. A precondition for perpetual peace is that human beings must
first establish, through an uncoerced exercise of the social self-governance of reason, specific forms of relationship that exhibit an explicit
intent to social union. Yet he then affirms in the essay "Toward Perpetual Peace" that the causal mechanism of nature will be the instrument for securing this concrete element of human destiny. Perpetual
peace will come about through the workings of the purposes of nature
that carry humanity along willy-nilly and do not wait for humanity to
form an uncoerced intent to social union but bring about the social
relations requisite for the establishment of perpetual peace though "the
mechanism of human inclinations" (*EF*, 8: 368/337).

An examination of this tension within Kant's account is of particular importance for the general interpretive thesis I have proposed
for the critical project, since the project of perpetual peace represents
the most concrete specification that Kant gives of what human beings
are required to do in virtue of their vocation as the juncture of nature
and freedom. This examination is also important for the second part of
this work, which will turn from the question of how to understand
Kant's critical project to the question of what import that project has
for us two centuries later. It is important because both the ethical
commonwealth and the project of perpetual peace represent Kant's most
mature efforts to articulate the social authority of the self-governance of
reason. As the remainder of this chapter will indicate, his efforts on both
counts are only partially successful, leaving in our hands, if we are
willing, the task of continuing the effort, first, to articulate the social

authority of reason and, second, to bring its governance to bear on the forms and the dynamics of human social relationships.

The following section will thus propose a way to resolve this tension within Kant's account of perpetual peace by locating it within the primary focus of the critical project on the vocation of humanity as the juncture of nature and freedom. The tension arises in virtue of the two irreducibly different ways—the theoretical and the practical— that the use of reason provides to human beings for rendering intelligible their dealings with the environing world, including their dealings with one another. From the perspective of the theoretical use of reason, the attainment of perpetual peace is intelligible only as the outcome of the causal determination of nature as it applies to the course of human events in history. From the perspective of the practical use of reason, however, the attainment of perpetual peace is intelligible only as the outcome of the exercise of human freedom: In the absence of an explicit human intent to the social union that enables the full exercise of the social self-governance of reason, the only perpetual peace that humanity will be able to attain is that of the graveyard.

Even though this tension in Kant's account can be resolved by noting that it arises in virtue of the two uses of reason—or, in Kant's technical language, that it arises as an antinomy of reason—this does not settle a more fundamental problem within his treatment of the social authority of reason. Accounting for this tension in terms of an antinomy makes it possible to take perpetual peace as a necessary object of the practical exercise of reason: We may validly hope that it will issue from the proper use of our moral freedom. It does not, however, sufficiently specify the forms or the dynamics of the human social relationships by which the human species concretely moves toward this goal. Put in terms of a concept that will play a major role in the second part of this work, resolving this tension does not provide a positive, concrete account of the social authority of reason. The third section of this chapter will thus look at what can be taken to be Kant's efforts to provide such a further specification: His account of the church as a concrete embodiment of an ethical commonwealth in terms of the noncoercive exercise of the social authority of reason. In this particular effort, Kant has only limited success because he is unable to specify in fully concrete terms how this noncoercive social authority functions in the governance of human social relationships. However, when this account of the noncoercive character of the social authority of reason is placed in the context of two concepts drawn from Kant's other efforts to articulate the social authority of reason—the public use of reason and the cosmopolitan perspective—greater prospects for concrete specification open up. The last two sections of this chapter will identify these prospects even while showing that Kant did not himself fully articulate them. As a result, even though these prospects each delimit key features of the social authority of reason, they still leave us with what is, at best, an incomplete account.

As the second part of this work will then argue, there are important lessons that we can—and indeed must—learn both from Kant's successes and from his failures in articulating the social authority of reason. The most important lesson, which will be the focus of chapter 6, is that the task of articulating the social authority of reason remains as urgent a task at the start of the twenty-first century as it was at the end of the eighteenth. Within his own context Kant was able to identify a number of the essential features that mark the proper exercise of the social authority of reason of which the most pertinent for us are, first, that it is noncoercive in character and, second, that it most properly functions within the context of an intent to social union. At the same time, Kant was unable to specify—with four notable and interrelated exceptions, that is, the public use of reason, the cosmopolitan perspective, the church as the ethical commonwealth, and the project of perpetual peace—the concrete forms of human social relationship in which the social authority of reason can be most fully exercised. Even the forms that he does specify are not fully articulated with respect to their concrete bearing upon the dynamics of human social existence. To put this point in terminology akin to his, he offers only the barest outline of how citizens of the ethical commonwealth are concretely to exercise the self-governance of reason with and toward one another. As chapter 7 will argue, however, even this bare outline can prove quite helpful for the efforts we need to make today not simply to articulate the social authority of reason but to enable it to take effective hold in the dynamics of contemporary society and culture.

Nature, Moral Progress, and the Antinomy of Perpetual Peace

An observation by Howard Williams on the relationship between *Religion* and "Toward Perpetual Peace" offers a useful point from which to start the examination of the tension between Kant's account of the ethical commonwealth and his proposal for perpetual peace:

> . . . at the international level Kant has unavoidably to look to the moral improvement of mankind as the only possible element that can ultimately ensure peace.
> The aim of perpetual peace cannot be achieved by political and legal means alone, so the success of Kant's plan for perpetual peace depends upon the moral progress of man. Political and moral progress converge therefore on the same goal which Kant outlines most fully in his essay *Religion within the limits of Reason Alone . . .*[1]

Williams is not the only commentator who has noted a connection between the moral world that Kant envisions in his exposition of an ethical commonwealth and the political order he encourages in his proposal for perpetual peace.[2] His remarks are particularly helpful, however, because they articulate a key point at which that connection becomes problematic, that is, the extent to which "the success of Kant's plan for perpetual peace depends upon the moral progress of man." Though that certainly seems to be Kant's view in the passage from *Religion* that stands at the head of this chapter, there are writings both before and after *Religion* in which Kant indicates with equal clarity that moral improvement is not so much the *instrument* for securing international peace but rather one of its important *consequences*. From "Idea for a Universal History with a Cosmopolitan Intent" (1784) down to *The Conflict of the Faculties* (1798), Kant consistently maintains that "providence" or "nature," working through strife, self-interest, and human inclinations, will ultimately secure world peace: ". . . nature itself *does* it, whether we will it or not (*fata volentem ducunt, nolentem trahunt*)" (*EF*, 8: 365/335; cf. *TP*, 8: 313/309). Achievement of peace among nations, "which is the halfway mark in the development of mankind" (*IAG*, 8: 26/21), then provides the conditions for definitive moral improvement.[3]

The relationship that Kant also enunciates in these writings between the moral and the civil realms in the establishment and maintenance of a national political order seems to confirm the view that he takes moral improvement to be a consequence, rather an instrument, of international peace. The establishment of a civil order of law does not depend on the moral realm, that is, the moral intentions or character of those who found it ("The problem of establishing a state, no matter how hard it may sound, is *soluble* even for a nation of devils" [*EF*, 8: 366/335]). What holds for a national political order also holds for international political order. Just as the self-interest of individuals is sufficient to motivate leaving the "state of nature," so too the self-interest of nations will be (eventually) sufficient to motivate leaving the international state of nature:

> Just as omnilateral violence and the need arising from it must finally bring a people to decide to subject itself to the coercion that reason itself prescribes to them as means, namely to public law, and to enter into a *civil constitution*, so too must the need arising from the constant wars by which states in turn try to encroach upon or subjugate one another at last bring them, even against their will, to enter into a *cosmopolitan constitution*. (*TP*, 8: 310/307)

Against the background of these other texts, understanding Kant's claim in *Religion* to be "that the moral improvement of mankind [is] the only possible element that can ultimately ensure peace" seems to make it quite contrary to the position consistently enunciated in his essays on politics and history. The fact that Kant does not even mention an ethical commonwealth in "Toward Perpetual Peace" seems also to lend support to the view that this claim is an anomaly. The later essay seems expressly to *exclude* pinning hope for world peace on the moral improvement represented by an ethical commonwealth. The guarantee for perpetual peace comes not from the establishment of a commonwealth of virtue but through something quite contrary—"the mechanism of human inclinations." "The spirit of trade" and "financial power" will apparently provide irresistible incentives for nations "to promote honorable peace" (*EF*, 8: 368/336)—incentives that Kant surely did not hold to be the *moral* one that alone is capable of bringing about the social relationships characteristic of an ethical commonwealth. We might thus conclude that the hope expressed in the claim from *Religion* that a "commonwealth of laws under virtue" will "assure the world of perpetual peace" is an aberrant moment in Kant's thought about the relationship between the inner moral world and the outer world of social and political dynamics in humanity's effort to attain the highest good and to extirpate radical evil.[4]

There are, nonetheless, good reasons for rejecting this conclusion and for affirming, on the contrary, that Kant's view in *Religion* that perpetual peace is contingent upon moral progress is consistent with the apparently contrary view in his other writings that full human moral progress requires the prior achievement of political progress. These reasons arise, moreover, from the very structure of the project of critique in its efforts to resolve the issue of the relationship between nature and freedom. The critical project arises in virtue of the unique position in which human beings find themselves in the cosmos. The reason with which human beings have been endowed by nature has a dynamism to comprehensive totality: To provide an account that will render fully intelligible the conditions of human existence. As the juncture of nature and freedom, however, human beings find that the dynamism of their reason provides two irreducibly different ways of rendering the conditions of their existence intelligible in such a comprehensive fashion: The theoretical and the practical. The first way provides an account in terms of the causally determined operations of nature; the second provides an account in terms of the exercise of moral freedom. Antinomies—opposition that appears to make the accounts we give in virtue of each use of reason irreconcilable, such that we must opt for one in preference to the other—arise and seem unresolvable, so long as we fail to attribute each account to the particular use of reason that generates it.

Kant does not structure his exposition of the tension within his account of perpetual peace as a formal antinomy such as the ones found in each of the three *Critiques* as well as in *Religion within the Boundaries of Mere Reason.* Yet in a number of places in his discussions of perpetual peace he clearly indicates it is a concept that we can and must treat in terms of both uses of our reason. Thus, in his discussion of the guarantee of perpetual peace, he explicitly affirms that "... here, we have to do only with theory (not with religion)" (*EF*, 8: 362/332), and then twice notes the significance of distinguishing these standpoints in treating the question of perpetual peace:

> Now we come to the question concerning what is essential to the purpose of perpetual peace: what nature does for this purpose with reference to the end that human being's own reason makes a duty for him, hence to the favoring of his *moral purpose*, and how it affords the guarantee that what man *ought* to

do in accordance with laws of freedom but does not do, it is assured he *will* do, without prejudice to this freedom, even by a constraint of nature. . . . When I say of nature, it *wills* that this or that happen, this does not mean, it lays upon us a *duty* to do it (for only practical reason, without coercion, can do that) but rather that nature itself *does* it, whether we will it or not (*fata volent ducunt, nolentem trahunt*). (*EF*, 8: 365/334)

In this way nature guarantees perpetual peace through the mechanism of human inclinations itself, with an assurance that is admittedly not adequate for *predicting* its future (theoretically) but that is still enough for practical purposes and makes it a duty to work toward this (not merely chimerical) end. (*EF*, 8: 368/337)

Thus, from the standpoint of the theoretical use of reason, perpetual peace is neither the sign nor the result of human moral progress; it is just an outcome of causal processes by which nature makes us do unwillingly what we willingly ought to do—but in fact do not. Nature, in guises of war-weariness and the spirit of commerce, will provide the incentive for nations, out of self-interest, to leave the international "state of nature" and establish a confederation to guarantee perpetual peace. Nature does not wait on our acknowledgment of a *moral* demand in order to effect this transition into a new political condition. Instead, nature utilizes our unsociable sociability to bring us to establish external conditions of peace, which will then be conducive to our eventually overcoming our self-incurred moral corruption.

Yet even as Kant provides a causal account of the attainment of perpetual peace from the standpoint of the theoretical use of reason, he also indicates that we can—and indeed must—consider it, from the perspective of reason's practical use, a moral demand upon our conduct: "yet reason, from the throne of the highest morally legislative power, delivers an absolute condemnation of war as a procedure for determining rights and, on the contrary, makes a condition of peace, which cannot be instituted or assured without a pact of nations among themselves, a direct duty" (*EF*, 8: 356/327). The conclusion of the *Rechtslehre* states this even more forcefully:

. . . What is incumbent on us as a duty is rather to act in conformity with the idea of that end, even if there is not the slightest theoretical likelihood that it can be realized, as long as its impossibility cannot be demonstrated either.

Now morally practical reason pronounces in us its irresistible veto: *there is to be no war*, neither war between you and me in the state of nature nor war between us as states . . . for war is not the way in which everyone should seek his rights. So the question is no longer whether perpetual peace is something real or a fiction, and whether we are not deceiving ourselves in our theoretical judgments when we assume that it is real. Instead, we must act as if it is something real, though perhaps it is not; we must work toward establishing perpetual peace and the kind of constitution that seems to us most conducive to it (say, a republicanism of all states, together and separately) in order to bring about perpetual peace . . . And even if the complete realization of this objective always remains a pious wish, still we are certainly not deceiving ourselves in adopting the maxim of working incessantly toward it. (*MdS*, 6: 354–355/490–491)

The language used here and in the "First Supplement: On the Guarantee of Perpetual Peace" (*EF*, 8: 360–362/331–332), where perpetual peace, from the standpoint of theoretical reason, is an "extravagant idea" [*überschwengliche Idee*] but "for practical purposes (e.g., with respect to the concept of the duty of *perpetual peace* and putting that mechanism of nature to use for it) is dogmatic and well founded in its reality," evokes those discussions in the *Critiques* about the antinomies human reason generates when we fail to distinguish properly its theoretical and practical uses (Cf. A 462–476/B 490–504; *CprR*, 5: 107–110/226–228). This suggests that the claim that perpetual peace is contingent upon the attainment of a commonwealth of virtue stands in contradiction to the claim that "nature guarantees perpetual peace by virtue of the mechanism of man's inclinations themselves" only so far as we do not distinguish them in terms of the use of reason from which they respectively issue; that is, it is a contradiction only to the extent that we do not recognize it as an antinomy generated from the different uses of our reason,

Kant's claim that nature, working through self-interest and human inclinations, will ultimately secure international peace is thus part of an account of the possibility of perpetual peace that issues from the *theoretical* use of reason. From this perspective the establishment of an international order to provide perpetual peace is possible only so far as it can be conceived of as issuing from causes such as strife, self-interest, and human inclinations. Such an account may not invoke moral determinants as causes in the establishment of this international order because, even if such moral determinants are present, they are aspects of human activity not accessible to reason in its theoretical use. Yet the possibility that we can conceive of the conditions for perpetual peace emerging from the causal processes of nature, without the assistance of moral factors is, on Kant's view, not without consequence for our moral use of reason. This possibility, as it is construed from the perspective of the theoretical use of reason, provides assurance that, in the long run, these conditions will finally obtain.

This "long run," however, is very long. Despite the confidence Kant professes in the eventuality of perpetual peace, the theoretical use of reason provides us only with its possibility—and only to the extent that reason cannot demonstrate the *impossibility* of our attaining it (*MdS*, 6: 354–355/490–492). So even as nature "guarantees" perpetual peace, we cannot predict—from the perspective of a theoretical account—when conditions for peace will be established: "In this way nature guarantees perpetual peace through the mechanism of human inclinations itself, with an assurance that is admittedly not adequate for *predicting* its future (theoretically)" (*EF*, 8: 368/337). Such a prophecy comes only from reason's practical use, but from this perspective, attainment of perpetual peace must be conceived, not as the necessary and inevitable long run outcome of the causal working of nature, but as contingent on our human moral effort and progress. As moral agents we cannot just wait for nature to provide it in the long run, since it is "a duty to work toward this (not merely chimerical) end" (*EF*, 8: 368/337).

The theoretical use of reason thus provides only the bare possibility that the causal working of nature will effect perpetual peace in "the long run." This, however, is not the only account of perpetual peace that reason can provide. Perpetual peace, which theoretical reason can show only to be not impossible, is the very same object that practical reason requires us to make actual as moral agents. The claim that "a commonwealth under laws of virtue . . . assures the world of perpetual peace" is thus one that arises—indeed, must arise—from the practical use of reason. It is a concrete way in which practical reason specifies the fulfilment of the human vocation to be the juncture of nature and freedom. Kant insists that the attainment of human moral destiny is a demand that arises from the practical use of our reason and that bringing it about—including, as an important stage on the way, perpetual peace—finally rests upon what human beings concretely do (e. g., *TP*, 8: 309–313/306–309; *EF*, 8: 356/327–328, 368/125; *MdS*, 6: 354–355/490–492). The establishment of a political order to assure perpetual peace is thus a concrete component in the attainment of human moral destiny, without, however, being identical to that destiny. We must make it our duty to attain perpetual peace as the "entire final end of the doctrine of right within the limits of mere reason" (*den ganzen Endzweck der Rechtslehre innerhalb der bloßen Vernunft*) and the "highest political good" (*[dem] höchsten politischen Gut* [*MdS*, 6: 355/492]).

These passages suggest that nature (or providence) can spur us unwittingly and unwillingly only so far along the path to our moral destiny. What theoretical reason provides in its claim that "nature guarantees perpetual peace by virtue of the mechanism of man's inclinations themselves," is neither unimportant nor contrary to the moral demand that we strive for perpetual peace. This theoretical claim clears ground for our recognition of the practical demand—and for action in accord with it—to bring into actuality the perpetual peace, which otherwise is just a theoretical possibility.[5] The moral demand that reason places on the formation of our action requires that we not take the attainment of the moral destiny of the human species as a foregone conclusion of the dynamics of history but rather as a task whose final shape and completion depend upon the properly ordered actions of human beings.

The resolution of this apparent antinomy that arises from reason's effort to render intelligible the possibility of attaining perpetual peace thus requires the recognition of the distinct sources in reason from which the two contrary claims issue. That, however, is not the whole story. The resolution of this antinomy, as is the case for the resolution of the other antinomies brought to light in the critical project, functions within the context of the affirmations of the primacy of the "interest" of reason in its practical (moral) use that Kant makes throughout the course of the critical project.[6] The resolution of this antinomy is not merely the solution of an intellectual puzzle. It also—and, indeed, principally—enables us to recognize the full scope of the moral demand that reason places on us. "There is to be no more war" is not a statement of a bare theoretical nonimpossibility. It is a *moral* possibility that is to be made actual by the decisions that human beings will make and the actions that ensue from those decisions.

Recognition that reason places on us this particular moral demand to strive for the end of war, however, does not fully settle the question of what human beings are concretely required to do in response to their vocation as the juncture of nature and freedom. In fact, since there are reasons—for instance, his judgment that reform properly comes from above, that is, from the sovereign—for taking the specific proposal that Kant elaborates in "Toward Perpetual Peace" to be addressed (perhaps ironically) to rulers rather than to the general citizenry, that text may not be the first place in which to look for an elaboration of how the social authority of reason may concretely function in ordering the dynamics of human social relationships. To do that, we must first return to Kant's discussions in Book Three of *Religion* in which he attempts to show how the social authority of reason bears upon the social relationships of all human agents who, by virtue of their exercise of the practical use of reason, stand to one another as fellow citizens of an ethical commonwealth. In the course of this discussion he provides the beginnings of an account of the forms that the social authority of reason is to take in the workings in the institutions of human society that provide the concrete context for social relationships. This account suggests that one concrete element of the intent to social union uniting citizens in an ethical commonwealth is a cosmopolitan hope that enables a commitment to work for perpetual peace.

The Ethical Commonwealth as "True Church": The Social Authority of Reason as Noncoercive

As Kant depicts the ethical commonwealth in *Religion within the Boundaries of Mere Reason* it represents the social form of the self-governance of reason that will enable humanity to attain the highest good and thereby to fulfill its vocation as the juncture of nature and freedom. In order to attain the highest good, however, humanity must overcome the radical evil it has brought upon itself through corruption of the self-governance of reason under the conditions of unsociable sociability. The overcoming of radical evil involves both an individual and a social dimension. The individual dimension, which Kant analyzes in Book One and Two, requires from each agent a moral conversion that

Kant places in what seems to be an atemporal logical space, a view that involves some difficulties.[7] In contrast, the social dimension for the overcoming of radical evil analyzed in Books Three and Four clearly involves particular sociocultural dynamics and arrangements of human life as they arise within the course of human history (*Rel*, 6: 93–95/129–130). He designates the concrete locus for this historical process of overcoming radical evil as "the church," which he carefully distinguishes into two forms: The variously organized and visible historical churches, which embody historical or ecclesiastical faith, and the true Church, in which pure religious faith (or true religion) is manifest (*Rel*, 6: 100–103/135–137; 115–116/146–147). The church, in both its forms, has a public and social character, but it is only through the latter, true church that the ethical commonwealth will finally and fully extend its domain over human activity (*Rel*, 6: 121–124/151–153).[8]

This distinction reflects Kant's view that the attainment of the highest good is contingent upon the fulfillment of two sets of interdependent conditions that provide the context for human moral conduct and social practices. First, there are the conditions constituted by the inner dynamisms and structure of human moral agency in accord with which persons autonomously govern their own individual conduct (*Rel*, 6: 98–100/133–134; *AP*, 7: 329–330/190–191); second, there are the conditions constituted by the external order in which human agents mutually regulate one another's conduct through social institutions and practice, most fundamentally by the establishment of a public order in which legitimate political authority devolves upon the state (*MdS*, 6: 340–342/480–481; *SF*, 7: 90–93/305–306; *CJ*, 5: 432–433/299–300). Reason has power to govern human conduct under both conditions; the extension of reason's effective governance throughout them both brings about the attainment of the highest good. Under the first set of conditions—as depicted in *Religion*—reason requires the moral conversion of individuals. This overcoming of radical evil in the will of individuals serves as a necessary condition for the moral progress of the human species (*Rel*, 6: 93–95/129–130). The second set of conditions suggests that such individual moral conversion alone is not sufficient for the full and definitive establishment of an ethical commonwealth. Under these conditions reason requires that the external order of human sociocultural practices also be given a shape and direction that exemplifies the overcoming of radical evil, that is, they must be formed to constitute an ethical commonwealth (*Rel*, 6: 105–106/138–139).

The problematic feature of Kant's depiction of the ethical commonwealth and the social governance of reason exercised within it is that he does not provide a full account of *the means by which* reason extends its social authority to govern conduct throughout the second set of conditions; that is, the external order of human conduct. The part of this account that Kant does provide, in *Religion* and elsewhere, pertains to the social authority of reason as it is exercised by the political institutions of the state. In this account, he marks off with precision a range of concrete human practice as the domain of right, that is, the domain subject to public legislation, enforcement, and adjudication by the authority of the state (*MdS*, 6: 230–232/387–389; 311/455). Marking off this domain of right makes it possible to set clear limits upon the exercise of political authority by placing it as a distinct form of the social authority of reason within the more encompassing domain of reason's moral governance of human conduct. The distinctive character of this political exercise of the social authority of reason is that it legitimately uses coercive power in the order of external human action.

The domain of political authority extends first of all over the external condition that Kant terms "the juridical state of nature" from which reason requires all agents to leave in order to constitute a "juridical-civil state" (*Rel*, 6: 95–96/130–132). Reason authorizes the use of coercion to enforce this requirement with respect to external civil status. Once in the juridical civil state, reason requires that all recognize the universal principle of right, that is, "Any action is *right* if it can coexist with everyone's freedom in accordance with a universal law, or if on its maxim the freedom of choice of each can coexist with everyone's freedom in accordance with a universal law" (*MdS*, 6: 230/387). This authorizes political authority to enforce the universal principle of right by the use of coercion in the regulation of a certain range of actions in the external order which "cannot coexist with freedom in accordance with a universal law" (*MdS*, 6: 231/387). The scope of this legitimation for political authority to use coercion, however, does not extend beyond this set of actions to other actions in the external order. Kant also holds that reason does not authorize the use of coercive power as a constraint upon the freedom of agents to set ends for their actions. "Now, I can indeed be constrained by others to perform *actions* that are directed as means to an end, but I never can be constrained by others *to have an end*: only I myself can *make* something my end" (*MdS*, 6: 381/513).

This last mentioned constraint on the use of coercion to enforce what reason requires holds even in the case when the universal principle of right is proposed as itself an end for agents to adopt. Kant is careful to note that, insofar as this is a principle for the governance of the *external* order of action, reason cannot coercively enforce its adoption *as an end* for that agent's action. All that reason requires from an agent is recognition of this principle as a law for external conduct that is enforceable, if needed, by the coercive authority of the state (*MdS*, 6: 231/388). This is so because Kant holds that the adoption of ends for action is properly a function of the inner order constituted by an agent's freedom. In that order, freedom is such that it cannot be subject to the governance of reason by external, coercive constraint. Conversely, reason functions properly in that order only when it functions noncoercively. Freedom is thus properly subject to reason only when reason is exercised as a form of the agent's self-governance—which means that freedom is itself nothing other than the self-governance of reason.

This constraint on coercion with respect to an agent's adoption of ends is thus fully in accord with Kant's understanding of the inner dynamism of human freedom. In setting ends for themselves, agents exercise freedom in the form of the self-governance of reason—and they do so even with respect to those ends that reason itself requires. In particular, one may refuse to adopt as one's own the end that reason in its practical use requires of all agents. This end that reason requires takes the form of the maxim to govern one's conduct as a self-legislating member of the kingdom of ends.[9] This means that, with respect to this end, one can even attempt to exercise the self-governance of reason in a way that is self-corrupting; that is, by forming a maxim through which one seeks to withdraw oneself from the jurisdiction of the self-governance of reason. This possibility of corrupting the self-governance of reason by a refusal to adopt the end reason requires of all agents is a constitutive feature of radical evil. But—and on this point Kant is insistent—neither the adoption, nor the refusal of this end on the part of individual agents can be brought about by coercion. Reason may not authorize the use of coercion to combat radical evil as it issues at this level of an agent's freedom. When individual agents in the exercise of their freedom undercut the self-governance of reason in the formation of their maxims, reason may not authorize the use of coercion to prevent this, even from the institutions and practices empowered to enforce the universal principle of right with respect to external conduct.

This constraint thus lies at the basis of Kant's judgment that even with the establishment of the juridical commonwealth, human beings remain in an ethical state of nature that they can leave only by entering, without coercion, an ethical commonwealth. The social authority of reason as it is legitimately exercised in the civil order by the institutions of the state cannot provide one of the conditions essential for the establishment of the ethical commonwealth. The social authority of reason, exercised in the form authorized to use coercion, cannot bring about the explicit intent to social union, even though this intent also is required as an end by the practical use of reason. Just as reason requires that each individual agent adopt (in the form of a maxim) the end of governing one's conduct as a self-legislating member of the kingdom of ends, it also requires that members of the ethical commonwealth adopt an end for their action. This end consists of the explicit intent to a social union that makes it possible to overcome the social consequences of radical evil and to attain the highest good for humanity. As in the case of the end that reason requires of individual moral agents, the adoption of this end cannot be coerced. The intent to social union as an end of action can arise only from the non-coercive exercise of the self-governance of reason (cf. *TP*, 8: 310–312/307–309).

At this point, however, Kant's account of the concrete dynamics of the social authority of reason in an ethical commonwealth seems to falter. It falters because Kant provides, at best, only a partial specification of the forms of the self-governance of reason that, by virtue of being both *uncoerced* and *social*, would make it possible first to establish an ethical commonwealth and then to sustain it in the course of human history. He invests true church with the noncoercive social authority of reason to accomplish its task and duty of establishing the ethical commonwealth. But he does not provide an adequate account of the *concrete social means* (or the *concrete forms of social relationship*) by which such a true church makes it possible for agents freely to adopt, as an end for their action, the social intent required for establishing and sustaining an ethical commonwealth. One characterization of these means that he provides is helpful only to the extent that it indicates what they are *not* to be like: They are not to take the form of the political institutions by which the social authority of reason governs a juridical commonwealth. The other model he provides—that the concrete form of social relationship that establishes an ethical commonwealth should be like a household or family—is positive, but proves to be unhelpful, as noted earlier in chapter 3. Familial relations as Kant describes them do not provide an adequate model for the noncoercive exercise of the social authority of reason that will enable an uncoerced intent to social union since, according to a later analysis he gives in the *Metaphysics of Morals*, they presuppose that the requirements arising from this relationship can legitimately be enforced by coercive power.

There is another matter on which Kant's account falters in addition to the inadequacy of its depiction of the means by which the true church makes it possible for agents to adopt freely the intent to social union needed to establish the ethical commonwealth. It also fails to specify fully the concrete forms of social relationship by which the true church then makes it possible for the social self-governance of reason to extend further over the range of concrete human conduct. This specification seems necessary for the ethical commonwealth to have the means to establish "the laws of virtue—a society which reason makes it a task and a duty of the entire human race to establish in its full scope" (*Rel*, 6: 94/130). Yet Kant's discussion of the true church provides neither a specific list nor a systematically detailed account of the kinds of external conduct or social practices that would exhibit the social authority of reason in a noncoercive form throughout the range of human conduct.

The Public Use of Reason: The Social Authority of Reason as Condition for the Intent to Social Union

Although Kant's account falters on these points, a case can be made that there are still elements within the account of the ethical commonwealth that can serve to articulate concrete forms for the noncoercive exercise of the social authority of reason. Identifying and utilizing these elements, however, requires making further links between the text of *Religion* and Kant's discussions of the concrete dynamics of history, politics, and culture. These are links that Kant seldom explicitly marks or brings to the attention of the reader. They are, instead, indicated by parallels in his argumentation and phrasing or suggested more obliquely in remarks Kant makes—sometimes in footnotes—to situate a particular concept, argument, or text within the larger context of the critical project. One consequence of the allusive way in which Kant makes these links is that he himself often fails to explore the possibilities they open up for delimiting in more concrete terms the forms by which the social authority can govern the dynamics of human social relationships.

By drawing these further links to Kant's other writings, we can identify two elements in Kant's account of the ethical commonwealth that are particularly important for an account of the social authority of reason. They are important not only because they allow us to render explicit points that Kant only allusively suggests. They are important because they also offer a useful and sound basis on which his effort to articulate the social authority of reason can be carried forward in our own day. The first of these elements emerges by connecting what Kant calls the public use of reason (*BF*, 8: 36–38/5–7; cf. *TP*, 8: 304/ 302; *SF*, 7: 19–20/248–249) to the concrete form that social authority of reason must take in order to make it possible for agents to adopt the intent to social union constitutive of an ethical commonwealth. The second one emerges by connecting the content of this intent to social union to what Kant terms a cosmopolitan perspective. Neither connection may be immediately obvious from reading just the text of *Religion*. Yet, as I shall argue in chapters 6 and 7, what Kant himself did not do to develop these elements of the social authority of reason in his account of the ethical commonwealth, we now need to do.

The human circumstances under which the practical exercise of reason requires that we work for the establishment of an ethical commonwealth instance the same dynamic of unsociable sociability that Kant describes under a variety of other headings. This dynamic constitutes the circumstances under which reason requires the establishment of a juridical commonwealth; within that juridical commonwealth, this dynamic in turn constitutes the circumstances that require the establishment of the social practices that will make possible the public use of reason. All of these, moreover, are instances of the fundamental human situation that the critical project seeks to address. In noting a deep connection between the problems of the cognitive and the political order that the critical project seeks to address, Onora O'Neill has aptly characterized these circumstances:

In either case [cognitive or political] we have a plurality of
agents or voices (perhaps potential agents or voices) and no
transcendent preestablished authority. Authority in either case
has to be constructed. The problem is to discover whether
there are any constraints on the mode of order (cognitive or
political) that can be constituted. Such constraints (if they can
be discovered) constitute respectively the principles of reason
and of justice. Reason and justice are two aspects of the solution of the problems which arise when an uncoordinated
plurality of agents is to share a possible world. Hence political
imagery can illuminate the nature of cognitive order and disorientation, just as the vocabulary of reason can be used to
characterize social and political order and disorientation. Kant
frequently characterizes skepticism as a failure of discursive
order, hence as anarchy; just has he characterizes dogmatism
(rationalism) as a form of despotism, a triumph of unjust discursive order.[10]

O'Neill's characterization just as readily applies to the circumstances
out of which reason requires the establishment of an ethical commonwealth. What may be of greater significance is that it also applies to
the circumstances that Kant had described in the first *Critique*, in the
section on the polemical use of reason regarding the very need for
critique. Critique is that by which reason comes to a free recognition
of its social nature. This suggests that the establishment of an ethical
commonwealth may represent nothing less than the final establishment
of the full social character of reason.

    If it is correct to connect the establishment of the ethical com-
monwealth with an understanding of critique as itself a form of reason's
acknowledgment of its own social character, then the significance of
the public use of reason for the establishment of the ethical commonwealth begins to emerge. This is so even though the actual text of
Religion is not one in which the notion of the public use of reason
plays a major role. In fact, given the events surrounding Kant's publication of this work, which occasioned a famous letter of rebuke from
the Prussian Emperor, it is more likely that any association between
this text and the notion of the public use of reason will focus more on
the details of Kant's conflict with the censors than on any conceptual
contribution that Kant's arguments within the text are seen to make to

the development of this notion. Yet the very fact that *Religion*—especially in Book Three—is directly concerned with "the problems which arise when an uncoordinated plurality of agents is to share a possible world" suggests that one will not have to dig very deeply to uncover a connection with the public use of reason. This is so because the public use of reason is precisely that form of uncoerced argumentative exchange that enables "an uncoordinated plurality of agents" to engage one another in common deliberation for the purpose of constructing a shared world.

The public use of reason—or, more precisely, the conditions that make possible the public use of reason—thus constitutes one form of concrete social dynamics that make it possible for human agents freely to adopt the intent to social union that is requisite for the establishment of an ethical commonwealth. Kant's notion of the public use of reason presupposes that we are capable, individually and collectively, of forming and taking a perspective on decision and action that concretely represents an intent to social union that will stand over and against the particular interests we have that fuel human unsociable sociability. In the case of the ethical commonwealth, the intent to social union that emerges from the public use of reason will be nothing less than the universal interest that reason takes in the social union that will enable humanity to fulfill its vocation as the juncture of nature and freedom. One way that Kant concretely articulates this intent to social union is through what he calls a cosmopolitan perspective, a notion to which we now turn.

The Ethical Commonwealth: The Social Authority of Reason as a Community of Cosmopolitan Hope

A cosmopolitan perspective is one of the most concrete ways in which Kant articulates the social authority of reason for his own late-eighteenth-century context. A cosmopolitan perspective means taking the viewpoint of a "world-citizen" upon the historical and cultural dynamics of human social and political interaction as it moves on a trajectory aimed at the destiny of the human race.[11] It functions, moreover, as a framework from which an answer—though admittedly not a full answer—can be made to the question that Kant identifies as "simultaneously practical and theoretical" (A 805/B 833): "For what may I hope?" From a cosmopolitan perspective one may specifically hope for that which Kant proposes as a necessary intermediate stage for humanity's reaching the moral destiny that is the object of a critically validated human hope. This intermediate stage is the establishment of a federation or league of nations which will provide the conditions for perpetual peace and thus for the eventual full attainment of the highest good as a social goal.[12]

Book Three of *Religion* begins with what may very well be Kant's most eloquent account of the unsocial sociability under which humanity must work out its moral destiny. Division One then elaborates the role of the church as an ethical commonwealth in the attainment of that moral destiny. It is of no little significance that the discussion of an ethical commonwealth in Division One concludes with two explicit references to concerns that inform Kant's account of a cosmopolitan perspective: First, in the long footnote to the next to last paragraph, Kant explicitly compares the problem facing the achievement of "this end of unity of the pure religion of reason" to the problem facing the achievement of a [single] cosmopolitan state (*Rel*, 6: 123 footnote/ 152–153); and second, in the final paragraph, Kant affirms the establishment of an ethical commonwealth as that which brings with it an assurance of perpetual peace to the world (6: 124/153).

These passages suggest a number of lines of connection that can be drawn through *Religion* and the essays of the 1780s and 1790s in which Kant tries to articulate a cosmopolitan perspective. This should not be too surprising in view of the fact that Kant wrote *Religion* and some of the key essays articulating a cosmopolitan perspective—the ones on theory and practice, perpetual peace, and human moral progress—within the same four year time frame (1792–95). The lines of connection that are most pertinent to Kant's efforts to articulate the concrete form for the exercise of the social authority of reason, moreover, run back to the three questions Kant formulates as a précis of the critical project: What can I know? What ought I do? For what may I hope? (A 805/B 833). This connection back to Kant's earliest published formulation of the scope of the critical project with respect to the unity of reason in its theoretical and practical uses is a key marker of the deeply embedded social character of the project.

In conjunction with one another, the ethical commonwealth and a cosmopolitan viewpoint each provide elements of a framework that enables moral agents to take their individual answers (i.e., the fidelity

of the conduct of their moral lives to the self-governance of reason) to
the second question:

What ought *I* do?

to have an effective bearing on the human destiny that is the outcome
of the course of history. That destiny provides a common and collective human answer to the third question:

For what may *we* hope?

Both these answers can be properly framed, however, only within the
context of a critically validated answer to the first question:

What can I know?

that delimits the proper range of claims that issue from the theoretical
and the practical uses of reason. All three answers together, moreover,
constitute a prelude to a fourth, anthropological question that Kant
makes explicit in his lectures on logic:

What is humanity?[13]

This final question, there is good reason to believe, is the controlling
question of Kant's entire philosophical career—and, of course, is
itself one way of articulating the project of resolving the issue of the
relationship between nature and freedom. For Kant, both the question and its answer lie precisely in the fact that humanity is itself the
juncture that unites nature and freedom even while preserving their
irreducible difference.[14]

Placed in this context, the notion of a cosmopolitan perspective is
an articulation of what Kant sees as the appropriate human response
to the status of our species as the unique juncture of nature and freedom. There is, on the one hand, the response that arises when we
consider the course of human history from the side of the theoretical
use of our reason. Nature, which has already thrust upon us the necessity of leaving the juridical state of nature to become citizens of a
particular state now also thrusts upon us—by virtue of the circumstances of our human existence as finite, needy beings on a planet of
finite resources—the necessity of taking the perspective of "world
citizen." Since nature gives us no choice but to live as social beings,
not only within the confines of a single nation, but also as members
of an assemblage of nations sharing one planet, we must learn to take
a perspective that looks out from and upon the whole human world.
Viewed in terms of the exigencies of nature, our human destiny—if
there be a common one—can only be along whatever path nature
carries us.

The cosmopolitan perspective, however, is not simply the out-come of the workings of nature. In fact, the workings of nature can provide us only with the kind of cosmopolitan perspective that arises for those who share a vantage point provided by our common destiny of the graveyard, an image that Kant uses with effective irony at the start of "Toward Perpetual Peace." If we wait for the workings of nature to bring about a social union that will make possible a common human destiny, we will find that destiny only in the death that is our common lot as mortals. Indeed, if we wait for nature to bring about the social union that its workings make appropriate for us as the juncture of nature and freedom, we may find ourselves cooperating in the attainment of that common fate by inflicting death on one another: Our unsociable sociability remains unregenerate, enabling war as the final and inextirpable social form of radical evil.

In contrast to this stands the cosmopolitan perspective that can and must be framed from the vantage point of reason's practical use. This perspective provides a form of comprehensive intelligibility to a matter—the trajectory of the whole course of human history—on which reason's theoretical use entangles itself and us in conflicts that are not merely dialectical but all too real. Only when formed from the work-ings of the practical use of reason can a cosmopolitan perspective provide us with a critically validated response to the question about the outcome of human history. Such a critically validated response is one that poses this question in terms of its moral intelligibility: What *ought we* do so that our being carried in history wherever nature takes us comports properly with the unique character of our human status as the juncture of nature and freedom?

When the question is posed this way, the response then turns on the possibility that human beings can and ought mutually to take moral responsibility with one another for the outcome of history. A cosmo-politan perspective is the critically validated social framework from which one may take human action (including one's own) to have ef-fective bearing upon the outcome of human history. We can effectively act as "world citizens" only on the basis of an uncoerced mutual recognition of one another *as agents of human destiny for one another*. This suggests that it is only to the extent that we place our action in the framework of a shared hope for a human destiny, which we work out in mutual recognition of one another's freedom, that we will be justified in taking our human destiny to move along a trajectory which we impart to it.

This suggests a way in which a cosmopolitan perspective gives concrete content to the intent to social union needed for the establishment of an ethical commonwealth. A cosmopolitan perspective that issues from the practical use of reason involves a form of mutual moral recognition of one another that is oriented to the outcome of what all of us will do so that we may together attain our destiny. This makes the intent to social union one that is oriented by the third of the Kantian questions, transposed into a social mode: For what may *we* hope?

As chapters 6 and 7 will show, the ethical commonwealth, the public use of reason, a cosmopolitan perspective, and Kant's project for perpetual peace are all features of Kant's account of the social authority of reason. Each of these features provides help in constructing an understanding of the authority of reason appropriate—and urgently necessary—to our own circumstances early in the twenty-first century. In our context, an authentically Kantian account of the social authority of reason may offer a way to envision the concrete forms of mutual moral recognition (or "social respect") that enable members of a polity—and a world—that is pluralist, multicultural, and multiethnic to engage one another in sustained, reasoned argument and common deliberation about the terms of living with one other, including the constitutive social ends that make them a polity and a global human community.

CHAPTER SIX

The Social Authority of Reason
and the Culture(s) of Post-modernity

Freedom, Coercion, and the Intent to Social Union

The political, social, and cultural circumstances of Kant's eighteenth-century world were considerably different from the ones that
face humanity at the outset of the twenty-first century.[1] Kant's Europe
was ordered by monarchy and mercantilism, a world in which class
and gender were taken for granted as appropriate determinants for life
prospects. It was a Europe already on a journey away from a culture
of unquestioned religious faith, even as the institutionalized forms of
Christianity and popular religiosity both continued to have important
social, cultural, and political functions. It was a Europe at the height
of colonial claim upon the Americas, moving to expand its influence
in Asia and poised to bring Africa under the sway of empire. It was
a Europe at the brink of an explosion of technological advances that
would make the term "revolution" as apt for the changes effected on
ordinary life as it was for the changes effected in political institutions
in the wake of the War of Independence in British North America and
the overthrow of the French monarchy.

Within Kant's own particular context as a citizen-subject of the
Prussian monarchy, he was considered—and, indeed, considered himself—an advocate of "enlightenment;" that is, of the principles that
eventually would enable reason properly to govern the full range of
human social dynamics in culture and political life. Though during
Kant's own lifetime there were some who considered him a dangerous
radical in view of his continuing sympathy for the ideals of the French

Revolution, he cast his own articulation of how principles of enlightenment apply to concrete human social dynamics in the language of reform rather than of revolution.[2] He envisioned it as reform set in motion from above, by the sovereign ruler, rather than from below, by the general populace—though the segment of the populace that is a "learned public" would play an important role in providing the conditions that enable reform to take proper effect (*TP*, 8: 298–300/298–299, 304/302; *MdS*, 6: 339–341/480–481; *SF*, 7: 89/305; 92–93/307–308). When viewed from the perspective of later history—especially one that takes into account not only the views Kant actually expressed by also how those views were then interpreted in subsequent debates about social and political order—Kant has been seen as an important figure in the development of liberal political thinking. Even though Kant advocated a number of concrete practices that seem at odds with political liberalism in many of its influential twentieth-century forms, he has been enshrined in the pantheon of liberal thinkers in view of the central role that he gives to human freedom, most prominently through his introduction of the concept of the moral autonomy of each human person.[3]

The interpretation of Kant's critical project set forth in the first part of this work acknowledges the fundamental importance of human freedom in Kant's thinking and the key role that freedom, understood principally as human moral autonomy, plays in the articulation of the enterprise he calls critique. Central to this project is an effort to elucidate human freedom in its relationship to the natural cosmos in which human beings find themselves placed. The all-encompassing issue for critique, I have argued, issues from the unique position in which human beings find themselves both as and at the juncture of nature and freedom. *At* the juncture of nature and freedom, human beings must acknowledge the irreducibly different character of the intelligibility that nature and freedom provide for the efforts we make to understand the structure and import of human existence: We are both embodied organisms fully embedded in the causal working of nature *and* moral agents endowed with the autonomy to shape the order of human relationship. From the acknowledgment of the irreducibility of these two ways of making sense of our human condition, Kant delimits each of them as spheres for the exercise of an appropriate use of reason: The speculative and the practical (moral). While this mutual irreducibility characterizes how human beings stand *at* the juncture of nature and freedom, it does not elucidate how human beings stand *as* the juncture of nature and freedom: Their intersection in humanity is neither a matter of pure contingency nor an automatic consequence of a preestablished harmony. Although this juncture is given, it is equally a juncture that humanity itself must bring about. *As the juncture of nature and freedom human beings are called upon to make themselves* and *the world of which they are part* a single unified reality for which the practical and the speculative are the two irreducible modes of making sense. Put in Kant's terms, human beings are called upon to exhibit in their dealings with one another and with the cosmos that the practical and the speculative uses of reason are uses of one and the same reason.

By tracing the development of Kant's account of the highest good against this background of the critical project's effort to elucidate the unique human place in the cosmos, I have argued that Kant comes to affirm social relationships as the dynamism through which human beings will most fully realize their vocation at and as the juncture of nature and freedom. Kant makes this affirmation most explicitly in terms of the notion of an ethical commonwealth, inasmuch as this designates the form of human social relationship through which the highest good of the human species is fully and definitively attained. I have also argued that, even though Kant introduces this particular concept at a late stage in his execution of the critical project, it is nonetheless a coherent and legitimate development of the fundamental moral and social trajectory that he imparted to this project from the outset, a trajectory that I have characterized as aimed at articulation of the social self-governance of reason. The need to make the social dimension of this trajectory explicit through the notion of an ethical commonwealth emerges more urgently as Kant explores how the social self-governance of reason is subject to the self-corruption he terms radical evil. While evil and human moral failure is not an entirely new topic for Kant's consideration in the critical project, his extensive treatment of it in *Religion within the Bounds of Mere Reason* shows most clearly how it bears directly on the ultimate success or failure of the critical project—and, even more important, how it bears on the fulfillment of the human vocation to be the juncture of nature and freedom. When radical evil is placed in conjunction with his other discussions of the unsociable sociability that provide the conditions for the self-corruption of the governance of reason, a telling image emerges to represent the ultimate failure of the social self-governance of reason: War. Armed conflict among human beings manifests radical evil in its fullness and brings about the ironic shadow of the perpetual peace that reason enjoins us to bring about with and for one another— the perpetual peace of the graveyard.

Over against war as the social form of radical evil, Kant sets an ethical commonwealth, which he identifies as the church ("the kingdom of God on earth"). He more concretely specifies, though only in part, the social dynamics by which the ethical commonwealth overcomes radical evil. One specification emerges in terms of the public use of reason that will provide conditions under which human agents can form the shared intent to social union needed to establish an ethical commonwealth; a second emerges in terms of a cosmopolitan perspective that sustains the hope needed for human beings to work together to establish the conditions for perpetual peace. Kant's efforts at concrete specification in these terms, however, are not fully successful. The public use of reason and a cosmopolitan perspective constitute appropriate social dynamics for the ethical commonwealth in that they are both instances of the social authority of reason exercised *noncoercively*. In delimiting them as elements of the social dynamics on an ethical commonwealth, Kant has thus successfully identified *the form in which* human beings are to exercise the social authority of reason in order to fulfill their vocation as the juncture of nature and freedom: As *a noncoercive power* that arises from a mutually free and shared intent to social union.

Exactly *how* this noncoercive power is to be instantiated in concrete social practices, however, remains unclear in Kant's account. One reason for this lies in the fact that he casts his account of the ethical commonwealth as the locus of the exercise of the noncoercive power of the social authority of reason primarily as a contrast to the coercive power that the state may—and indeed sometimes must—use in its legitimate exercise of the social authority of reason. This contrast is a negative one in that it more clearly articulates what the noncoercive exercise of the social authority of reason is not, but provides little concrete specification of what it is. That it is not to be like the exercise of the civil power of the state is clear. What it is, on its own terms, however, is not.

The fact that Kant does not clearly fill in the positive side to this contrast is not the only factor that makes this part of his account of the social authority of reason incomplete. Another difficulty arises from the fact that such an account needs to provide it with concrete specification on two levels. The first bears upon the exercise of the social authority of reason with respect to the very establishment of the state and of the ethical commonwealth; the second bears upon the exercise of the social authority of reason once the state and the ethical commonwealth have been established as frameworks for ordering human social dynamics. In specifying the public use of reason and a cosmopolitan perspective as forms of the noncoercive social authority of reason, Kant's account succeeds, at least in part, in supplying what is needed at the second level. These forms, however, cannot provide what is needed at the first level, especially for the establishment of an ethical commonwealth. As a result, Kant's account again leaves us only with what is, at best, an indication of what the exercise of the social authority of reason may *not* be. As we shall see below and in the next section, the *lacuna* at this level is a serious one, both for Kant's project as well as for my own effort to bring his account of the social authority of reason to bear upon our contemporary circumstances. He has left unanswered the crucial question of the concrete means by which the social authority of reason will bring about the shared intent to social union without which there can be no ethical commonwealth.

To see the extent of the problem that Kant's account leaves unresolved, we need to see look at the two levels at which there is need to provide specification of concrete form for the exercise of the social authority of reason. At the first level, according to Kant's account, coercion is authorized by reason in the founding of civil society in view of what he sees as an *a priori* requirement of reason that every human agent be under the jurisdiction of *some* civil society. He takes this to mean that the establishment of civil society rests upon the authorization reason gives to compel human agents to leave what he terms the juridical state of nature. The coercion is purely external and as such, it cannot effect an intent to social union in any agent. It should be noted that Kant does not understand this "juridical state of nature" as an historical description of an asocial condition in which human beings once lived. It is rather a way of articulating the claim that the most basic requirement that civil order makes of human beings is such that no one can claim exemption from the external jurisdiction of all civil order.

In contrast, even though it is also an *a priori* requirement of reason at this same level that every human agent leave the ethical state of nature, reason cannot authorize that this latter requirement be enforced by coercion. This is so because the requirement to enter an ethical commonwealth, unlike the one to enter civil society, does not bear upon agents in their external relation to one another but on the intent with which they stand in relation to one another. This intent issues from an agent's power to set ends for oneself, and thus comes about only in virtue of the agent's own exercise of freedom; such intent cannot issue from coercion. In consequence, Kant needs to articulate in concrete terms how reason, by noncoercive means, brings about in each and every agent the intent to social union constitutive of an ethical commonwealth.

As noted in chapter 5, Kant does provide at least two specifications of the noncoercive exercise of the social authority of reason: The public use of reason and a cosmopolitan perspective. The question that then needs to be raised is whether these, either individually or jointly, will be sufficient to bring about the intent to social union needed to establish an ethical commonwealth. The answer, unfortunately, seems to be no. Neither seems able *to bring about* the intent to social union that establishes an ethical commonwealth inasmuch as they each seem to presuppose that such intent *is already operative* in the social dynamics they each designate; that is, in the argumentative exchange among those engaged in the public use of reason and in the hope for perpetual peace that serves as the horizon of the cosmopolitan perspective. Rather than being forms of the social dynamic that founds an ethical commonwealth they seem to be indicators that it is, to at least some degree, already extant. This also seems to preclude the possibility that, even taken jointly, they could provide an adequate account of the social dynamics requisite to enable human agents freely to form the mutual intent to social union necessary for initially establishing an ethical commonwealth. Their conjunction would not obviate the problem in that they presuppose the very intent their conjunction is supposed to bring about.

In consequence, both the public use of reason and a cosmopolitan perspective are more likely candidates for exhibiting the noncoercive exercise of the social authority of reason on the second level at which Kant's contrast operates. Given the framework provided by the establishment of civil society, in which reason authorizes the use of coercion to enforce the universal principle of right with respect to actions that "cannot coexist with the freedom of everyone in accord with universal law," the public use of reason and a cosmopolitan perspective *open up an area of social and public "space" for exhibiting the social authority of reason in noncoercive form.* This is no small accomplishment, even though Kant's account of how these forms concretely function tends to be sketchy; for example, he does not indicate in sufficient detail what institutional structures and practices might be appropriate in fostering or extending the public use of reason to make it effective in the dynamics by which matters of public policy are decided.

One reason why Kant fails to do so, at least in this particular case, seems to lie in his preference for reform "from above" (*SF*, 7: 92–93/ 307–308). It may also be connected with his (perhaps ironic) confidence that sovereign rulers will rise to the level of practical wisdom in recognizing and redressing injustice that their constitutional role requires of them. As we shall see in chapter 7, Kant's articulation of both of these forms remains instructive for our own efforts to articulate the workings of the social authority of reason in a contemporary setting. Yet the very possibility of their functioning effectively within the concrete workings of human social dynamics, be it in Kant's day or our own, rests upon a resolution of the more fundamental issue that lies at the heart of Kant's account of an ethical commonwealth: How is a shared intent to social union to be brought about by reason—and to be brought about in the only manner that is fitting for reason and for the human agents who exercise the self-governance of reason, that is, noncoercively?

This issue lies at the very core of Kant's critical enterprise, inasmuch as I believe that Kant's identification of human freedom with the practical use of reason is an affirmation that *the most fundamental form of the social authority of reason is and must be noncoercive.* This affirmation of *both* the *social* and the *noncoercive* character of the authority of reason runs so deep, moreover, that it extends even to the most fundamental condition for the exercise of reason's social authority. Although reason *requires* from us the recognition of the social character of its practical us, it cannot *force* such recognition from us. Such recognition must issue as a free assent and it is this assent that constitutes the "intent to social union" constitutive of the ethical commonwealth.

This issue is important, however, not merely for an understanding of Kant's critical project. It is important—in fact, of central importance—for the shaping of human social and cultural dynamics for the twenty-first century. This is so because we currently find ourselves faced with the possibility that, from the dynamics of the informational, economic and technological "globalization" that seems to be emergent as a successor culture to modernity, the desirability, the necessity, and even the possibility of an intent to social union has radically been called in question. Equally called in question is whether such an intent, if indeed possible, can be brought about or—in a phrase more apt in a so-called "postmodern" context—can be authored by the exercise of a human reason that is social and non-coercive. It is to the emergence of such questioning that we now turn.

Globalization: Unsociable Sociability in Worldwide Context

"Globalization" is a term that can be used to designate a wide range of phenomena affecting human lives and culture in the contemporary world and is thus open to a wide range of analyses and construals. As shorthand for the processes, practices, and technologies that have made it possible for human beings to communicate instantaneously with one another at any time and from almost any place, globalization of this kind might immediately seem to be a development that comports well with Kant's notion of a cosmopolitan perspective and one that would make possible a worldwide extension of the public use of reason. We have every reason to think that Kant would have welcomed the still growing repertoire of electronic technology that enables human beings to transact their business, collaborate in scientific research, share advances in knowledge, and expand and deepen their acquaintance with the rich array of human life practices and culture. At the same time, we have every reason also to think that Kant would have been alert to the manner in which any of the activities and practices we might group under the term globalization are subject to the human dynamic that he terms unsociable sociability and could thus be employed in service of the self-corruption of the social self-governance of reason. Like any other human dynamic, globalization is susceptible to the subtle self-serving inversion of moral maxims that Kant terms radical evil. Kant would further insist, I believe, that, from the perspective of critique, an appropriate understanding of the natural and social dynamics at work in globalization must show how the exercise of reason in its practical use is to put them in service of humanity's vocation as the juncture of nature and freedom. Critique should enable us to show how both the workings of nature harnessed in service of globalization and our human engagement in direction of that enterprise enter into the attainment of the highest good as a social goal.

In this section I propose to describe and examine certain features of globalization from the perspective afforded on its social dynamics by the notion of unsociable sociability and by the possibilities it contains for exhibiting radical evil. In the course of this analysis, I will argue that we cannot assume that globalization carries with it an intent to social union of the kind necessary for the establishment of an ethical commonwealth or—put in terms of a related concept—that it either automatically or of itself extends the range or effectiveness of the social authority of reason. In fact, my argument will continue, there may be good reason to think that globalization can be just as readily put in service of a dynamic of social fragmentation that undercuts the social authority of reason. As the third section of this chapter will indicate, a globalization that intersects with practices expressive of the shattered selves of so-called postmodernity puts the very possibility of a shared intent to social union in question. At this juncture, the only authority "reason"—if it may be called that—may exercise socially is coercive power, because this is a juncture at which both reason and human sociality are no more than shifting constructs and temporary configurations of particularities locked in a struggle over what appears to be the only lasting reality of our human social dynamics: The wresting of recognition from the other. At the conclusion of this discussion, I will indicate that Kant's notion of a shared intent to social union has embedded within it an alternative to the dynamics of the combative wresting of recognition from one another: The social respect that ensues from full mutual recognition of one another is one that reason *requires*, without paradox, that we *freely* give to one another as moral agents bound to one another by a destiny of shared responsibility for our common humanity.

The very fact that globalization is a term open to being given a wide array of meanings and to having varied assessments placed upon any one of those meanings can serve as a useful clue to the issues of chief concern for this section. The usefulness of placing globalization as the focus, and a shifting one at that, for an array of meanings and evaluations is that it suggests that it functions as a conceptual construct that instantiates particularly well some key social and intellectual dynamics at work in the contemporary world. By this I mean that whatever range of reference globalization may have—for instance, to expanding regional and worldwide links among economic enterprises, or to the development of communication technologies that place more and more people in immediate direct contact, or to a greater awareness of the complex mechanisms by which apparently local and small scale events interlock with others to have wider and more long-range impact—those references typically fall within a grid of meanings and valuations framed on grounds that are shifting between the still largely dominant culture of modernity and the nascent culture of postmodernity.

This means, on the one hand, that certain dynamics at work in globalization can be read in continuity with Kant's cosmopolitanism, as a further step on a trajectory in which recognition of mutual economic interdependence will play a central role in bringing about a world political order that will more effectively reduce the risk of armed conflict among its member states. Placed in the grid of meanings and valuations to which Kant's own moral philosophy made a significant contribution, the dynamics of globalization can effect a recognition of a common humanity and makes possible wider acknowledgment of a broad range of rights that pertain to each and every person simply in virtue of being human. On this reading globalization involves significant opportunities for deepening and widening of the application of universal moral principles of justice and fairness, while at the same time giving due recognition to the rich array of human cultural differences.

This way of reading the dynamics of globalization, however, is not the only one. In fact, it is articulated from a grid of meanings and valuations that stands radically challenged by dynamics that, from a different grid of meanings and valuations, also seem to be at work in the processes of globalization. From this other grid, globalization provides a horizon, more adequate than what the abstract Enlightenment universality of cosmopolitanism could offer, for recognizing and highlighting, not the commonality and universality connecting human beings to one another, but the particularity that makes each human being and set of human circumstances unique. On this reading, the import of globalization lies in the new possibilities it can provide for the full articulation of human uniqueness and particularity: The establishment of new forms through which human beings can make links with one another and have direct access to the output of the full range of human knowledge, labor and creativity will make possible a more complete expression of the uniqueness of each individual within an ever more closely linked web of connections.

These two readings of globalization are not, of course, the only ones. On could, for example, offer a reading that seeks to resolve at least some of the tension between these two by way of a construct such as "the global village," which suggests a context in which the concern for the extension of human commonality and universality can be made compatible with the concern for affirming the depth and variety of human particularity. There are arrays of conceptual and imaginative grids that can be applied from the perspectives of economics, anthropology, politics, religion, cultural studies, communications, ecology—indeed from almost every of form of human inquiry—precisely because the effects of globalization have the potential for affecting every area of human life and affecting it "deep down."

From the perspective of this inquiry into the social authority of reason, the aspect of globalization that is of most central concern is precisely the way in which its actual dynamics and the imaginative and conceptual constructs by which we articulate those dynamics bear upon our modes of understanding of human connectedness and our human differences. This accounts for my selection of the two particular readings of globalization briefly outlined above: They bring to the fore two quite different possibilities for construing our human connectedness and our human differences that emerge from the process of globalization. One sees globalization as providing new possibilities for deepening affirmations of human connectedness; the other sees it making possible a more radical and complete affirmation of human differences. As I shall argue below, these possibilities are not entirely new inasmuch as embedded within them are the polarities of our unsociable sociability, and these polarities are not resolvable as simply as a construct such as the global village might suggest. Globalization provides a new context that radically challenges ways of engaging these polarities that minimize difference at the expense of connectedness or, conversely, connectedness at the expense of difference. In addition, to the extent that certain dynamics within globalization bring into question the very possibility that an intent to social union can be effected by the noncoercive social authority of reason, they require us to exhibit, more fully than Kant was able, the concrete social dynamics that make possible the establishment of an ethical commonwealth.

Within the context of globalization, the question of whether forming an intent to social union of the kind necessary to establish an
ethical commonwealth is even possible is a question about the extent
to which our recognition of our connectedness and our difference can
properly be considered to be an exercise of reason: Are they accorded
adequate and proper recognition principally *in consequence of* the
noncoercive exercise of the social authority of reason? It is also a
question about the social and the noncoercive character of such an
exercise of reason: Is the recognition we appropriately give our connectedness and our differences one that reason *requires* of us even as
it also specifies that such recognition fully comports with reason only
if it is *freely* and *reciprocally* given?[4] Finally, it is also a question
about the character (or, to use a term that, though apt, is suspect in
many quarters, about the "nature") of our human connectedness and
our human differences: What is the character of this connectedness
and these differences such that an exercise of *reason* functions as the
proper form of their acknowledgment?

When analyzed from the perspective of unsociable sociability,
globalization can be seen to exhibit the same tension within its own
dynamics that Kant identified as the source from which the need for
critique arises: The inner conflict within reason itself precisely about
how to deal with the recognition of our human likeness and difference
(see chapter 4, "War: The Social Consequences of Radical Evil"). Even
as globalization makes it possible for human beings to forge new and
more complex links among themselves, to see more clearly the range of
already existent connections that tie human activities to one another and
to the processes of nature, and to allow awareness of the possibilities of
interconnection to feed back into the shaping of daily practice, it also
allows us to construe the most basic form of human connections to be
constructs increasingly amenable to determination by the exercise of
arbitrary human choice. Even as globalization expands the possibilities
for acknowledging our likenesses and their power to draw us together,
it also enables us to construe them in ways that allow us to reserve a
"right" to withdraw from the claims they place upon us. In each case,
globalization, as a form of the dynamic of unsociable sociability, provides new possibilities for exhibiting the exception made in one's own
individual (or group) favor that lies at the heart of radical evil.

Even as globalization makes it possible for human beings to recognize, articulate, and better appreciate the character of their differences, be they of language, race, gender, culture, social practice, be

they among individuals, or among communities, it also makes it increasingly possible for individuals or groups of individuals to determine *which* differences they are willing allow to impinge upon their own lives, even as the recognition of certain differences is accepted as subject to coercive enforcement in the political order. Consider, for instance, what seems to be the persistence of racist and sexist attitudes even in societies that have developed extensive bodies of legislation and forms of public regulation, especially in the last half-century, to eliminate the impact of these attitudes in the operation of an extensive range of social, economic, cultural, and political practices. In the contemporary context of a globalization that provides everyone with access to instantaneous worldwide communication, the possibilities for the articulation, reenforcement, and wider dissemination of such attitudes exponentially multiply. One need not be, moreover, overtly or consciously racist to exhibit this bifurcation: Globalization, to the extent that it helps to provide circumstances for a healthy economy in already prosperous nations, makes it all the more possible for persons and groups to order their lives so as to ensure the least possible impingement of such difference on their life practices. An example of this would be the continuing pattern of *de facto* residential segregation by race that remains common in the United States.

In its crudest form, such a construal allows us to take any form of connection that we have with other human beings or with the processes of nature to be subject to "on/off" control that is finally determined by what the person at the switch happens to want. Conversely, it allows us to allocate difference into two distinct zones for recognition. In one zone, the exercise of the coercive power of the political order is acknowledged as appropriate for ordering the public consequences of such recognition—or nonrecognition. In the other zone, recognition of difference is construed as yet another matter for the exercise of choice, a matter of taste, or acceptance of the force of social custom. Thus globalization enables us, on the one hand, to acknowledge more fully our differences and to recognize the claim they make upon us to be held in a respect whose power lies precisely *in the way it connects us even in difference.* Yet, on the other hand, it also enables us more easily to demarcate the places in our lives that we seek to keep exempt from the claims of difference and the respect that ensues upon these claims.

The way that the dynamics of connectedness and difference play out in the processes of globalization are themselves affected by the particular economic, cultural, and historical circumstances in which the organizational and technological conditions that make globalization possible have emerged. Abstracted from those circumstances, globalization alone does not pose any more of a threat to the social authority of reason—nor offer greater opportunity to extend that social authority—than predecessor movements (e.g., industrialization) that have had long-range impact upon human social organization and dynamics. Like those predecessor movements, the results are likely to involve both loss and gain, with the particular forms of loss and gain emerging from the larger matrix of human activity of which globalization now plays a part. I have already suggested that the radical nature of the challenge that globalization poses to the social authority of reason arises from its intersection with other powerful dynamics at work in an era in which the shape of what has hitherto been known as modernity seems itself to be undergoing major change. With respect to the social authority of reason, the most significant of these intersecting dynamics bears upon the manner in which we construe our human connectedness and our human differences.

As I shall argue in the next section, the current mode of modernity—be it transitional or not—has put in play a set of conceptual and cultural dynamics that bring into question the very possibility that human beings can form a shared intent to social union based upon the noncoercive exercise of the social authority of reason. These dynamics, moreover, have had a role in the concrete shape that globalization has so far taken and to that extent they serve to entrench the dynamics of unsociable unsociability more deeply into globalization rather than make it more amenable to the social authority of reason. One consequence of this is that it moves the challenge that this contemporary form of unsociable sociability presents to the social authority of reason back to a level that Kant himself was only partially successful in articulating: These are the crucial questions about the precise character of the shared intent to social union without which there can be no ethical commonwealth and about the concrete means by which the social authority of reason noncoercively brings about this shared intent.

The Leveling of Meaning: Connectedness and Difference in the Culture(s) of (Post)modernity

Like "globalization," the terms "modernity" and "postmodernity" can be used to designate a wide range of phenomena affecting human lives and culture in the contemporary world and are open to a wide range of analyses and construals. My goal in this section is not principally to add yet another analysis to what has burgeoned into a bewildering array of diagnoses, attacks, defenses, praises, and denunciations of either modernity and its still adolescent off-spring (or, might I cautiously suggest, younger sibling), postmodernity. I propose rather to work along a vein that has already been well prospected by commentators such as Charles Taylor and George Steiner in order to locate certain features of the forces currently at work in shaping human social dynamics that bear most directly on the question of the social authority of reason.[5] As the discussion of the previous section has already indicated, these features concern a direction we seem to be taking in the construal our human connectedness and our human differences and the form of human social dynamics in which such construals are exhibited.

The central claim I will advance in this section is that the features of our modern/postmodern cultures that most fundamentally challenge the social authority of reason are those that enable—and indeed encourage us—to view our connectedness and our differences as a contingently shifting interplay of complex, though ultimately partial, links and gaps, an interplay whose significance, if any, is conferred—also only contingently—from individual vantage points that themselves move along the flux and vectors of temporality. Once this shifting interplay is seen as it is, moreover, the exercise of "reason" stands unmasked as a set of persistent efforts to "fix" the interplay from one or another vantage point. This enterprise of reason can be successful, moreover, only to the extent that one vantage point can be made to prevail—ideally as the only one possible, but at least as the one that can be taken to provide the widest and most comprehensive point from which to fix the interplay. Making one vantage point prevail, however, inevitably and necessarily requires those who appeal to "reason" to place no constraint in principle upon the possibility of exercising it coercively.

That one particular vantage point prevails as reason—even over a long period of time, as has been the case in the modern era in the West—does not have its basis, however, in any authority intrinsic to its particular vantage point as "reason." It rests, instead, upon the exercise of a social power that through sometimes subtle, sometimes overt coercive means brings others to take the vantage point that has prevailed as "reason" to be one that serves their own interest. The "authority" of reason in this sense is surely social in that its proper functioning requires that there be acknowledgment of an interconnection among agents; but the interconnection does not itself arise from the recognition of an authority that is intrinsic to that connectedness with respect to the exercise of "reason." What holds this connection together, instead, is a dynamic of mutual coercion that will enable the victors not only to claim their interest as the interest of all but also to secure the assent of all—including those who lose—to that claim.

This modern/postmodern reading of "reason" as merely the mantle of an extrinsic authority that cloaks long-term victors in the interplay of contending interests has become a quite influential factor in shaping contemporary intellectual culture, but it also represents a dynamic that can be seen to have been at work in the wider range of Western culture well before the term "postmodern" became current.[6] It is a dynamic that is not altogether novel—and neither, I suspect, are many of the postmodern articulations it has been given. Nietzsche does have legitimate claim to be recognized for drawing attention to the need for this dynamic to be unmasked and to be faced without illusion. Other significant earlier articulations of key elements in this dynamic can also be found in (among others) Machiavelli, Hobbes, and David Hume, who, on this point at least, could well claim recognition as "proto-postmoderns."[7] One might even go farther back—to Democritus, Epicurus, and Lucretius—and recognize articulations of this dynamic in their ontology of the atomistic flux of particulars.

Kant, of course, recognized a form of this dynamic at work through his articulation of the notion of unsociable sociability. Unsociable sociability is a dynamic that recognizes the social authority of reason, but only in its coercive form. Because unsociable sociability accepts conflict and war as inextirpable from human social interaction, it cannot elicit from us any sure hope for perpetual peace and thus makes it pointless to work for it. Unsociable sociability is thus not the dynamic that will give human social interaction the form required to fulfill humanity's vocation as the juncture of nature and of freedom, let alone the external sign of its fulfillment, an international order securing perpetual peace among nations. Unsociable sociability does not provide for the full exercise of the self-governance of reason that constitutes its social authority. This full exercise becomes possible only as the self-governance of reason is extended over the dynamics of unsociable sociability not merely through the establishment of civil society with its coercive power to exercise the social authority of reason but also through the establishment of an ethical commonwealth made possible by the recognition that the social authority of reason in its most complete form is noncoercive.

The establishment of an ethical commonwealth is thus made possible by the recognition that reason is thoroughly social in its practical use. This recognition, moreover, cannot be exacted coercively, because the social authority of reason at this most fundamental level arises as a mutual and inclusive recognition of each and every human agent's freedom. Unsociable sociability, since it limits our horizon of recognition of the social authority of reason to its legitimate coercive forms, cannot by itself provide the framework for such recognition. The establishment of an ethical commonwealth is thus itself the framing of a horizon of understanding for human social dynamics, beyond that of unsociable sociability, through which full scope can be given to the noncoercive exercise of the social authority of reason.

Although we can draw lines tracing the lineage of philosophical articulations and analyses of unsociable sociability at least as far back as the first stirrings of modernity, a contemporary extension of them is pertinent because the process of globalization contains elements that seem to possess a cultural power capable of embedding this dynamic even more deeply across an extensive range of human practice. Among the most powerful of these elements stands the image that seems to have fully captured the contemporary world's economic imagination: The competitive marketplace driven by consumer choice. As with the terms globalization, modernity, and postmodernity, the marketplace and its dynamics are amenable to multilayered and multivalent construals. Many of these construals function in terms of theories that function as predictive models of economic practice. Although my account does not seek to engage these theories in their predictive function, I hope it will suggest the need for holding them to stringent conceptual and imaginative accountability with respect to assumptions embedded in them about the character of human sociality and rationality. The relevance of the marketplace to my effort to extend Kant's account of the social authority of reason into contemporary discussion arises, instead, from the imaginative horizon it provides of the cultural dynamics of exchange: Against this horizon, exchange is most efficiently and rationally made in terms of commodification; that is, of setting a value in terms of a "price" for something's possession or use. The import of the marketplace with respect to globalization is that this image of exchange through commodification—as it extends into more and more forms of human practice—brings with it the peril of leveling human connectedness and human differences to a function of exchange valuation. It makes it possible—indeed, it makes it easy and convenient for us—to take the very links and gaps that globalization allows us better to notice as the weaving of the fabric of human life and activity to be just one more set of items with a capacity to be "priced" by reference to one set or another of exchange value tokens.

Not all of the processes involved in globalization, of course, are directly moved by these dynamics of the exchange commodification of the marketplace. In fact, those that bear kinship with a cosmopolitanism of the kind envisioned by Kant—such as those that enable the respectful and freely offered cultural and intellectual hospitality he sees as one of its essential components or those that widen the public use of reason as a form of exchange in which the parties hold themselves accountable to one another for the testing of whatever view is put forth—can be seen to run athwart the dynamics of exchange commodification. The reason for this, as I shall argue below, is that cosmopolitanism enables us to construe our human connectedness and our human differences in terms of a depth, strength, and variety that escapes the only imaginative and conceptual grid that the image of marketplace exchange can provide—the play of impervious and bounded points schematized in terms of linear connections and intervals. Nonetheless, the image of the marketplace seems to have become so powerful that it constricts the range of human activities in which we can retain full confidence about the resilience of their inner social dynamics to resist even rhetorical—let alone actual—incorporation in the dynamics of the consumer marketplace.

Consider, for instance, the transformation, which started to take place during the last three decades of the twentieth century in the United States, that has turned what was once a primarily "entrepreneurial" practice of the medical profession into one component of a health care "industry." This shift, it is important to note, is not the introduction of marketplace dynamics into practices in which they had not been previously operative; in fact, one ironic consequence of this shift from solo practitioner to corporate operation in the provision of medical care has been to make us considerably more alert to the often masked way in which marketplace dynamics had previously shaped medical practice. The shift, rather, concerns *which* dynamics are to have the determining role in shaping the concrete forms of medical practice. Before this shift, these have been the dynamics arising from traditions of medical training and practice in which the provision of health care was construed as taking place within a framework of social relationships that defined the physician's professional responsibility primarily as ordered to the patient's well-being and presumed that such well-being was best secured in a relation of mutual trust. The very fact that it now has become commonplace to speak of a health care "industry," with neither surprise, irony, or chagrin, suggests the extent to which there is already significant cultural acceptance of a commodification of medical practice. We—at least in the United States—seem to have become comfortable with construing health care as yet one more product for inclusion in the consumer's "market basket," even as the provision of health care for those who find themselves priced out of the market continues as a neuralgic problem for many individuals and communities. The social context in which health care is provided is increasingly determined in terms of the organizational forms and contractual models of successful business practice; and, concomitant with efficiencies of scale, there also seem to be larger opportunities for lucrative medical fraud.[8] An analogous transformation seems to be at work in education, particularly at postsecondary levels, where models drawn from the financial and organizational practices of business have are shaping a new administrative *lingua franca* and affecting the manner in which the activities of instruction, research and service are conducted and assessed.[9]

This brief consideration of the impact that the dynamics of exchange commodification seems to be having on the practice of medicine is offered as merely suggestive with respect to the power that these dynamics, gathered under the image of the marketplace, can exercise in shaping a construal of an important area of human social interaction. It no longer seems odd to consider the practice of medicine as a business, and to many, such as investors in the vast range of for-profit entities that have become essential components of "the health care industry," the practice of medicine can readily be taken to be *only* a business. This consideration, moreover, has not taken into account the ways in which the vectors of globalization may play themselves out in the practice of medicine. There are elements to a globalization of medicine that may very well function as countervailing factors to a simple exchange commodification of health care, such as the wide and rapid dissemination of pertinent new methods of diagnosis and treatment, almost instantaneous access to a patient's medical history from any point on the globe, or the possibility for rapid deployment of personnel, equipment, and medicine in response to calamities such as a major earthquake. Yet there are also elements that can function to reinforce the power of the dynamics of exchange commodification to shape the practice of medicine. Behind the reports of a clandestine market in organs for transplant lurks the possibility of a future legitimation, in at least some contexts, of open commercial trade in human body parts—a possibility that could take a quantum leap closer to actuality if and when the technology for organ-specific cloning is developed. It also may not be accidental that, of the enterprises directly connected with the practice of medicine, those concerned with pharmaceutical research and production, including the field of genetic modification, have an enormous stake in the successful globalization of their ventures.[10]

The issues that arise in just this one area in which the dynamics of exchange commodification intersect with those of globalization help us to locate more precisely the character of the challenge facing a Kantian account of the social authority of reason in the contemporary world. As I have already noted, the target of this challenge is quite clear: The very possibility that there can be *a concrete intent to social union* that can be *shared* by all moral agents precisely insofar as this intent is *formed* from the *noncoercive* exercise of the *social authority of reason*. What we now need to pinpoint is precisely *how* the possibility is placed in question by this particular convergence of these powerful forces at work across the range of contemporary culture. As the rest of this section will show, this possibility is brought in question by the social practices emergent in this convergence that have the effect of leveling our human connectedness and our human differences down to forms of transient contingency devoid of the capacity to bear enduring meaning.

These practices constitute a horizon for rendering human connectedness and differences intelligible against a flux of contending particularities—an intelligibility that will inevitably be incomplete, transitory, and fragmented. Whatever meaning these connections and differences can bear arise in function of a horizon of intent, imagination, and choice that is both bounded and bonded to the interplay of limited and particular individual interests that even though they may converge and coalesce for long periods of time eventually will fracture back into the immediacy, contingency, and transience of particulars. Our connectedness is never more than mere alliance, and always subject in principle to renegotiation; our differences can never be affirmed in the fullness of their difference, since to do so would be to relinquish one's power to declare, precisely over against them, what they are. Against this horizon for construing our connectedness and difference, there is no concrete intent to social union that can be shared by all moral agents, since any concrete intent to social union arises from the contingent convergence of particular interests. Neither is there a noncoercive form of the exercise of the social authority of reason, since any authority intending to be of inclusive scope over the interplay of particular needs must be exercised coercively.

The challenge is thus not that the dynamics of exchange commodification or the image of the marketplace are themselves intrinsically problematic with respect to the shared intent to social union needed for the noncoercive exercise of the social authority of reason in an ethical commonwealth. Nor does the challenge arise from something that is intrinsically problematic about the new and complex possibilities that globalization provides for identifying and construing our connectedness and our differences. The challenge arises, rather, in virtue of an intellectual and social dynamic that has historically been a vector in the trajectory of these phenomena as they move with us toward the cusp between modernity and its aftermath. It is a continuation of the vector that Kant himself recognized as the dogmatized forms of empiricism and skepticism that provided the context for his efforts to bring self-discipline to reason in its seemingly self-opposing efforts to render the human place in the cosmos intelligible, both theoretically and morally. (see, e.g., A 462–476/B 490–504, A 739–769/B 766–797). Kant recognized this vector as, ironically, one of the ploys by which we use reason, in the name of one of reason's own interests, to avoid the discipline of self-governance that is required by the very social nature of reason. This is also the vector along which radical evil—that is, the self-corruption of the self-governance of reason—takes social form because this vector takes the deepest form of our human social dynamics to be the contention of particularities that constitutes us all as conscripts in a never ending state of war. It is a vector along which lie a proliferation of modernist anxieties, nihilist exaltation and despair, fideist and atheist contentions and, more recently, postmodernist shrugs of indifference—the last of which contains the most radical challenge to the reason and its social authority in that it puts aside, with little trace of regret, the enterprise of rendering our human circumstances intelligible in favor of making one's own (brief) way through the world comfortably or at least with minimal bother.

Even though radical evil lies along the trajectory described by this vector, it is important to note that Kant's own analysis and assessment of this vector affirms the legitimacy of its concern to give full recognition to the complexity of the interplay of particulars. Radical evil, we must remember, is not wickedness, evil affirmed and chosen for its own sake. It is corruption, though of a most subtle kind—corruption that is self-incurred, in the form of the self-deceit than makes exception in one's own favor and enfolds such exception under the mantle of reason. Skepticism and empiricism can function as legitimate articulations of what he terms the speculative interest of reason—so long as they also acknowledge that are subject to the "tribunal" of a critique that is fully public and social. This suggests that Kant could just as readily acknowledge the legitimacy of later developments along this vector that draw our attention to the indeterminacy of such interplay and to what postmodernism has tellingly come to term its "interruptions"—so long as they acknowledge that they, too, are subject to the same critical tribunal. What Kant would not acknowledge as valid, however, are claims in which "interruption" and contention are then dogmatized so as to make them the only modes of interplay among particulars. The basis, moreover, for Kant's rejection of this—and, in fact, of every form of dogmatism—is that this vector eventually turns us away the very social dynamic that makes it possible for us to discipline reason to the exercise of its own self-governance. It is a vector that entails the denial of a principle that is most basic to critique: That reason is thoroughly social. It is a vector along which lies the strongest temptation to be complicit in the radical evil that is the self-corruption of reason. We enlist reason in service of the denial of the fundamentally social character of its exercise and authority.

The main thrust of this challenge to the social authority of reason does not run only along a conceptual vector delimited by philosophical forms of skepticism in continuity with the kind Kant sought to engage. A far more significant vector is one now being delimited by a dynamic of immediacy in contemporary culture that narrows the imaginative and conceptual construal of our human connectedness and differences to horizons framed only in terms of immediacy, transience, and contingency. Much of this dynamic seems to arise precisely in virtue of a convergence of technologies and skills central to the processes of globalization; for example, networks of instantaneous global communication, virtually unlimited capacity for the storage and retrieval of information, new forms and techniques to organize and present information, with forms of social interaction modelled on the image of a marketplace in which contention, cooperation, risk, loss, and gain are fueled by calculations for winning as large a share of the "action"—be it wealth, power, admiration, fame—as one can. Although the motivating elements in this dynamic can hardly be considered new—they are, indeed, key ingredients in the dynamics of unsociable sociability—what is new is that they may now be played out against a frame of reference in which we can negotiate our way through matters of human connectedness and human difference with power to acknowledge or to dismiss them—to "click" them on or off—literally at our fingertips. What is new here is the immediacy with which connectedness can be made or broken, and with which difference may be noted or ignored.

There are ironies in this dynamic of immediacy that Kant would not miss noting: The human knowledge and skills that make it possible for us to enlarge the complexity and the scope of our connectedness with one another, have also made it possible for us to level our connectedness down to the linear simplicity of discrete moments of transactional exchange. Our imaginative construal of the content of what connects us begins to be modeled on the means that now so easily enable us to make—or to break—so many connections with one another: Encoded packets of instantly transmittable information. There is a parallel irony here in our construal of difference: Even as our connectedness is leveled to linearity, our differences are leveled to the sheer multiplicity of contingent particularity. The knowledge and skills that make possible an articulation of difference as difference in ways that are potentially richer than any that were available in previous eras, have also made it possible for us to level difference down to the contingent coalescence of particularity that wins its meaning not as difference but as effective power against other congeries of particularity. As connectedness becomes linear, difference becomes punctual. The trajectory that began from a reaction to a Cartesian dualism that split the cosmos of matter in motion from the interior punctuality of the thinking self sets us down in a world that hauntingly remains within the confines of Cartesian coordinates. It is a world on which connection and difference can be fully located by digitized sets of surface coordinates and on which they need not possess depth on their own since that can be constructed virtually from further coordinates. In such a networked world, there need not be any shared intent to social union: All one needs is the capacity to "log on"—and whether one does, or does not, or whether one "logs off," makes no difference with respect to attaining a shared social goal for humanity.

The language I have just used is intentionally parodic of the electronic digitalization of information that has become the instrument of globalization and the tool that has enabled the markets of finance and credit to replace those of physical commodities as the primary engine driving the world's economy. Parody, however, can be used to make a serious point—and in this case, the point is that we can readily make participation in a fully "networked" and "digitized" world that seems to be emerging as both means and outcome of a globalized marketplace an effective way to thwart the possibility of the shared intent to social union necessary for the establishment of an ethical commonwealth and for the full exercise of the social authority of reason. The way we do so is precisely by allowing the ease of connection and disconnection, the rapidity with which we can move from difference to difference, to create the illusion that our human connections and differences function the same way. They can quite readily become matters of mere human contrivance and construction, matters that no longer matter once they are "off the screen." Our use of these tools of globalization and marketplace exchange make it easy for us—in the absence of a contemporary counterpart to "critique"—to conceal from ourselves the depth in and through which we all must eventually work with each another in order to sustain our fundamental human connectedness throughout the whole range of our human differences.[11]

Where, then, does this situation leave us with respect to the shared intent to social union that is necessary for the establishment of the ethical commonwealth and to the noncoercive exercise of the social authority of reason required to call forth this intent from our freedom? The account of human social interactions and relationships that emerges from the dynamics I have been describing in this chapter would make of such intent yet one more mere "construction" out of human particularity, but with a horizon to a universality that will inevitably require coercion for its attainment. Though it would concede the possibility of a intent to social union shared among particular agents, such intent itself remains always particular, never universal, always within the particular confines of specific historical societies and communities. To extend it universally would go counter to the freedom of individuals or of particular communities to choose the shape of their own destiny, to decide with whom and for whom to share an intent to social union. To bring about such intent universally would be to override the freedom to choose and to act in one's own favor and in behalf of one's own—and to override freedom in that way is to authorize coercion against freedom.

Because this account makes quite clear the nature of its fundamental challenge to the social authority of reason, it should also be quite clear what Kant's reply to this challenge would be. This account pleads for the very thing that Kant would consider to stand most fundamentally against the authority of reason: That one reserve a "special" place for oneself and for those most like oneself within the most fundamental set of human social relationships—the moral world that is constituted by free and full recognition of one another's moral agency—in which there are *no* special places, least of all places that can be unconnected at will from *moral* commerce with the rest of humankind. The account invokes reason—in the guise of freedom to choose in one's own favor—over against the universal intent of reason that is embedded in one's very status as a moral agent. This account challenges the social authority of reason because it challenges the fullness of the social scope of our human reason that, without paradox, *requires* us *freely* to bind ourselves to every other human by mutual recognition of one another's moral personhood and of the shared responsibility that it entails that we work together to shape a common destiny as humankind.

As I shall show in chapter 7, this account places in question what I term the "social respect" that human moral agents owe to one another as the fundamental form of mutual moral recognition. Such social respect, I shall argue, is precisely that which constitutes the intent to social union requisite for the establishment of an ethical commonwealth. In the course of delimiting the elements of social respect, my argument will show what makes it possible as a shared intent to social union against the challenge offered by the vector of contemporary culture that denies in theory but, even more pointedly, in practice the possibility of such an intent. Showing that this shared intent is possible, however, does not yet complete the task that I set to do at the outset of this work. I must also identify at least some of the forms of social respect that our current circumstances require of us as a concrete exhibition of this shared intent to social union. This further and final step is needed to vindicate the social authority of reason because the in-practice denial of such an intent has emerged not only in the intersection of dynamics of exchange commodification with those of globalization but also in the forms of our engagement with one another for purposes of determining the policies, practices, and institutions in which we share responsibility for the civil, social, and cultural life of our communities, be they local, national, regional, or global. At this level, the social authority of reason comes under challenge on the very field in which Kant sees us working out the fulfillment of our vocation as the juncture of nature and freedom: The shaping of a human culture suited to the social interaction of moral agents bound in mutual respect for one another's freedom. In order to do this final task, I will show how Kant's notions of the public use of reason and cosmopolitanism offer the basis for articulating the dynamics of human social relationship that make it possible to extend the social self-governance of reason over these contemporary—and radically challenging—forms of unsociable sociability.

CHAPTER SEVEN

The Unfinished Task of Critique:
Social Respect and the Shaping of a Common World

The Interest of Reason: Critique as the Socialization of Reason

Chapter 6 sketched out elements of an emergent culture in which the processes of globalization take place within a landscape framed by horizons that manifest the fracturing of the hitherto dominant modern understandings of what constitutes us as human. I argued that this convergence of globalization with a fractured understanding of our human commonality has made it possible for a dynamic of immediacy to challenge the social authority of reason by denying, in practice, the very possibility that human agents freely can form a concrete intent to a social union that is fully universal. The source of such a denial lies in the way in which practices expressive of this dynamic of immediacy encourage us to narrow down the imaginative and conceptual possibilities of construing our human connectedness to a field constituted by the transient interplay of contingent particularities. Human agents seem to find themselves inescapably enmeshed in historical and cultural particularity that allows, at best, for only partial commonalities constructed on the contingent convergence of particular interests. This renders deeply problematic the possibility for construing our commonalities in terms of concepts of an enduring human nature that had once constituted a *lingua franca* for self-understanding. The result is that, despite the new possibilities that globalization offers for enlarging the scope of our human connectedness,

139

any intent to a social universality founders upon the need to keep clear the space that difference needs in order to affirm the power of its particularity within the interplay of immediacy.

This dynamic has emerged from a trajectory that has had as one of its major vectors the deeply rooted modern concern for the liberty of human beings. Put in terms of the language of liberty, this dynamic affirms the radical particularity of the freedom of individual human refusal over against the possibility of a fully universal intent to social union. Human freedom loses its significance once it abandons the very possibility of saying the "no" that issues from its own unique particularity to claims made upon it in the name of a social universality. From the perspective of individual liberty, social universality inevitably contains the possibility for overriding the very particularity on behalf of which liberty is exercised. Particularity thus must stand constantly ready to affirm itself in its immediacy—and the emergent global culture provides greater scope to such an affirmation by providing new power to make and to break, at will, at any time, our connectedness with one another.

In the context of the historical development of philosophical articulations of this concern for liberty, it may seem strange to identify Kant as a champion of a fully universal intent to social union over against these apparently new possibilities for the exercise of individual liberty. His formulation of the notion of moral autonomy has been rightly understood as a major milepost on the modern journey to attain full recognition of liberty as definitive of our human make-up. As such, autonomy seems to function precisely as the boundary line with respect to a universal intent to social union, the immovable place from which the "no" of particularity can most clearly be uttered. As I have argued throughout most of this work, however, such a construal of autonomy misses the extent to which Kant's own account of this notion is firmly rooted in an understanding of the social character of human moral agency and, thus, of the freedom through which that agency is exercised. Kant not only articulates the notion of autonomy in terms of the fundamentally social concept of law, he takes it to function most properly with reference to that community of moral agents he terms a kingdom of ends and to be ordered to a social goal, the highest good, as its proper object. This social character of moral agency and of human freedom is, in its turn, rooted in Kant's understanding of reason as itself having a fundamentally social character.

The social character of reason, however, is something that we come to recognize fully only through the activity Kant terms critique: Critique is the exercise of a self-discipline that enables us to exhibit the fully and thoroughly social character of reason. In consequence, the case against the denial of the very possibility that human agents freely can form a concrete intent to a social union that is fully universal is one that properly begins by returning to the very grounds on which Kant argues for the necessity of the enterprise of critique.

Kant sees critique as necessary inasmuch as there is a dynamic within the human exercise of reason that resists being drawn into the ambit of the full sociality of reason; that is, into the reciprocal relationship of inclusive argumentative exchange in which all interlocutors stand in full mutual accountability to one another. No one holds privileged place in such an exchange, even as all acknowledge that all have voice in such an exchange. Against such inclusive argumentative mutuality, Kant perceives an element within the human exercise of reason in virtue of which we each seek to privilege our own view by placing it outside of the dynamics of holding one another fully accountable for what we claim in the name of reason. In Kant's terminology, we each seek to privilege our own particular interest individually over against the interest of reason. In so doing, however, we fail to recognize the interest of reason as precisely that which constitutes an interest that we can claim precisely as *ours*; that is, the interest that we all *mutually* claim precisely in virtue of our recognition of one another as inclusively accountable to one another in the exercise of reason. To the extent that we fail to recognize the fully social character of reason and of the interest that arises from this, we seek to set reason against itself—and in so doing, we set ourselves against one another.

In order to see this, we need to return to Kant's description of this tension interior to our human exercise of reason in the "Doctrine of Method" of the first *Critique*, where he presents it in terms of an analogy with the exit from an atomistically construed state of nature into a civil society constituted by a set of ordered social relationships. His use of this analogy provides one significant indication that he sees this tension within our use of reason to be connected with the drama of unsociable sociability played out in human culture. As he presents this analogy, critique functions to transform this tension so that it supports rather than subverts the efforts of human inquiry in the attainment of humanity's unique destiny as the juncture of nature and freedom. Critique does so precisely by placing that tension within the larger horizon formed by recognition that human reason is fully social in character. Recognition of the full social character of human reason, moreover, constitutes a crucial element in construing why Kant takes the interest of reason to require of us the free adoption of a fully universal and inclusive intent to social union.

At the very heart of the dynamics through which human inquirers come to recognize the full depth of the social character of reason when it is put to theoretical use lies the question of a willingness (or an unwillingness) to accord to one another proper recognition in such inquiry. This recognition is possible only in terms of an intent to social union that forms the horizon of theoretical inquiry by requiring each one to stand in full and inclusive mutual accountability to one another. Within the ambit of the theoretical use of reason, a refusal properly to accord such recognition takes form either as dogmatism or as skepticism. Each form represents one side of what is ultimately a mutual failure to recognize that exercise of human reason must discipline itself to the acknowledgment of the fully social character of its theoretical use. Each denies this social character by seeking to take full possession of the full field of reason's inquiry by driving off the other. This dynamic of coercive antagonism arises from mutual failure to recognize that they each must exercise the self-discipline of critique upon the scope of what they claim on behalf of the issue of their inquiry. This self-discipline places them within a horizon of inquiry formed by an intent to social union, already implicit in their use of reason, that makes it possible for each to play a proper, mutually limiting role on the field of inquiry.

It is important to attend to the fact that, in using this analogy of an exit from the state of nature into civil society to characterize how critique brings about recognition of the full social character of the use of human reason, Kant does not take this self-discipline to bring about the *elimination* of dogmatism or skepticism from the dynamics of human inquiry. Instead of elimination, critique brings about a mutual self-recognition that they each represent only a partial interest at work in the full dynamics of human reason applied to theoretical inquiry. They are partial both in the sense that they each represent only a part of the full interest of reason and in the sense that they each function as partisan combatants, seeing to vanquish an opposing position seen as dangerously inimical. Critique will function to overcome both forms of partiality. It will place the first form of partiality within the more comprehensive context provided by attention to the full interest of reason. It will disarm the second form of partiality by showing that the perception of dangerous mutual hostility rests upon a self-generated illusion. In both cases, critique does so by drawing our attention to the fully inclusive social character that is required for the proper use of human reason. Recognition of the use of reason as universally inclusive is precisely the means that secures the possibility of engaging one another in the enterprise of critique: "The very existence of reason depends upon this freedom [of critique], which has no dictatorial authority but whose claim is never anything more than the agreement of free citizens, each of whom must be able to express his reservations, indeed even his *veto*, without holding back" (A738–739/B 766–767; see also A 752/B 780).

In line with this placement of the opposition between dogmatism and skepticism as representative of partial interests at work within the dynamics of a human inquiry that needs to be seen in its inclusive social context, Kant later characterizes their relationship to critique as stages in the development of reason from childhood to maturity:

> The first step in matters of pure reason, which characterizes its childhood, is **dogmatic**. The just mentioned second step is **skeptical**, and gives evidence of the caution of the power of judgment sharpened by experience. Now, however, a third step is still necessary, which pertains only to the mature and adult power of judgment. . . . this is not the censorship but the **critique** of pure reason. (A761/B 789)

Like the processes of human maturity, however, such growth to maturity in the human use of reason requires a proper social context to foster it correctly. Within the ambit of speculative inquiry, this social context is provided by conditions that make it possible for the argumentative exchange between dogmatism and skepticism to be conducted not as a form of armed conflict in which the victory of one side entails the defeat of the other, but as a form mutual self-correction within a common horizon that is provided by the self-discipline of critique. Kant advises: "Thus let your opponent speak only reason, and fight him solely with weapons of reason. . . . The conflict cultivates reason by consideration of its object on both sides, and corrects its judgment by thus limiting it" (A 744/B 772).

A bit later he once more significantly reaffirms the social character of the context that critique provides for such an argumentative exchange to take place. Critique makes it possible for the human disunion represented in the conflict between dogmatism and skepticism to be overcome inasmuch as it provides the discipline needed for the overcoming of self-imposed illusion:

> Reason also very much needs such a conflict, and it is to be wished that it had been undertaken earlier and with unlimited public permission. For then a mature critique would have come about all the earlier, at the appearance of which all of this controversy would have had to disappear, since the disputants would have learned insight into the illusion and prejudices that have disunited them. (A 747/B 774)

Kant then immediately notes "a certain dishonesty in human nature" (A 747/B 774) that leads to duplicity in human communication—even in the theoretical use of human reason "where human beings have far fewer hindrances to and no advantage at all in forthrightly confessing their thoughts openly and honestly" (A 749/B 777). Such duplicity is a tactic by which one tries to carve out a place for oneself on the field of contention that is not subject to argumentative accountability. This suggests that the practices of human communication will play a crucial role in determining whether and how we can form a concrete intent to a social union that is fully universal and thus bring about conditions for exercising the social authority of reason in ways that are appropriately noncoercive.

Kant's discussion of the resolution of this conflict that takes place within the theoretical use of reason also anticipates in a number of intriguing ways his later discussions of the conditions for establishing perpetual peace and an ethical commonwealth. Kant presents each of these notions as a particular form of social relationship through which human beings will be able to bring the dynamics of "unsociable sociability" under the full governance of reason. It is not insignificant that Kant uses images that involve the occupation of space to exhibit the process by which our relations to one another will be brought under the full governance of reason. This is a movement through which space that had been seen only as a field of contention is reenvisioned as a common ground upon which we can live and even flourish in our differences. Unsociable sociability begins to lose its grip upon our imagination and action to the extent that we begin to recognize that because we *must* share common space, be it the metaphorical space of an intellectual "battlefield" or the real geographical space of earth's finite globe, we *can* find mutually acceptable ways to do so. Although Kant does not himself explicitly connect these later discussions with this section of the first *Critique*, nor explore the ramifications of his own spatial imagery, the resemblances are striking enough to suggest the appropriateness of taking them all to be articulations of the enterprise of critique precisely as it is ordered to bring about a recognition of the thoroughly social character of the exercise of human reason.

It is not only the speculative use of reason that stands in need of critique to bring about recognition of the social character of reason out of what seems like an intractably divisive conflict within reason itself. At the heart of the dynamics through which human agents come to recognize the full depth of the social character of their practical use of reason Kant finds us deeply involved in the drama of unsociable sociability that is played out upon the stage of human history and culture. On one side of our unsociable sociability is a dynamism by which we seek to enlist reason in privileging the interest that arises in virtue of one's own particularity over against any claim made upon it in behalf of human connectedness: Because I am who I am precisely in my differentiation from all others, no other—be it individually or collectively—may lay legitimate claim against me. I can withdraw to a space that is wholly "mine," declaring it unconnected to that of any other. We exercise reason here to validate our separateness and differences.

On the other side of our unsociable sociability is a dynamism that enables us to recognize that it is precisely our human connectedness that provides the framework for making sense of interaction among our varied human particularities. Over and against the interests we take on behalf of our individual particularities (in virtue of which we seek for ourselves such things as property, power, and recognition), there is an interest we take—or which the circumstances of our human existence force us to take—in making and having a *shared* world; that is, a common field of activity in which we can each and all pursue our particular interests. We exercise reason to constitute a shared framework as the very condition of possibility for the recognition of the otherness and difference from which our particular interests arise and upon which they come into contention. Reason enables us to constitute a framework of (implicit) *mutual* recognition that makes possible, when our interests contend, my recognition that my resistance against your claim exhibits the interest that arises from my particular otherness over against yours, and *vice versa*. This framework, moreover, opens a horizon within which there is the possibility of settling contention among particular interests. On this side, we exercise reason to validate a human connectedness within which we can both recognize particularities in contention and envision the possibilities for bringing such contention to settlement.

Kant's affirmation of an interest of reason that is not simply a particular interest of any one of us, nor merely the aggregate of all of those interests, is one that crucially differentiates his account of the authority possessed by human reason in virtue of its autonomy from many later accounts that invoke Kant as a patron saint of liberalism. Central to Kant's own liberalism is the claim that in the use of our reason we are capable, individually and collectively, both of forming and taking a perspective for making decisions and for guiding actions that concretely represents, both over against our own particular interests and beyond alliances that bring together interests of the like minded or the commonly situated, the universal interest of humanity. This claim is crucial because it differs in a important way from a claim often at least implicitly operative in liberal political cultures—such as those in North American and Western Europe—that take human liberty, particularly of each individual, as the primary value to be protected and promoted in the institutions and practices that give order to public life. This claim, in contrast to Kant's, holds that human beings both are and can be driven *only* by particular interests which, of their very nature, are partial and not universal.[1] There is no "interest" of reason that can be considered to be over and above these particular human interests in such a way as to constitute an interest common to us all.

The partiality and particularity of these interests is a consequence of their being conceived as part of an account of agency in which rationality and rational choice is simply instrumental to the fulfillment of an agent's desires and preferences. Although there have been numerous ingenious efforts (of which utilitarianism remains in practice the most influential) to show that such desires and preferences can be enlarged to include the interests of others, such accounts still take the rationality of even those enlarged interests to rest upon their relationship to the particular interests of individual selves. Such enlarged interests are, of course, morally praiseworthy and socially useful, but they are genuinely rational only to the extent that agents see the fulfillment of others' desires and preferences as (ultimately) serving their own. Interests are enlarged by the joining of particular sets of interests; but there is no such thing as humanly common interest[2]— that is, one that bears upon all humanity both individually and collectively—that is more than the sum total of sets of interests instrumental to the desires and preferences of particular agents and that is capable of generating a concrete basis for determining actions.

This presupposition has the wisdom of some experience behind it. We have learned very well to discern and unmask how partial and particular our interests can be with respect to class and gender and race and all the elements of social location. We have learned how destructive exercises of human power arise when such partial and particular interests don the mask of universality. These are insights that have played a role in making plausible views that confine our human circumstances and the very makeup of our humanity to a horizon of particularity. Kant would most likely agree with much of the wisdom articulated in these insights, though not with the conclusion that they then require us to constrict the scope of what can be claimed on behalf of the interest of reason. He has no doubt about the power of partial and particular interests to fuel our action. He even holds that, as unpromising as they seem in the light of moral considerations, these partial and particular interests constitute the basic materials out of which we must construct our sociocultural world (*AP*, 7: 327–330/ 188–190). But I think that he would also claim that this does not give us the whole picture. The very possibility of using the material of our particular interests to construct a shared field for any human activity— our desires for acquisition, for power, for recognition, etc.—presupposes that we can take an interest that genuinely represents an inclusively universal standpoint that is proper to the exercise of human reason. Onora O'Neill puts this point well:

. . . Kant has grounded the authority of reason in considerations about the conditions for its having universal scope. Reasoning is a matter of following patterns of thought or adopting principles of action that all others can follow or adopt. If we aspire to reach only local and like-minded audiences there will be shared assumptions enough from which to reason. But the reasoning undertaken will be no more than a private use of reason, and its conclusions will be comprehensible among the (at least partially) like minded. *If we seek to reach beyond restricted circles*, with shared authorities, or shared assumptions that can carry the burden of conditional reason-giving, *we have to use principles of thought and action that all members of a wider, potentially diverse and specified plurality can follow.* (Emphasis added)[3]

Kant's affirmation that embedded within the use of human reason is the possibility of taking a standpoint that represents the inclusively universal interest of reason thus has direct bearing upon the question that the dynamics of contemporary culture have raised about the establishment of the social authority of reason: Can human agents freely form a concrete intent to a social union that is fully universal? In this context, showing that it is possible for us to take such an inclusive and universal interest is fundamental for the establishment of the social authority of reason and for determining the means by which such authority is enforced. Kant's claims that there is such an interest and that we can and must take such an interest are thus claims about how we establish and recognize the authority of reason in the field of human social interaction that is constituted by the exercise of our freedom. More specifically, these are claims about whether and how the authority of reason can serve as the basis for envisioning and constructing a *shared* world in which moral agents freely accord one another due recognition of one another's autonomy.

In order to understand Kant's claims about this "interest of reason" and its bearing on the social authority of reason we must keep in mind the way Kant views our fundamental human circumstances. The "peculiar fate" of humanity that gives rise to the need for critique is that we are beings who stand as and at the juncture of nature and freedom. Even as we stand under constraints of nature by which we already and of necessity share a world that connects us to one another in a nexus of causal interaction, we are nonetheless able, by the exercise of our freedom, to give moral shape to our connections with one another in the world that nature constrains us to share. The moral shape that we give to the world will thus be a function of the extent to which we exercise the governance of reason upon relationships to one another. On the one hand, nature gives us no choice but to have an interest in a shared world; that is, in the circumstances of our human existence as finite, needy beings on a planet of finite resources and limited space for our habitation. On the other hand, as Kant sees it, there is an interest that reason has—and that we can freely adopt—for us to share this limited world with one another not merely as a matter of "natural" necessity, but as a matter of a free, noncoerced mutual recognition of one another, a recognition that has its roots in the mutual exercise of our freedom as practical reason, rather than in the service of any of our particular interests (*Rel*, 6: 94–95/130, 97–98/132–133; *AP*, 7: 328–329/188–189; cf. *CJ*, 5: 448–450/314–316). Put in its simplest terms, Kant sees our human circumstances as requiring us to share a world, even as our reason makes it possible for us to determine in mutual freedom *what kind of (moral) world it will be* that we share.[4]

As a result, the shared moral world we ultimately shape by the use of our freedom will mark the success—or the failure—of our efforts to fulfill our human vocation to be the juncture of nature and freedom. The interest of reason bears upon the shaping of the world of social relationships that issues from the exercise of human freedom. In such a world, moreover, the social relationships that most adequately express the interest of reason will be those in which the authority of reason can be recognized and exercised in the manner most appropriate for beings who mutually acknowledge one another's freedom, that is, noncoercively. Put in terms of the notion of an ethical commonwealth, these are precisely the social relationships that would issue from the free mutual adoption of the universal and inclusive intent to social union upon which an ethical commonwealth is founded.

As Kant sees the interest of reason functioning in the course of history and in the development of culture, it provides us with a dynamism to universality and inclusivity for shaping a shared world for the exercise of freedom. This interest of reason provides a driving force for the cosmopolitanism that he advocates, and is deeply implicated in the exercise of the public use of reason. The interest of reason gives form to the intent to social union that establishes an ethical commonwealth and it enables us to envision the conditions that make perpetual peace possible. Cosmopolitanism, the public use of reason, the ethical commonwealth, and the conditions for perpetual peace are all notions that arise along the social trajectory of the critical project. They arise as articulations of the socialization of reason that the discipline of critique seeks to effect and they all require us to consider the questions of *how extensive* are we prepared to make this shared world of mutual freedom and *with whom* are we prepared to share it. These issues were urgent enough in Kant's day. They have gained increasing urgency in a contemporary world where demands for the recognition of plurality and difference have not only become more insistent but are increasingly recognized as articulating a deep and legitimate moral claim.

The interest of reason, in each case, is that our answers to these questions, as they are embodied in the organization and the practice of our social relationships, become ever more universal and inclusive. The interest of reason requires that our social practices enlarge the horizons of our human connectedness and the transparency of our communication even as we recognize the finitude of our human condition that is manifest in the very differences that make it challenging for us to share the limited space of our planet. Moreover, because the social relationships that most adequately satisfy the interest of reason are those in which the authority of reason is exercised and acknowledged noncoercively, the manner in which we are both to establish and to enlarge such a shared world for the human interaction constituted by the exercise of our freedom must itself be noncoercive.

By placing Kant's claims about the interest of reason in the context of the socialization of reason brought about by the discipline of critique, we can now discern better how the interest of reason contrasts with our partial and particular interests. For Kant, the dynamism of reason is inclusive and its authority is noncoercive; in contrast, the dynamism of our partial and particular interests is exclusive and their authority to sway others is coercive. As a result, a field for common human interaction constructed on the basis of our partial and particular interests can be inclusive only to the extent that we can coerce into it others who do not share those interests with us. Just as the cultural dynamics of immediacy and particularity would have it, such a field of interaction cannot fully be inclusive, since it brings others into its ambit by the exercise of the hegemony of coercive power, not of the authority of reason. On the other hand, it cannot be universal: If our recognition of these interests as partial and particular restrains us from coercing others onto the field of our interests, all we have constructed is a tribal circle, an enclave of particularity that does not exhibit the dimensions of a world in which all may share. The particularity of each field of interaction would set the authority of reason within arbitrary and contingent limits.

In contrast, the interest of reason constitutes a horizon for our engagement with one another that goes beyond that provided by the immediacy of any of our particular interests, as genuine and as demanding as they may be. On Kant's account, over and against the particular interests we bring with us in our engagement with one another, and in virtue of which we seek for ourselves such things as property, power, and recognition, there is an interest we take—or, more precisely, which the exercise of our reason, in consideration of the circumstances of our human social existence, requires us to take— in constituting a shared world of action for one another through the exercise of our freedom (*Rel*, 6: 94–95/130, 97–98/132–133; *AP*, 7: 328–329/188–189; cf. *CJ*, 5: 448–450/314–316). The interest of reason requires of us a commitment to engage one other in an ever-enlarging circle of communication, inquiry, and argument to find and to construct an enduring and inclusive world for social interaction on the basis of mutual respect for one another's freedom. This commitment to engage one another in the enterprise of constituting a shared world for interaction with one another in freedom exhibits reason's interest, since that interest is not simply a particular interest of any one of us, nor merely the aggregate of all of those interests, but *an inclusive and universal interest in the freedom of each of us and of all of us*, the freedom that most fundamentally constitutes us as members of the human species.

Engagement with one another in a common enterprise to constitute a shared world for interaction with one another—that is, the establishment of an ethical commonwealth—can thus be considered the full social expression of what Kant terms the interest of reason. The world that the exercise of our reason requires we construct with and for one another through our freedom is ordered to the goal of establishing an ethical commonwealth. Kant's claim that there is such an interest of reason thus exhibits the fundamentally social character of his identification of human freedom with the moral autonomy exercised in our practical use of reason. Because the exercise of human autonomy is a function of the interest of reason, it requires that all moral agents can and must take such an interest in the constitution of such a common world for interaction in freedom with one another. In order to constitute a common world of action for one another, we must be ready to accept the social authority of reason as the basis for determining the terms for living with one another in the world we have so constituted. This suggests that acceptance of the social authority of reason *as the basis for the project of constituting a common world for the mutual exercise of freedom* is fundamental to forming the fully universal and inclusive intent to social union on which an ethical commonwealth can be established. If this is so, then the issue of whether such an intent is possible, given the dynamics of immediacy and particularity that are at work in shaping an emergent globalized culture, turns on vindicating the claim that the exercise of human freedom is itself fundamentally ordered to the project of constituting a fully and inclusively shared world for human interaction. The vindication of the social authority of reason and, with it, of the possibility of freely adopting a fully universal and inclusive intent to social union, thus involves nothing less than showing that the practical use of reason constitutive of our human freedom is fully social.

Constituting a Shared World: Human Freedom as Social Respect

If the account of the interest of reason given in the preceding is correct, it means that the fundamental issue in the critical project is not simply the authority of reason but, as Onora O'Neill has argued, the authority of reason *precisely as social.* Delimiting the social authority of reason was an important task for Kant because he saw it as the only adequate basis from which human beings can be morally empowered to construct a principled social ordering of human existence—and without such a principled ordering of its own existence and activity, humanity would fail to attain the destiny unique to it as the juncture of nature and freedom. At stake, therefore, is the validity of the claims that reason has social authority and that its authority is noncoercive: Does such social authority constitute the basis on which we exercise our freedom so as to give order to the dynamics and practices that constitute our social relationships to one another? Does such social ordering ultimately rest upon a coercive power that must eventually be pressed into service to enforce the demands arising from the contention of particular interests? Or is it possible for the social ordering of human existence to issue from an exercise of human reason that enables us to stand in relationships of full, inclusive, and mutual recognition of one another's freedom?

Kant clearly answers the final question affirmatively by articulating the interest of reason in social terms and, from that, positing the possibility of establishing an ethical commonwealth on the basis of a fully inclusive and universal intent to social union. His affirmation seems based upon a confidence in the power of human reason that, two centuries later, seems to many to be at least out of proportion, if not out of place. As many contemporary intellectual perspectives view the contention of human particularities and partial interests, reason is one more particular vying for a place from which to extend and exercise a sway that will turn out—as do all such efforts eventually—to be impermanent and incomplete. We are now supposed to know, thanks to Nietzsche and other "unmaskers" of modernity, that Kant's effort to curb the pretensions of human reason by the power of reason was flawed at the outset by his unwillingness or his inability to recognize that the hegemonic dynamic of reason he tried to limit by "critique" cannot be curbed by *any* form of self-discipline. Given the perspective that the distance of two hundred years provides, Hume's dictum that reason is slave of the passions seems a more apt caption upon the mayhem human beings have wrought on one another throughout the twentieth century and into the twenty-first than any of Kant's invocations of the critique of reason as the tribunal to adjudicate the contentions that run deepest in our human makeup.

What, then, is to be said in vindication of the social authority of reason that Kant's critical project attempted to articulate as a mark of what he was confident enough to call "an age of enlightenment"— though not an "enlightened" age (*BF*, 8: 40/8)? Does an age in which all authority has become suspect as a mask for the exercise of coercive power on behalf of interests that are all irreducibly partial and particular provide any space for human reason to claim even a modicum of authority, let alone primary authority to govern the ordering of our social relationships with one another? In the rest of this section, I will outline what I believe can function as an initial step for answering these questions. This first step involves articulating the notion of the "social respect" that human beings are to accord to one another in virtue of their freedom. The purpose of so doing is to show that such reciprocal recognition of freedom among moral agents is the fundamental form of the social authority proper to the exercise of human reason. The social respect that issues from the practical use of reason—that is, from the exercise of the autonomy constitutive of our human moral freedom—thus constitutes the horizon within which the project of constituting a common world for interaction may take place.

Articulating the notion of social respect as the fundamental form of the social authority of reason is only the initial step, however, because, as I hope my argument will also show, a full answer is possible only in actually undertaking a reordering of our human social dynamics to accord with the social respect we owe one another. Such reordering would serve to make them loci for communication that makes more transparent the multiple forms of human connectedness that run through even our deepest plurality and difference. In Kant's terminology, whereas unsociable sociability forms the horizon over against which the human social dynamics of the contention of partial interests take place, social respect is the horizon that reason constitutes in the exercise of our moral freedom for the social dynamics of an ethical commonwealth. We remain enclosed within a horizon of unsociable sociability—and thus within an ambit in which even reason must ultimately resort to coercive power to enforce its authority—so long as we refuse to recognize that our freedom provides us with the capacity to constitute a larger and far more appropriate horizon for the mutual exercise of our freedom. This horizon, moreover, is one that provides the possibility for a noncoercive exercise of the authority of reason. This horizon is constituted by the social respect that exhibits an inclusively universal intent to social union. This horizon of social respect enables us to bring the dynamics of unsociable sociability under the self-governance of reason proper to our human vocation to be the juncture of nature and freedom. But—and this is the reason why only the actual undertaking of a reordering of human social dynamics provides a full answer to the challenge to the social authority of reason presented by contemporary culture—such a horizon cannot be framed except through the mutual exercise of human freedom. It is a horizon that we have the power to frame, but which can only be framed in the very adoption of a universally inclusive intent to social union that is required by the full recognition of one another's freedom in the form of social respect.

In speaking of unsociable sociability and of social respect as "horizons" for our human social dynamics, I am thus trying to mark off a crucial element for understanding the kind of answer that then develops from this first step. At issue in the question of the social authority of reason are not merely the *actual* social circumstances in which human beings interact with one another. At issue are the social circumstances that through the exercise of moral freedom *we can both envision as possible and are willing to make actual*. The language of horizon is thus intended to suggest that the exercise of the social authority of reason requisite for the establishment of an ethical commonwealth is a function the construal of human possibilities that Kant designates as "hope." Kantian hope is constituted by our *willingness* to *imagine* that *what we ought to make possible* for one another through the mutual exercise of our freedom *is precisely what we can make possible*. This means that hope is more than a mere envisioning of possibilities. It is an envisioning of possibilities that enables us to give our human action a trajectory that it would not have taken in the absence of that hope.

In this context, Kant's remarks at the conclusion of the *Rechtslehre* are particularly instructive for the connection they make between what the exercise of freedom makes it possible for us to envision and our willingness to undertake what is envisioned:

> . . . What is incumbent on us as a duty is rather to act in conformity with the idea of that end [i.e., perpetual peace as the "highest political good"] even if there is not the slightest theoretical likelihood that it can be realized, as long as its impossibility cannot be demonstrated either.
>
> Now morally practical reason pronounces in us its irresistible veto: *there is to be no war*, neither war between you and me in the state of nature nor war between us as states . . . for war is not the way in which everyone should seek his rights. So the question is no longer whether perpetual peace is something real or a fiction, and whether we are not deceiving ourselves in our theoretical judgments when we assume that it is real. Instead, we must act as if it is something real, though perhaps it is not; we must work toward establishing perpetual peace and the kind of constitution that seems to us most conducive to it (say, a republicanism of all states, together and separately) in order to bring about perpetual peace . . . And even if the complete realization of this objective always remains a pious wish, still we are certainly not deceiving ourselves in adopting the maxim of working incessantly toward it. (*MdS*, 6: 354–355/491)

As Kant is quite clearly aware, the theoretical "nonimpossibility" that the workings of nature could bring about the conditions for perpetual peace among nations seems hardly sufficient to constitute grounds for bringing us to work for it. Indeed (as noted in chapter 5), the perpetual peace that nature brings is just as likely to be that of the graveyard as that of an international political order. All that such theoretical nonimpossibility supplies is space in which the full significance of the exercise of our human freedom toward the goal of perpetual peace becomes evident. Perpetual peace will not come in the absence of human willingness to hope for it *precisely in a way that construes it as a goal that we are able to effect*. It will not come about until and unless we are willing to envision that it will come about precisely in virtue of the exercise of our freedom. In the absence of such hope, perpetual peace becomes in fact impossible—not because it is of itself impossible but because we have denied *that its possibility is something we can effect through our human freedom.*

This Kantian focus on hope with respect to the possibility of perpetual peace indicates something quite ironic about the denial of the social authority of reason that arises from our own contemporary cultural context. This denial is not about what the exercise of our reason authorizes us to *think* about our social relationships, but it is more a denial of what the exercise of our reason authorizes us to *imagine* and to *will* about those relationships. The denial that reason has a social authority that requires us to adopt freely an intent to universal and inclusive social union, is equivalently a claim that we can neither imagine nor will the circumstances under which human beings could freely and mutually establish a fully inclusive, universal, noncoercive set of social relationships for the mutual exercise of their freedom. From Kant's perspective, reason authorizes us to ask: What is the basis for such a denial? What *requires* us to take such relationships as lying *beyond our power to effect*? Are we *inevitably* bound by past human failures to establish and successfully foster such relationships? If we rule them out as beyond our powers, of course we will be unwilling to bring them about; but if we enlarge our imagination to encompass them as relationships that we have the power to effect, then we indeed make it possible for us to work toward making them actual. As in the case of perpetual peace, the fundamental denial is of the possibility of hope—such an intent to social union is not in itself impossible; *we make it impossible* by denying that we can effect it through the exercise of our human freedom.

If this is correct, then the first step toward constructing a response to this denial—that is, articulating the notion of the social respect that human beings owe to one another as the fundamental form of the social authority of reason—must attend to more than just a conceptual reconstruction of Kant's account of the conditions constitutive of an ethical commonwealth in terms of this notion of social respect. It must also provide a basis from which one can then envision concrete possibilities for shaping human social dynamics. These possibilities will be ones that, in virtue of the hope exhibited in social respect for one another, we are able to envision coming to actuality precisely out of the mutual exercise of freedom: They will never come to actuality were we to abandon hope in *our* making them possible. If such possibilities can be shown, then answering the challenge the dynamics within contemporary culture present to the social authority of reason will then finally rest upon what we are, in fact, ready to do to make them actual. As I will suggest in the concluding section of this chapter, a good test case for showing such a possibility can be found in Kant's project for perpetual peace: The best way to ensure that it will never come to be is precisely to abandon hope that it is something that human beings can actually bring about.

Before doing that, however, there is still the unfinished business of articulating the notion of the social respect that human beings are to accord to one another in virtue of their mutual freedom and showing how such social respect exhibits the social authority proper to reason. The basic elements for articulating this notion have already been laid out in the prior discussions of critique as the process by which we come to recognize the thoroughly social character of the exercise of human reason, of the interest of reason as constituting the horizon for the mutual construction of a shared world, and of hope as the basis for effecting possibilities to shape the trajectory of our human action. Kant presents these elements against the background of the circumstances in which we find ourselves necessarily placed in working out the destiny of our species as the juncture of nature and freedom. These circumstances consist in two basic, unavoidable and irreducible "facts." One of these may be considered a "fact of nature": We have no choice but to live as social beings—and to live as social beings within the limited confines of the surface of the earth. The other may be considered a "fact of reason": As moral agents, we have freedom to set ends for ourselves—ends that, in view of our social circumstances, will stand in complex modes of connection with the ends freely set by others.

In thus seeking to work out our destiny between these two facts, the manner of our living together as social beings must be shaped so that it befits our moral freedom precisely as the freedom of social beings. Critique is essential to this effort to work out our destiny in that it disciplines us to the social character of the reason through which we construe the world both as a nexus of causal interaction and as a field for the exercise of our moral freedom. Critique provides us with this discipline by enabling us to acknowledge an interest of reason that is not just the sum total of the particular interests that are engaged in our efforts to construe the world and to make it a field for the exercise of our freedom. By enabling us to give due recognition to the interest of reason, critique thus makes it possible for us to locate the exercise of our freedom—which, we must remember, Kant identifies with the exercise of reason as practical—as fundamentally belonging to the social world constituted by the mutual acknowledgment we are to give one another as legislative members of a kingdom of ends. We exercise our freedom to set ends for ourselves as part of a community of moral agents that is in principle universal and inclusive and is constituted by a mutual recognition of one another's freedom. Thus the intelligibility of moral freedom as the power of setting ends for oneself is itself embedded in a social context of inclusive and universal mutual recognition among a community of moral agents.

This provides us with fundamental elements for articulating a notion of social respect as, first of all, a mutual moral recognition of one another's freedom by which we acknowledge that we constitute, for and with one another, a community of moral agents. This first articulation of social respect can be understood as the way in which we mutually acknowledge that the exercise of freedom by each one of us must exhibit the interest of reason inclusively in the freedom of each and every moral agent. This articulation, however, does not yet take into full account the specific circumstances under which we, as finite moral agents at and as the juncture of nature and freedom, exercise this freedom. It shows social respect as it functions in a kingdom of ends, but not yet as it functions for agents for whom their membership in a kingdom of ends must be brought to bear upon their circumstances of unsociable sociability. This first articulation of social respect bears upon the mutual recognition of freedom for agents in a context in which the social relationships made possible by the mutual exercise of freedom are fully given in that mutual recognition. This is social respect as it would function in a kingdom of ends that has already become a kingdom of grace. It is social respect as it would function for all rational moral agents, but it does not yet specify how it would function under the concrete circumstances in which human moral agents are constrained to exercise their freedom. In consequence, a further articulation is needed, and for this articulation Kant's notion of hope is crucial.

The circumstances of unsociable sociability in which human moral agents exercise their freedom are such that the social relationships that the mutual exercise of freedom makes possible are not fully given. Full mutual moral recognition of one another is, instead, a hard won accomplishment. In fact, there is a minimal form of mutual moral recognition, one that is required for the exercise of freedom in civil society, which needs to take only an "external" form. This form of mutual moral recognition does not engage our freedom at its core of its self-determination, but only places constraints on the scope of our outer conduct. In this form of mutual moral recognition, the authority of reason functions in a limited manner that can be adequately envisioned from a horizon constituted merely by the contention of particular interests. It places a constraint on a certain range of our social relationships and this constraint, so long as we remain within that horizon of the contention of particular interests, can be legitimately enforced by coercive power. Kant formulates this constraint as the "Universal Principle of Right":

Any action is *right* if it can coexist with everyone's freedom in accordance with a universal law, or if on its maxim the freedom of choice of each can coexist with everyone's freedom in accordance with a universal law." (*MdS*, 6: 230/387)

Kant sees this principle as central to his distinction between the manner in which the authority of reason can be enforced on the one hand, as a matter of civic law and, on the other, as a matter of morality. It has also been taken to mark out the distinction between law and morality as isomorphic with the distinction between the "public" and the "private" spheres of human existence. While I believe that this parallel is mistaken, that issue need not be addressed here.[5] For the purpose of articulating the notion of social respect, all that we need to note here is that Kant does not take the establishment of civil society and the external form of mutual moral recognition consequent upon it to be the full and final exhibition of the interest of reason in our human freedom. Recognition of the interest of reason makes it possible for us to envision a horizon of interaction with one another in which mutual moral recognition is not simply grudgingly exacted from us through coercive power but instead issues from the full willingness of our moral freedom.[6] The mutual moral recognition that the interest of reason requires of us will thus be complete only as the outcome of a common task that inclusively engages the freedom of each and every moral agent. This common task is nothing other than first envisioning the possibility of our constituting, on the basis our freedom, a shared world for the mutual exercise of our freedom, and then, on the basis of the hope that such envisioning provides, engaging one another in the project of making this shared world an actuality. What we so envision is the universal and inclusive intent to social union that establishes an ethical commonwealth.

The full articulation of social respect thus places it within the ambit of Kant's construal of hope and the bearing such hope has upon the trajectory of our action. It is possible for us to *have* the social respect for one another that enables us to have the mutual intent to social union needed for the establishment of an ethical commonwealth *only to the extent that we construe it as a real possibility for our freedom.* As in the case of perpetual peace, it is not a question of "whether perpetual peace is something real or a fiction, and whether we are not deceiving ourselves in our theoretical judgments when we assume that it is real. Instead, we must act as if it is something real, though perhaps it is not." Similarly, "we must work toward establishing" such perpetual peace ". . . even if the complete realization of this objective always remains a pious wish, still we are not deceiving ourselves in adopting the maxim of working incessantly toward it." What brings about full social respect for one another's freedom and the consequent possibility of engaging one another in a common task of constituting a shared world is *the concrete exercise of human freedom to accord one another such full social respect.*

The possibility of such full social respect thus turns upon envisioning it as a possibility that we can make actual through the concrete exercise our human freedom. Social respect, an inclusive and universal intent to social union, an ethical commonwealth, perpetual peace, will surely never come to be once we have convinced ourselves that these lie beyond the range of what is possible for our human freedom. *If we are convinced that these are ends that we human beings can never realize, we will cease to set them before ourselves as ends and thus guarantee that they will never be realized.* This suggests the insidious nature of the challenge that the dynamics of immediacy and contingent particularity present to the social authority of reason: They narrow the social authority of reason by scaling down the horizon of the hope of what is possible through the exercise of our human freedom. Since an inclusively shared human world as a field for the mutual exercise of freedom can never be, there is no reason to work for anything other than whatever series of transient satisfactions might suit the shifting interplay of my own interests in their (perhaps) regrettable but no doubt ineluctable partiality. Since human difference and plurality are incommensurable, claims for a normative universality expressive of substantive human connectedness are, at best the articulation of chimerical ideals, at worst—and far more likely—a mask for hegemonic erasure of difference.

This challenge that the dynamics of immediacy and contingent particularity present to the social authority of reason is as much a challenge to the moral imagination by which the social authority of reason empowers us to hope as it is a challenge to the conceptual coherence and adequacy of the very notion of the social authority of reason. In consequence, an important line of response to this challenge needs to be charted by engaging in an imaginative reconfiguration of social practices; the aim of such an imaginative configuration is to enlarge the horizons of these practices in directions that exhibit how it is possible for human freedom to effect concretely a trajectory toward inclusive universality that fully respects the bounds of our human pluralities and differences. Such imaginative reconfiguring of social practices was one of the dynamics at work in the civil rights movement in the United States in the 1960s; loosening the suffocating grip of racist imagination upon civic life was made possible in part by actions and practices that concretely exhibited what that imagination had deemed impossible and unthinkable regarding communication, connection, and respect between individuals and communities across racial differences that previous practices had tried to entrench as an unbridgeable divide. More recently a similar dynamic has functioned in the truth and reconciliation process in South Africa. These examples suggest, perhaps more convincingly than any abstract argument, that the dynamic of the social authority of reason is to engender an efficacious hope—that is, a hope that can guide us to shape our social practices in ways suited to the construction of an inclusively shared world that fully respects the bounds of our human pluralities and differences.

Perpetual Peace: Reconstituting a Horizon of Hope for a Shared Human World

The central conclusion that I propose to draw from the analysis and argument offered in this and chapter 6 is that the contemporary challenge to the social authority of reason bears most centrally on the possibility of framing a common answer on the part of humanity to the last of the three questions—transposed into the plural—that Kant formulates to articulate the interest of reason: For what may *we* hope? One measure of the cultural distance that we have traveled in the two centuries that separate us from Kant is that a strong case could be made for the proposition that Kant himself framed a far more robust and confident answer to that question—particularly with respect to humanity as a species—than much of our contemporary culture would allow us to do. Even as the culture of globalization offers a tantalizing horizon for the fulfillment of hopes for an individual's immediate life prospects, those same dynamics can just as readily induce forgetfulness of the need for—let alone the possibility of—a common horizon of hope for the humanity connecting us all. The challenge is not so much that the implicit answer to the question "For what may *we* hope?" that arises from the dynamics of immediacy is likely to be "Not much." It is rather that the possibility of raising the question of hope for our common humanity *does not even occur.* In place of the anxiety and despair that has lurked at the edges of a declining modernity, a culture of postmodernity seems far more likely to offer a shrug of indifference to concerns about the prospects of humanity. Despair is a possibility only when hope matters—and there are dynamics at work in the emergent global culture that suggest that, indeed, it doesn't.

Within this context, a useful focus for illustrating the consequences of this conclusion can be found by considering the hope that Kant argues the exercise of our reason requires us to have for an international order that would provide the conditions for perpetual peace. He alludes to this in a number of his writings in the 1780s and 1790s and offers a detailed outline of such an order in the 1795 essay "Toward Perpetual Peace: A Philosophical Project." His proposal for perpetual peace is a useful focus not so much for the details it provides for an international federation of nations but for the way in which it portrays perpetual peace as an object of hope that is necessary for providing a certain trajectory to the determination of actions that we undertake in concert with one another. As long as we keep it in view as an object of our hope, perpetual peace among nations becomes possible. It is seen as possible precisely as an outcome of human actions taken, in view of this hope, to establish an international political order. In the absence of such hope, actions to establish an international order to make perpetual peace possible will not be taken, with the result that the only perpetual peace that can be brought into being is that of the graveyard.

The hope that reason requires us to have for perpetual peace is, of course, one that Kant places in the context of the larger set of circumstances in which we find ourselves as and at the juncture of nature and freedom. The workings of nature have a role to play in the attainment of the human destiny that we must work out in view of our unique status in the cosmos. Kant thus indicates in a variety of places that the attainment of our human destiny as the juncture of nature and freedom—including important stages on the way, such as perpetual peace—is an outcome of causal processes by which nature (or, as he will sometimes call it, "providence") does often make us do unwittingly and unwillingly what we willingly ought to do—but in fact do not.[7] Nature need not wait for the exercise of human freedom to effect conditions conducive to the attainment of human destiny. Nature even utilizes our "unsociable sociability" to spur us to the development of the culture and the civil order that provide external conditions conducive to attainment of our human moral destiny (e. g., *IAG*, 8: 24–26/ 34–36; *CJ*, 5: §83, 429–434/297–301; *TP*, 8: 310–313/307–309; *AP*, 7: 322–325/183–186; 328–331/188–191).

Yet even as he affirms the role of nature, Kant is equally insistent that the attainment of human moral destiny is something the use of our reason demands of us. Bringing that destiny about, including perpetual peace as a stage on the way, finally rests upon what human beings concretely do (e. g., *TP*, 8: 312–313/308–309; *EF*, 8: 355–357/327– 328, 368/336–337; *MdS*, 6: 354–355/490–492). Nature can spur us unwittingly and unwillingly only so far along the path to perpetual peace and our moral destiny: The moral demand that reason places on the formation of our action requires that we not take the attainment of perpetual peace or of the moral destiny of the human species as a foregone conclusion of the dynamics of nature. It is rather a task whose final shape and completion depend upon the properly ordered actions of human beings—and the ordering of such actions is a function of the hope that such human action will be effective in the attainment of these objects of hope. As a result, the particular human social, cultural, and political dynamics over which human beings can exercise control in accord with the self-governance of reason will have a decisive impact upon the trajectory along which humanity moves toward the attainment of a goal such as perpetual peace.

It may be easy to overlook the fact that Kant places the project of perpetual peace within the context of the hope that arises from the practical use of reason because he places principal responsibility for acting in accord with such hope not on all citizens but on the sovereign monarchs of the Europe of his day.[8] Within Kant's own historical context, "Toward Perpetual Peace" is an ironic, perhaps even a sardonic, plea for enlightened political leadership in the matter of international relations based precisely on the hope that the exercise of leadership by kings and princes has power to make a new order among nations possible. Although monarchs no longer wield political sovereignty in our world, Kant's essay retains its sharp moral bite, since there apparently continues to be little effective will for peace among the politically powerful. In our context, however, the moral bite of his proposal is not only for the leaders of nations. We are in a position to recognize more clearly than Kant did that the moral exercise of our reason places the demand to strive for peace upon members of every polity, but especially upon citizens of nations with a republican (representative) form of government (*EF*, 8: 349–351/322–324, 355–356/327–328; cf. *TP*, 8: 310–312/307–309). Political leaders will be far more likely to show an effective will for peace and then act upon it only when it is first voiced as the will of those on whose behalf they exercise their leadership.[9]

A set of considerations similar to those Kant offers on behalf of perpetual peace can be offered on behalf of social respect and an inclusively universal intent to social union. Like perpetual peace, these goals will remain impossible hopes just and only so long as we consider them to be impossible. As Kant was sage enough to notice, however, their impossibility is not theoretical: "their impossibility cannot be demonstrated." There is nothing incoherent in envisioning human beings freely according one another a mutual moral recognition that is effective in ending the practices and the social dynamics that disempower or disenfranchise fellow human beings because of their race, religion, gender, or cultural heritage. Neither is there anything incoherent in envisioning, for instance, Albanians and Serbs in Kosovo from learning to accord one another the mutual moral recognition capable of finally effecting the reconciliation necessarily for living together, in full respect for their cultural and religious differences, in a single civil society.[10]

Such a list could go on at length. For Albanians and Serbs, one can also read Indians and Pakistanis, Protestants and Catholics in Northern Ireland, Israelis and Palestinians, Hutu and Tutsi, urban poor and affluent middle-class—indeed, the whole array of divisions present in the social dynamics of human life at the start of the twenty-first century. Yet the point to be made here is simple. If anything makes mutual social respect "impossible" across these divisions, it is not the inexorable causal workings of a nature not subject to human direction, it is not a set of circumstances that lie beyond the power of human beings to alter. Mutual social respect, and the concrete social dynamics that would follow from it are not impossible to imagine; it seems rather that because they are difficult to achieve, because their achievement will likely require all parties to alter often deeply entrenched particular interests to construct a common interest, it is easier to *declare* them unthinkable or impossible rather than to exercise the imagination and will to make them actual. They are difficult to achieve because they require both individual and common commitment to overcome what are the real sources that block the social respect that arises from the interest of reason in a fully inclusive and universal acknowledgment of human moral freedom: Narrowness of imagination and recalcitrance of will. They are difficult to achieve because they require a form of moral courage that is empowered only by a willingness to act upon the possibilities opened up by a horizon of social respect. In Kant's terms, the "impossibility" is one that resides precisely in our capacity to say "no" to that dynamic of the moral exercise of our reason that orders us to mutual moral recognition. It is a form of radical evil, with the consequence that such "impossibility" is one for which we can be held accountable—or, to frame this in terms proper to the social authority of reason, it is an "impossibility" for which we must finally hold one another accountable.

What I have argued for so far in this section may still seem quite abstract in that it has not yet specified new forms for social practice or advocated particular reforms of existent political, economic, or cultural institutions to make it possible for the social authority of reason to extend more fully over the social dynamics of our human existence. Specification of this kind has not emerged, however, because the social respect that arises from making an inclusively universal intent to social union the object of our hope primarily frames a new horizon for our human interaction. It does not itself directly specify new practices. To that extent, it exhibits the "formality" of Kant's ethics, though like other Kantian formalities of the practical use of reason it proves to be quite robust with respect to the determination of action. It provides a horizon in virtue of which we can then engage one another in a deliberative exchange that will enable us to determine together the concrete shape of the practices of freedom appropriate to our mutual membership in an ethical commonwealth.

As a result, even though the horizon of social respect does itself not directly specify forms of social practice, it does allow us to specify a framework for the deliberative exchange in which we engage one another on questions about shaping such practices to accord with the mutual recognition and exercise of freedom. In Kant's terminology, this framework is constituted by the principles that make possible the "public use of reason." It is a framework within which we take on a mutual commitment to provide for one another a public, social setting for mutual communication for purposes of establishing common bases for decision and action. Such a social setting then makes it possible to conduct an inclusive deliberative exchange to seek out and identify, as a basis for decision, relevant common interests in which all have a stake. In the absence of such a framework, we are far more likely to turn any deliberative exchange in which we engage simply into another expression of an "unsociable sociability" that pays no heed to the possibility of framing deliberation in terms of an enduring common interest. Deliberative exchange will serve simply as an arena for the articulation and adjudication of the contention among the particular and partial interests that we each bring with us without raising our sights to the possibility of conducting reasoned argument aimed at reaching agreement about matters of fundamental common concern. Little or no room can be made or given for appeal to relevant common interests large enough to allow particular clashing interests to make themselves subordinate in the making of decisions and the shaping of policy. As former Senator Robert Dole succinctly noted, such a common interest has become hard to find in our legislative processes: "Republicans figure out what is best for them, and Democrats figure out what is best for them, and nobody figures out what is best, period."[11]

I would thus propose a reappropriation of Kant's notion of the public use of reason as a key step to renew the social authority of reason in a polity where cultural, economic, and ideological fissures run increasingly wide and deep. The purpose of this reappropriation would be to provide a framework for ongoing public deliberation on matters of policy and practice in which the "interest of reason" *can emerge from the course of our deliberation* as the appropriate basis for determining policy and practice. Such interest can emerge, however, only to the extent that our engagement with one another in such deliberation is shaped by the horizon provided by social respect. That horizon places two requirements upon our deliberation, without which the interest of reason is unlikely to emerge. The first requirement is that we must bring to our deliberations a common recognition of the two "facts" that constitute our circumstances as the beings who stand at the juncture of nature and freedom: Our circumstances as free rational beings are such that we have no option but to live together in society and that we can do so in the manner that befits our freedom only to the extent that we come to uncoerced agreement about the terms of our living with each other. The second requirement frames the horizon of the common *hope* that we, as rational agents, must also bring to the deliberation: That *it is within the power of the exercise of our freedom to make agreement possible* in our deliberation about the terms of our living with one another.

There is a particularly important consequence that follows from this second requirement of a common hope. This common hope specifies the way in which the public use of reason exhibits the distinguishing mark of autonomy as it is properly exercised by agent-members of a realm of ends: In such a realm one claims no special place for oneself, but only the due recognition for one's own freedom that one mutually owes to every other agent-member. This means that the function of the public use of reason is to enable us to achieve and recognize, as a basis for action, common interests that we cannot simply presume to be exactly identical with any of the particular interests any of us may have initially brought to the argument. The whole point of the public use of reason is not to have one or another particular interest prevail over the others as the outcome of a zero-sum game. To do so would be to fix unsociable sociability as the final horizon for the social interaction of human freedom. The point of the public use of reason is, instead, to place deliberative exchange in an arena in which the proper outcome is not the victory of one set of interests over another but the emergence, out of our deliberative engagement with one another, of the shared and inclusive interests for decision and action that all can freely acknowledge as fitting for agents who acknowledge one another's freedom.

Placed within this horizon of Kant's notion of hope, the public use of reason may seem a quite daunting enterprise in the context of an emergent culture of globalization that multiplies the possibilities for continuing contention among competing interests and increasingly envisions that contention on the model of the market place. We find ourselves in a social and cultural context that, despite its readiness to use the language of global awareness and human interconnectedness, seems to find questions of a common human destiny to have less urgency and force than they apparently had for Kant and his Enlightenment contemporaries. A culture increasingly ordered to the dynamics of marketplace choice does not seem to require an authority rooted in the social matrix of human existence, let alone an authority of human reason forged and ratified in the self-discipline of an ever widening circle of human dialogical and argumentative exchange. The culture of marketplace choice does not seem to require that we engage one another in sustained, reasoned argument about the terms of our living with each other, about the constitutive social ends that make us a polity, and even less about what ends our common humanity might make incumbent on us. These are all matters on which much contemporary argument may be "in public" but is by no means argument that engages us in "the public use of reason." Against a horizon in which such debate over such matters simply becomes one more arena in which particular interests compete for ascendancy, public argument about them—be it in legislative processes, political campaigns, or whatever is the current "hot" forum for sampling public opinion— becomes just one more element of strategy in a "zero-sum" game where there have to be losers in order for there to be winners. In argument conducted in the absence of a horizon of social respect and hope for the emergence of agreement, the only game in town gets played under the rules of hegemonic power.

As I have argued throughout the course of this work, Kant's understanding of the unique status humanity has as the juncture of nature and freedom leads him to affirm that our freedom makes it possible for us to envision and to effect a quite different social dynamic for dealing with one another about the fundamental terms of living with one another in society. Our freedom provides a horizon of hope that encourages continuing engagement with one another in reasoned argument about the terms of our living with each other, about the constitutive social ends that make us a polity, and about ends our common humanity makes incumbent on us—not under the dynamic of unsociable sociability, but of an ethical commonwealth. In contrast to the deliberation conducted solely within a horizon furnished by unsociable sociability, engagement in the public use of reason stands under conditions of social respect that enable us to put aside the social dynamics that require us always and inevitably to divide into winners and losers. Arguments set within the conditions for the public use of reason are not put forth as tactics in a zero-sum game. Instead, the fundamental function of such arguments is to determine a course of action on the basis of a mutual achievement and recognition of common interest rather than on the expected satisfaction that one course of action might give to any set of particular interests articulated in the course of argument. Claims that finally satisfy the norms of the public use of reason do not give "victory" just to those who may have first proposed them. They stand, instead, as an accomplishment of all who have participated in the argumentative process through which they have successfully passed.

Engagement in the public use of reason conducted against the horizon of social respect thus requires a threefold commitment from its participants. The first articulates the hope that the exercise of mutual freedom makes possible. It is the commitment to work together to make agreement possible. The second articulates one's autonomy as one that bears no special privilege in a realm constituted by mutual acknowledgment of freedom. It is the commitment to let one's own position and the interests that shape it be fully subject to argumentative analysis, challenge and criticism by others, thus rendering them open to possible qualification and revision. The third articulates the intent to an inclusively universal social union. It is the commitment to persevere in the mutual effort of deliberation to make agreement possible even when none has yet emerged. These commitments are no more than an articulation of the conditions that make deliberation about the terms of our living with one another morally intelligible in the light of the interest of reason and of the two facts that frame our human circumstances. It makes no sense to deliberate with one another about these matters, unless we expect the outcome of deliberation to bring us to agreement. If we do not envision such agreement, we then remain within the horizon of unsociable sociability and these matters continue to be ones in which only particular interests compete for ascendancy. In this case, deliberation can no longer claim to involve the public use of reason. It is nothing more than a mask for the interplay of power, so any agreement reached in its course simply represents a moment in the current vector of competing and clashing powers.

There is a deep moral bite to these commitments when placed against the context of the dynamics of immediacy, commodification, and competition operative in the emergent culture of globalization. These commitments require a shift in the horizon from which one views the purpose, the process, and the outcome of deliberative exchange among human beings about the terms of their living with one another. We engage in public use of reason not, as the dynamics of contention would have it, to attain ascendancy for our particular interests but to reach agreement on how to shape a shared world. We understand the process not, as the dynamics of commodification would have it, to be mere bargaining over loss and gain, but to be mutual communication to attain shared understanding. We seek outcomes that are not, as the dynamics of immediacy would have it, just temporary realignments of interests for better positioning in the inevitable next round of contention but stable transformations of our interests from the particularity of contention to the inclusivity of mutual respect. Agreement that arises out of our engagement with one another in the public use of reason is thus a function of mutual recognition of the full moral equality in which we stand with one another, rather than a self-protective demarcation of the narrow spaces where we find that the greatest number of particular interests currently overlap.

As with just about every element of Kant's work that has moral bite to it, the most fundamental significance of the public use of reason has to do with its role in disciplining us to that self-governance of reason through which the self-corruption of radical evil may be extirpated. As a result, the shifts in horizon required by the commitment to engage one another in the public use of reason can quite rightly be understood as the social counterpart to the moral conversion from radical evil that Kant sees as necessary for individual moral agents. In its social form the self-corruption of radical evil manifests itself as the horizon against which human social dynamics cannot but take the form of contention, struggle, and finally war. The final form of this self-corruption is the abandonment of hope that transformation of these dynamics lies within human power—an abandonment of hope that then makes it pointless to try to engage with one another in the construction of a shared world. The best we can do is cobble together for our own protection whatever fragments are at hand without illusion that the result will or has to fit into the inclusive patterns of intelligibility and significance that constitute a "world" to share fully with others. Since we are ultimately incapable of constituting a fully shared human world with one another, we must always reserve the right to place our particular interests above that of anyone else's. There can be no such thing as an interest of reason nor, *a fortiori*, the social authority of reason.

Kant's critical project is an articulation of considerably higher expectations for human beings, both individually and as a species. He takes us to be capable of a mutual moral recognition that requires us, in the concrete circumstances of finite human existence, to engage one another in argument and activity to construct a common world. Kant is not so naive as to think that the construction of such a common world will be easy, or that it will ever be fully finished. He nonetheless sees it as a task we cannot shirk. As we cannot extricate ourselves from the social circumstances of our human existence, we are under the exigency of constructing together terms for our living with one another in a shared world (*Rel*, 6: 93–100/129–134). Despite what the dynamics of immediacy, contention, and commodification would have us believe about ourselves, there are compelling reasons for taking on the higher expectations Kant has articulated. The circumstances of our human existence as needy, limited beings on a planet of finite resources currently press upon us more and more urgent questions about our willingness and our ability to share this particular world—in the literal sense as a global space for living—with fellow human beings and, indeed, with our fellow living beings. The basis for our sharing of this world merely as a place of survival, let alone as a possible field for human interaction on the basis of freedom, may no longer be sustainable merely on the dynamisms of unsociable sociability by which those currently dominant wittingly or unwittingly force others to share the world on terms dictated by their interests—until, of course, some other gain the ascendency.

These dynamics of the contemporary world would hardly surprise Kant since they manifest the latest turn of the interplay between the interest of reason and unsociable sociability. Increasing awareness of our global interdependence accords well with the cosmopolitan perspective that issues from the interest of reason. The continuing fierce and often fatal struggle for domination among particular interests in which those best able to marshal the power of coercion win—for a time—shows the continuing power of unsociable sociability to shape the dynamics of our relationships with one another. Kant, indeed, couples a quite bleak portrayal of the struggle for domination by means of coercion with an almost serene expectation of its eventual resolution through acknowledgment of global interdependence. He expected that we would eventually weary of the destruction we inflict upon each other and, in our exhaustion, see the wisdom of setting out on our own in the direction toward which the interest of reason has been pointing us. A quick overview of the misery and death that has ensued from the conflict of particular interests in the waning years of the last century and the opening years of the current one suggests that Kant sadly overestimated the possibility of our wearying of war.

That, however, need not require us to belittle his confidence that we can make the interest of reason our own; in fact, it makes all the more urgent the need to commit ourselves to search with one another through mutual engagement in the public use of reason for those common bases on which we can share this world with one another. One element of our peculiar fate as free but finite rational beings who must live in society is that, even in the absence of any guarantee that we will reach agreement, we must ever stand in hope of reaching agreement. We therefore need to persevere in engaging one another in argument about the terms of our living with one another. In this case, as in the case of our individual possibility of overcoming radical evil, Kantian hope is not an empty velleity but a disposition to persevere in conduct befitting our moral freedom. Anything else is unworthy of our vocation as free beings.

Notes

Chapter One

1. See, for instance, Frederick C. Beiser, *The Fate of Reason: German Philosophy from Kant to Fichte* (Cambridge, Mass.: Harvard University Press, 1987); *German Idealism: The Struggle Against Subjectivism 1791–1801* (Cambridge, Mass.: Harvard University Press, 2002); G. Felicitas Munzel, *Kant's Conception of Moral Character* (Chicago: University of Chicago Press, 1999); Susan Neiman, *The Unity of Reason: Rereading Kant* (New York; Oxford: Oxford University Press, 1994); Onora O'Neill, *Constructions of Reason: Explorations of Kant's Practical Philosophy* (Cambridge: Cambridge University Press, 1990); Andrews Reath, Barbara Herman, Christine M. Korsgaard (eds.), *Reclaiming the History of Ethics: Essays for John Rawls* (Cambridge: Cambridge University Press, 1997); Roger Sullivan, *Immanuel Kant's Moral Theory* (Cambridge: Cambridge University Press, 1989); Richard L. Velkley, *Freedom and the End of Reason: On the Moral Foundation of Kant's Critical Philosophy* (Chicago; London: University of Chicago Press, 1989); John Zammito, *The Genesis of Kant's Critique of Judgment* (Chicago; London: University of Chicago Press, 1992); *Kant, Herder and the Birth of Anthropology* (Chicago; London: University of Chicago Press, 2002).

2. See, for instance, Barbara Herman, *The Practice of Moral Judgment* (Cambridge, Mass: Harvard University Press, 1993); Thomas Hill, *Dignity and Practical Reason in Kant's Moral Theory* (Ithaca: Cornell University Press, 1992); Jane Kneller and Sidney Axinn, (eds.), *Autonomy and Community: Readings in Contemporary Kantian Social Philosophy* (Albany: State University of New York Press, 1998); Gordon E. Michalson, Jr., *Kant and the Problem of God* (Oxford: Blackwell, 1999); Patrick Riley, *Kant's Political Philosophy* (Totowa, NJ: Rowman and Littlefield, 1983); Friedo Ricken and François Marty (eds.), *Kant über Religion* (Stuttgart: Kohlhammer, 1992);

Philip J. Rossi and Michael J. Wreen, (eds.), *Kant's Philosophy of Religion Reconsidered* (Indianapolis: Indiana University Press, 1991); Howard L. Williams, *Kant's Political Philosophy* (Oxford: Blackwell, 1983).

3. Among the major—and divergent—philosophical and theological studies in English revisiting the Enlightenment and its relation to "modernity" have been: Richard Bernstein, *Beyond Objectivism and Relativism: Science, Hermenutics and Praxis* (Oxford: Blackwell, 1983); Michael Buckley, *At the Origins of Modern Atheism* (New Haven: Yale University Press, 1987); Louis Dupré, *Passage to Modernity: An Essay in the Hermeneutics of Nature and Culture* (New Haven: Yale University Press, 1993); Alasdair MacIntyre, *After Virtue* (2nd edition, Notre Dame: University of Notre Dame Press, 1984); John Milbank, *Theology and Social Theory: Beyond Secular Reason* (Oxford: Basil Blackwell, 1990); Iris Murdoch, *Metaphysics as a Guide to Morals* (London: Chatto and Windus, 1992); Susan Neiman, *Evil in Modern Thought: An Alternative History of Philosophy* (Princeton: Princeton University Press, 2002); Richard Rorty, *Philosophy and the Mirror of Nature* (Oxford: Blackwell, 1980); George Steiner, *Real Presences* (Chicago: University of Chicago Press, 1989); *Grammars of Creation* (New Haven: Yale University Press, 2001); Charles Taylor, *Sources of the Self: The Making of the Modern Identity* (Cambridge: Cambridge University Press, 1989); *Modern Social Imaginaries* (Durham and London: Duke University Press, 2004). They represent, however, only the tip of the iceberg: There is now extant a vast range of literary, cultural, philosophical, and theological studies that attempt to describe, analyze, and assess the "modernity" for which the Enlightenment, according to many of these studies, is a significant source.

4. See, for instance, James Schmidt, (ed.), *What is Enlightenment?: Eighteenth-Century Answers and Twentieth-Century Questions* (Berkeley; London: University of California Press, 1996); Roy Porter and Mikulas Teich, (eds.), *The Enlightenment in National Context* (Cambridge: Cambridge University Press, 1981).

5. Ernst Cassirer, *Kant's Life and Thought*, trans. J. Haden (New Haven and London: Yale University Press, 1981), 391, quotes a remark from a letter of Goethe to Herder: "Goethe remarked bitterly in a letter to Herder that Kant has disgracefully 'slobbered on' his philosopher's cloak 'with the blot of radical evil so that even Christ would be entitled to kiss its hem.' " The letter is dated June 7, 1793, (*Goethes Briefe*, Vol. 2, *Briefe der Jahre 1786–1805*, ed. Karl Robert Mandekow. Hamburg: Christian Wegner Verlag, 1964, 166). The original has "so that even *Christians* (*Christen*) would," not "so that even *Christ* would" ("damit doch auch Christen herbeigelockt werden, den Saum zu küssen").

6. W. H. Walsh's entry on Kant in *The Encyclopedia of Philosophy*, Vol. 4., ed. Paul Edwards (New York: Macmillan, 1967) is representative of

the interpretation of Kant's view of religion that prevailed for much of the twentieth century: In seventeen pages of text, Kant's philosophy of religion is treated in two paragraphs, the notion of radical evil is summarized in one sentence, and the conclusion drawn is: ". . . he had certainly meant to suggest that many of the beliefs and actions of practicing Christians were without value, if not positively immoral. Indeed, the originality and continuing interest of his work on religion connect directly with that fact" (322).

7. See, however, Paul Guyer, "The Strategy of Kant's *Groundwork*," in *Kant on Freedom Law, and Happiness* (Cambridge: Cambridge University Press, 2000), 223–227, which locates a fundamental link between the argumentative structure of the *Groundwork* and the later doctrine of "radical evil."

8. In the last section of *The Conflict of the Faculties* (1798), "An Old Question Reconsidered: Is the Human Race Constantly Progressing?"

9. A carefully crafted argument for this interpretation has recently been offered by Michalson in *Kant and the Problem of God.*

10. In the *Critique of Pure Reason*, Kant describes the "the ideal of the highest good" more in the global terms of God's power to effect the totality of the moral world than in terms of the proportioning of happiness to virtue for individuals; it is "the idea of such an intelligence, in which the morally most perfect will, combined with the highest blessedness is the cause of all happiness in the world, insofar as it stands in exact relation with morality (as the worthiness to be happy)" (A 811/B 839). In the *Groundwork*, the highest good is referenced to the will as "good in itself"; it is the only unconditioned good (and thus the condition for every other good) though not "the sole and complete good" (*GMM* 4: 396/52); even "the concept of God as the highest good" is referenced to "the *idea* of moral perfection that reason frames a prori and connects inseparably with the concept of a free will" (4: 409/63). In the *Critique of Practical Reason*, Kant then goes on to identify the highest good in terms of the proper proportioning of happiness to virtue for individuals (5: 110–113/228–231). As will be noted in chapter 3, his later understanding of the highest good places it in a larger social context that seems to be anticipated in part in the earlier discussion of the first *Critique*.

11. Cf. Susan Nieman's thoughtful reflection on 9/11 in *Evil in Modern Thought: An Alternative History of Philosophy*, 281–288. She perceptively observes that after the events of 9/11, "We face new dangers. But they are not, I submit, new forms of evil" (283).

12. Cf. Robert B. Pippin, "On the Moral Foundations of Kant's *Rechtslehre*," in *The Philosophy of Immanuel Kant*, ed. Richard Kennington, Studies in Philosophy and the History of Philosophy, Vol. 12 (Washington, DC: The Catholic University Press of America, 1985), 142: "If what we

might loosely call the 'highest good' form of reasoning is inherently involved in why duties of justice are duties at all, then the famous post-Kantian extension of a concern for justice into social as well as political institutions could be seen as wholly consistent with *Kantian* premises."

Chapter Two

1. Katrin Flikschuh, *Kant and Modern Political Philosophy* (Cambridge: Cambridge University Press, 2000), 12–79, offers an extensive criticism of the tendency of contemporary liberal political philosophy claiming Kantian lineage, such as that exemplified by Habermas and Rawls, to avoid metaphysics, even that of Kant himself.

2. Lewis White Beck, *A Commentary on Kant's Critique of Practical Reason* (Chicago: University of Chicago Press, 1960), 11, cf. 200.

3. It not unlikely that readers acquainted with Kant's work only through surveys of the history of modern philosophy or even of Kant's own work think of the major divisions of the first *Critique* to be constituted by the Transcendental Aesthetic and the Transcendental Logic with its own subdivisions into the Transcendental Analytic and Transcendental Dialectic. These, however, are themselves all subdivisions of the first part of the work, which Kant titles "The Transcendental Doctrine of Elements."

4. *Kant and the Experience of Freedom* (Cambridge: Cambridge University Press, 1993), 4.

5. Cf. "Reason and Politics in the Kantian Enterprise," *Constructions of Reason,* 23–27, in which she argues that "the Categorical Imperative is the supreme principle of reason," and "Reason and Autonomy in *Grundlegung* III," *Constructions of Reason,* 57: "Reason has no transcendent authority; it can only be vindicated by critique, and critique itself is at bottom no more than the practice of autonomy in thinking."

6. Iris Murdoch, *The Sovereignty of Good* (New York: Schocken, 1971), 80, has expressed this reading of Kantian autonomy in exemplary fashion: "How recognizable, how familiar to us, is the man so beautifully portrayed in the *Groundwork*, who confronted even with Christ turns away to consider the judgment of his own conscience and to hear the voice of his reason. . . . [T]his man is with us still, free, independent, lonely, powerful, rational, responsible, brave, the hero of so many novels and books of moral philosophy. . . . He is the ideal citizen of the liberal State, a warning held up

to tyrants . . . Kant's man had already received a glorious incarnation nearly a century earlier in the work of Milton: His proper name is Lucifer."

7. There has been a considerable amount of discussion about the role of the third section of the *Groundwork*, both with regard to its role within the overall argumentative structure of that work as well as its relationship to the arguments elucidating freedom that Kant later offers in the *Critique of Practical Reason*. Some useful summaries are found in Louis White Beck, *A Commentary on Kant's Critique of Practical Reason* (Chicago: University of Chicago Press, 1960), 170–75; Roger Sullivan, *Immanuel Kant's Moral Theory*, (Cambridge: Cambridge University Press, 1989), 81–90; Allen W. Wood, *Kant's Ethical Theory* (Cambridge: Cambridge University Press, 1999), 171–182.

8. The construal of Kant's distinction between the sensible and the intelligible, particularly when he articulates it in term of the notions of "phenomenon" and "noumenon" has been a matter of controversy from the time of the earliest reception of Kant's critical philosophy. A full-scale argument for the position I am taking—viz., that Kant is not a metaphysical dualist with respect to the "world" that humans engage through the various activities in which reason is ingredient—is beyond the scope of this work. A good starting place for such an argument is articulated by Onora O'Neill in "Reason and Autonomy in *Grundlegung* III," 59–63.

9. Kant makes use of this distinction in his 1770 dissertation, *De mundi sensibilis atque intelligibilis forma et principiis*, which is often considered to be a major step toward the formal articulation of his critical project. That work, however, does not yet fully link the use of this distinction with the need for reason to place limits upon its use of "transcendent ideas."

10. ". . . it is admittedly required that his reason have the capacity to *induce a feeling of pleasure* or delight in the fulfillment of duty and thus there is required a causality of reason to determine sensibility in conformity with its principles. But it is quite impossible to see, that is, to make comprehensible a priori, how a mere thought which itself contains nothing sensible produces a feeling of pleasure or displeasure" (*GMM*, 4: 460/106).

11. "This feeling (under the name of moral feeling) is therefore produced solely by reason. . . . But what name could one more suitably apply to this singular feeling which cannot be compared to any pathological feeling? It is of such a peculiar kind that it seems to be at the disposal only of reason, and indeed of pure practical reason" (*CprR*, 5: 76/201–202). It is not accidental, I believe, that in the same work Kant accords a similar singular status to his claim about "the fact of reason" (*CprR*, 5: 31/165).

Chapter Three

1. G. W. F. Hegel, *The Philosophy of History*, trans. J. Sibree (New York: Willey, 1944), 21.

2. The controversy between "liberals" and "communitarians" over a range of issues in political and social philosophy is one where this issue has been recently been played out—though usually without much consideration of the question whether either of the contending views adequately represent Kant's own thinking. Both sides have commonly taken it for granted that Kant's reading of moral agency—and, *a fortiori*, the autonomy that is its central conceptual element—is an individualist one (or, as some parties to the controversy have termed it, a "thin" account of moral agency.) Cf. Katrin Flikschuh, *Kant and Modern Political Philosophy*, Chapter One, "Kantian Metaphysics in Contemporary Liberalism," 12–49, for a useful typology that indicates how, despite significant differences, all sides function from within an individualist reading of Kantian autonomy—and metaphysics!

3. "Reason and Politics in the Kantian Enterprise," *Constructions of Reason*, especially 17–24.

4. As noted in chapter 2 n.5, O'Neill argues in "Reason and Politics in the Kantian Enterprise," *Constructions of Reason*, that "the Categorical Imperative is the supreme principle of reason" (24). Later in the same essay (27) she observes "Critique of reason is possible only if we think of critique as recursive and reason as constructed rather than imposed. The constraint on possibilities of construction is imposed by the fact that the principles are to be found for a plurality of possible voices or agents who share a world. Nothing has been established about principles of cognitive order for solitary beings." In the following essay, "The Public Use of Reason," she argues that for Kant "a wholly private ground of reason is no more a possibility than a Wittgensteinian private language" (37).

5. Cf. Alan Donagan, *The Theory of Morality* (Chicago and London; University of Chicago Press, 1977), 1–9; Roger Sullivan, *Immanuel Kant's Moral Theory* 4–6; Allen W. Wood, *Kant's Ethical Thought*, 19–20 for brief accounts of the role that ordinary moral judgment or, in Donagan's terms, "common morality," plays in Kant's moral philosophy.

6. For discussions of this social dimension, see Sharon Anderson-Gold, "Ethical Community and the Highest Good," *Proceedings of the Sixth International Kant Congress* II/ 2. ed. Gerhard Funke and Thomas M. Seebohm (Washington, DC: Center for Advanced Research in Phenomenology, 1989), 231–242: Burkhard Tuschling, "*Rationis societas*: Remarks on Kant and

Hegel," *Kant's Philosophy of Religion Reconsidered*, ed. Philip J. Rossi and Michael J. Wreen (Indianapolis: Indiana University Press, 1991), 181–205; Allen W. Wood, "Unsociable Sociability: The Anthropological Basis of Kantian Ethics," *Philosophical Topics* 19 (1991), 325–351. An earlier discussion that reads Kant's account of good in terms of the social character of the human is Lucien Goldmann, *Immanuel Kant* (London:1971), an English translation of *Introduction á la philosophie du Kant* (Paris: Gallimard 1967); that work is a revised and expanded version of Goldmann's dissertation, which in both its German original and initial French translation has titles that highlight the social dimension: *Mensch, Gemeinschaft und Welt in der Philosophie Immanuel Kants* (Zurich, 1945) and *La communauté humaine et l'univers chez Kant* (Paris: Presses universitaires de France, 1948).

7. This discussion has been ably summarized by Jaqueline Mariña in "Making Sense of the Highest Good" *Kant-Studien* 91 (2000), 329–355.

8. Kant's definition of this "kingdom" (Reich) is "die systematische Verbindung verschiedener vernünftiger Wesen durch gemeinschaftliche Gezetze," which Gregor translates as "a systematic union of various rational beings through common laws."

9. Part of the particular cognitive opacity with respect to moral conduct results from what Kant holds to be a more general opacity of self-knowledge on the part of embodied and finite rational beings. This more general opacity is not of immediate concern to the analysis offered here.

Chapter Four

1. One instance: Even though Ernst Cassirer's treatment of the issues raised in *Religion* is quite sensitive to the bearing they have on basic concepts of Kant's critical philosophy, he nonetheless passes the following judgment, in *Kant's Life and Thought* (New Haven: Yale University Press, 1981), 381, on the work as a whole: ". . . Kant's book on religion cannot be measured by the same standards as his fundamental, critical work. It is not on a par with the writings on the foundation of his system, with the *Critique of Pure Reason* or of *Practical Reason* or the *Foundations of the Metaphysics of Morals* or the *Critique of Judgment*." For a more positive assessment, see Allen W. Wood, "Rational Theology, Moral Faith, and Religion," in *The Cambridge Companion to Kant*, ed. Paul Guyer (Cambridge: Cambridge University Press, 1992), 394–416.

2. This criticism is not necessarily hostile to religion, even though it has been (and continues to be) put to polemical use against religion.

In assessing the force of this criticism, however, it is important to keep in mind the extent to which the understanding of an adequate "moral life" undergoes transformation during the course of the Enlightenment and post-Enlightenment discussion. For a very helpful analysis of these various transformations, see Charles Taylor, *Sources of the Self: The Making of the Modern Identity* (Cambridge: Cambridge University Press, 1989).

3. This perspective does not have to be conceived as peculiarly "modern." Within Western philosophical thinking, it can properly claim to have roots in the kind of questions raised (and, significantly, not answered) in Plato's *Euthyphro.*

4. Gordon E. Michalson, in *Kant and the Problem of God* has argued for an even stronger thesis: Kant takes a conceptual direction that best fits with the stream of Enlightenment and post-Enlightenment thought that leads quite directly to an explicitly atheistic denial of God.

5. Gordon E. Michalson's earlier work, *Fallen Freedom: Kant on Radical Evil and Moral Regeneration* (Cambridge: Cambridge University Press, 1990) located "wobbles" in *Religion,* which indicate elements of Kant's thought that stand in tension with the more "typically" Enlightenment views he held.

6. These presuppositions, however, may be more characteristic of certain modern, post-Enlightenment reductive programs, than they are of the varied forms of Enlightenment thought on the relationships among religion, morality, and the attainment of human destiny.

7. See especially chapters 4 and 5 of *Fallen Freedom,* 73–106.

8. Consider, in contrast to the struggle that Kant sees entailed in our dealing with radical evil, the confidence he expresses, in the *Critique of Practical Reason,* that "not even the most common human understanding can fail to see at once, in an example presented to him . . . that he can never be expected to obey anything but the pure practical law of reason alone" (*CprR,* 5: 92/214). See, however, Jacqueline Mariña, "Kant on Grace: A Reply to his Critics," *Religious Studies* 33 (1997), 379–400, for an analysis that, correctly in my judgment, sees the question of grace in *Religion* arising at a level prior to that of moral conversion; as a result, Kant's position comes much closer to Augustine's than it does to Pelagius'. See also Elizabeth Cameron Galbraith, *Kant and Theology: Was Kant a Closet Theologian?* (San Francisco: International Scholars' Publications, 1996), who argues that Kant's view on a number of theological matters is close to that of Erasmus.

9. This is by no means an innovation: deeply embedded in the Hebrew roots of Christianity is a concern for the salvation of the people.

10. Mariña's article cited above (endnote 8) argues that the issue of conversion is not the primary locus for Kant's treatment of grace. Helpful earlier discussions of a possible role for grace include James Collins, *The Emergence of Philosophy of Religion* (New Haven: Yale University Press, 1967), 178–181; Michel Despland, *Kant on History and Religion* (Montreal: McGill-Queen's University Press, 1973), 228–236; Gordon E. Michalson Jr., *Fallen Freedom*; Leslie A. Mulholland, "Freedom and Providence in Kant's Account of Religion: The Problem of Expiation," in Rossi and Wreen, *Kant's Philosophy of Religion Reconsidered*, 77–102. For a clear exposition of a Pelagian reading of Kant see Nicholas Wolterstorff, "Conundrums in Kant's Rational Religion," in Rossi and Wreen, 40–53.

11. Although no argument is proposed here for taking this to be a particularly apt way of articulating Kant's understanding of the supreme principle of morality, there are at least three features of Kant's discussion in the *Groundwork of the Metaphysics of Morals* from which support for this interpretation can be derived: 1. It comports with the formal primacy that Kant gives to the "universal law" formulation; 2. It is consistent with Kant's insistence that one has a grasp of the supreme principle of morality even as one adopts a maxim that is contrary to it; and 3. It offers a general description that seems appropriately to capture Kant's claim that his formal articulation of this principle merely makes explicit what is already present in ordinary moral experience—specifically, that concern with the "dear self" is what leads us morally astray.

12. In connection with this, it is significant that the very first "preliminary article" that Kant articulates precisely concerns the parties to a peace treaty making tacit reservations in their own favor: "No treaty of peace shall be held to be such if it is made with a secret reservation of material for a future war" (*EF*, 8: 343/317).

13. As Guyer and Wood note in the introduction to their translation of the *Critique of Pure Reason* in the Cambridge Edition of the Works of Immanuel Kant (18), the neglect may arise "perhaps because the 'Doctrine of the Elements' is so long and the arguments already surveyed are so exhausting."

14. Hannah Arendt has argued: "In the center of Kant's moral philosophy stands the individual; in the center of his philosophy of history (or rather, his philosophy of nature) stands the perpetual progress of the human race, or mankind. (Therefore: History from a general viewpoint.) The general viewpoint or standpoint is occupied, rather, by the spectator, who is a 'world citizen' or, rather, a 'world spectator.' It is he who decides, by having an idea of the whole, whether, in any single, particular event, progress is being made" (*Lectures on Kant's Political Philosophy*, ed. Ronald Beiner, Chicago: University of Chicago Press, 1982, 58).

15. A more complete examination of these and other parallels between the ethical commonwealth and the international federation of nations to secure perpetual peace would, I believe, be of use in dealing with the much larger question of the role that anthropological considerations take within Kant's account of the critical use of human reason. For a discussion of this larger issue see Holly L. Wilson, "Kant's Integration of Morality and Anthropology," *Kant-Studien* 88 (1997), 87–104; Allen W. Wood, "Unsociable Sociability: The Anthropological Basis of Kantian Ethics," *Philosophical Topics* 19 (1991), 325–351. Sharon Anderson-Gold, *Unnecessary Evil: History and Moral Progress in the Philosophy of Immanuel Kant*, Chapters 4–5, 53–84, frames this issue in terms of role of culture and history in the development of the critical use of reason.

Chapter Five

1. *Kant's Political Philosophy*, 261. See also 278: "Finally, the success of Kant's whole political philosophy rests on the hope and moral presupposition that the human race will improve ethically. The long term hope for peace rests on the commitment of mankind to the objective spelled out by Kant in the categorical imperative, namely, never to treat each other simply as means but always as ends."

2. Such discussions can be found in Lucien Goldmann, *Immanuel Kant*, trans. Robert Black (London: NLB, 1971); Pierre Laberge, "Das Radikale Böse und der Völkerzustand," *Kant über Religion*, ed. Friedo Ricken and François Marty (Stuttgart: W. Kohlhammer, 1992), 112–123; Howard Williams, *Kant's Political Philosophy*, 260–268.

3. See also The *Conflict of the Faculties* where Kant refers to war as "the source of all evil and corruption of morals" (*der Quelle aller Übel und Verderbnis der Sitten* [7: 86/155]), "the destroyer of everything good" (*den Zerstörer alles Guten* [7: 91/165]) and "the greatest hindrance to morality" (*das größte Hindernis des Moralischen* [7: 93/169]). In that same essay, to the question at the head of Section 9, "What Profit Will Progress Toward the Better Yield Humanity?" he answers: "Not an ever-growing quantity of morality with regard to intention, but an increase of the products of legality in dutiful actions whatever their motives" [7: 91/165]).

4. This is Despland's view: ". . . after 1793 the only wing of his disjunction between political and moral progress was the pessimistic one: Kant was looking for the kind of political progress of which even devils are capable. . . . Kant never returned after 1793 to the notion of the philosophy of

the history of religion, that is, a philosophy of history that encompasses religious and moral progress" (*Kant on History and Religion*, 278).

5. See Joseph M. Knippenberg, "The Politics of Kant's Philosophy," in *Kant and Political Philosophy*, ed. Ronald Beiner and William James Booth (New Haven: Yale University Press, 1993), 180–186.

6. This affirmation is controversial, not the least because it bears upon one of the most vexing issues within the critical project that Kant seems not to address in full: What constitutes the *unity* of the finite human reason that has these two uses, the theoretical and the practical? At times, Kant seems to take this unity as given, at other times, he offers what seem to be at least partial arguments for it; Susan Neiman remarks, "Precisely concerning the nature of reason, Kant's writings reveal inconsistencies and unclarities that can only suggest that he himself has not yet acknowledged the magnitude of the task he had undertaken" (*The Unity of Reason: Rereading Kant*, 3). A plausible argument can be made that part of the reason Kant writes the *Critique of the Power of Judgment*—a work that he seems not to have envisioned, even as late as the writing of the *Critique of Practical Reason*, as an element of critique—is a recognition that the question of the unity of reason needs to be addressed in a more explicit fashion than he previously had done: ". . . in the *The Third Critique* Kant made his most strenuous effort to achieve the unity of reason" (John H. Zammito, *The Genesis of Kant's Critique of Judgment*, 345). The question of the unity of reason also bears upon other long-discussed issues about the meaning, coherence, and adequacy of key concepts around which Kant structures the critical project, such as the distinction—and the relation—between the sensible and intelligible. Susan Neiman's study mentioned above examines some of the key issues.

7. Kant seems well aware that there are difficulties involved in his account. He articulates the difficulties, but does not solve them, with the quite apt saying that "a revolution is necessary in the mode of thought [*Denkungsart*] but a gradual reformation in the mode of sense [*Sinnesart*]" (*Rel*, 6: 48/92]. A key difficulty has precisely to do with the relationship between apparent timelessness of revolution and the necessarily temporal character of the reformation. These difficulties do have systematic significance for a number of key elements in the critical project, but they are not directly relevant to the present discussion. An important canvassing of these issues is found in Michalson, *Fallen Freedom*. See also Gene Fendt, "Innate Corruption and the Space of Finite Freedom," *American Catholic Philosophical Quarterly* 68 (1994), 179–201; Philip Rossi, "Moral Struggle and Moral Conversion in Kant's Religion," *Akten des Siebten Internationalen Kant-Kongresses*, ed. G. Funke (Bonn: Bouvier, 1991), 283–293.

8. Some essays that note the role Kant gives to the church in relation to moral progress are: Hans Michael Baumgartner, "Das 'ethische gemeine Wesen' und die Kirche in Kants 'Religionsschrift,' " in *Kant über Religion*, F. Ricken and F. Marty, ed. (Stuttgart: Verlag W. Kohlhammer, 1992), 156–177; Philip Rossi, "The Social Authority of Reason: The 'True Church' as the Locus for Moral Progress," *Proceedings of the Eighth International Kant Congress*, II/2, ed. Hoke Robinson (Milwaukee: Marquette University Press, 1995), 679–685; Nancy Sherman, "The Virtues of Common Pursuit," *Philosophy and Phenomenological Research* 53 (1993), 277–299; Allen W. Wood, "Rational Theology, Moral Faith, and Religion" in *The Cambridge Companion to Kant*, Paul Guyer, ed. (Cambridge: Cambridge University Press, 1992), 394–417; and "Unsociable Sociability: The Anthropological Basis of Kantian Ethics," *Philosophical Topics* 19 (1991), 325–351.

9. That the set of maxims Kant formulates as ones suitable to serve as "practical law"—that is, as the forms of the "categorical imperative"—can *also* be articulated as constitutive of *the end that reason requires* of moral agents is a point that often is overlooked. This is especially true of those accounts of Kant's moral philosophy that pit the "formality" of its "deontology" over against approaches to moral philosophy in which "teleology" allows "material" specification of moral principles; cf. Barbara Herman, "Leaving Deontology Behind," *The Practice of Moral Judgment* (Cambridge, Mass: Harvard University Press, 1993), 208–240. This connection between the form of maxims suited to serve as practical law and the end that reason requires of moral agents is also at the root of two aspects of Kant's discussion in the *Groundwork* that are often seen as problematic: First, the claim that the various formulations of the categorical imperative are equivalent; second, the content of the concept of a rational agent as an "end-in-itself."

10. "Reason and Politics in the Kantian Enterprise," *Constructions of Reason: Explorations of Kant's Practical Philosophy*, 16.

11. Though Kant's discussions of a "cosmopolitan perspective" comprise a heterogeneous set of texts and touch on a variety of topics, a feature common to one important set of them is a referencing to an historical trajectory, which has as its goal the attainment of human destiny: for example, in "An Idea for Universal History" (1784), the "cosmopolitan state" is "the perfect civic union of the human species," which is "nature's supreme objective" (8: 28–29/38); the discussion of cosmopolitanism in the *Critique of the Power of Judgment* (1790) occurs in §83, "On the Ultimate Purpose that Nature Has as a Teleological System" (5: 429–434/297–301); similarly, the discussion in "Theory and Practice" (1793) is embedded in a discussion in which Kant affirms the practical necessity of presuming the continuing moral progress of humanity (8: 310–311/307–308). In *Anthropology from a Prag-*

matic Point of View (1798) the establishment of a cosmopolitan society is envisioned in terms of "a regulative principle, [directing us] to pursue this diligently as the destiny of the human race" (7: 331/191). There are passages in which Kant does not explicitly associate what is cosmopolitan with an historical trajectory toward human destiny; these discussions, however, seem concerned only with that aspect of a cosmopolitan perspective that can be articulated as enforceable articles of international law: rights of hospitality and commerce (cf. *MdS*, 6: 352–353/489–490; *EF*, 8: 357–360/328–331).

12. In connection with this, it is important to note that Kant takes the attainment of "perpetual peace" to be the highest *political* good (*MdS*, 6: 355/ 492), but it does not of itself constitute the full attainment of human destiny he designates, without qualification, as the highest good.

13. *Lectures on Logic*, trans. and ed., J. Michael Young (Cambridge: Cambridge University Press, 1992), 538.

14. See Kant's letter to C. F. Stäudlin of May, 4, 1793, in *Kant: Philosophical Correspondence 1779–1799*, trans. and ed. Arnulf Zweig (Chicago: University of Chicago Press, 1967), 205.

Chapter Six

1. For an overall picture of political and social institutions in Kant's Prussia, see C. B. A. Behrens, *Society, Government and the Enlightenment: The Experiences of Eighteenth-century France and Prussia*, (London: Thames and Hudson, 1985).

2. For Kant's positive view of the French Revolution, see Manfred Kuehn, *Kant: A Biography* (Cambridge: Cambridge University Press, 2001), 340–343. An earlier treatment of Kant's view, G. P. Gooch, *Germany and the French Revolution* (New York: Russell and Russell, 1966 [c. 1920]), 276–277, gives details of a rumor that circulated in 1796 that Kant had been invited, through Abbé Sieyès, to come to Paris as an adviser on constitutional law.

3. For brief overviews of Kant's continuing influence in liberal political thinking, see William A. Galston, "What Is Living and What Is Dead in Kant's Practical Philosophy," *Kant and Political Philosophy*, ed. Ronald Beiner and William James Booth (New Haven and London: Yale University Press, 1993), 207–223; Patrick Riley, "The Elements of Kant's Practical Philosophy," *Kant and Political Philosophy*, 9–37. For interpretations of the role that Kant's account of autonomy has played see Paul Fairfield, *Moral Selfhood in the Liberal Tradition: The Politics of Individuality* (Toronto: University of

Toronto Press, 2000); Lewis Hinchman, "Autonomy, Individuality and Self-Determination," *What Is Enlightenment: Eighteenth Century Answers and Twentieth Century Questions* (Berkeley: University of California Press, 1996), 488–516.

4. This question is meant to suggest a parallel to the ones Kant poses in the *Critique of Practical Reason* in his effort to articulate the fundamental law of practical reason. In both cases, the fundamental law will be one that *reason* requires, and thus has the *necessity* appropriate to a principle of reason, yet it is also a principle that requires *uncoerced* acknowledgment by moral agents—and is thus a principle of freedom. It is a principle that is, without the expression being oxymoronic, a *law* of *freedom*. Put in Kant's terms, this expression "law of freedom" is an articulation of the principle that "freedom and unconditional practical law reciprocally imply each other" (*CprR*, 5: 29/162).

5. George Steiner, *Real Presences* (Chicago: University of Chicago Press, 1989); Charles Taylor, *Sources of the Self: The Making of the Modern Identity* (Cambridge, Mass: Harvard University Press, 1989).

6. In 1964, long before the terminology of the postmodern has gained widespread currency, John Courtney Murray, S. J., in *The Problem of God: Yesterday and Today* (New Haven: Yale University Press, 1964), devoted the final section of a chapter to "The Godless Man of the Post-Modern Age" (101–121). He noted two types, one of whom is "of the [Marxist] Revolution," the other is "of the Theater." His discussion of the latter is remarkably prescient of crucial elements that have emerged in intellectual culture during the forty years since the publication of that work.

7. Hobbes is at least as clear-sighted as Nietzsche in recognizing that this dynamic is that of ceaseless war. Machiavelli is astute enough to see that the coercion necessary to enforce effectively an external form of social union can be exercised by quite subtle as well as overt means. Hume, however, may be the most instructive for our circumstances in that he represents this dynamic as one that we can best learn to live with by cultivating a range of civilized practices that distract our attention way from it.

8. See, for instance, "Falsifying Records, Endangering Patients," *The New York Times*, May 17, 1999; Laura Landro, "Informed Patient: Knowing When to Say 'No' to Tests," *Wall Street Journal*, February 13, 2003; Julie Appleby, "Medco probe leads to lawsuit: Accused of risking safety of patients," *USA Today*, September 30, 2003.

9. See Derek Bok, *Universities in the Marketplace: The Commericalization of Higher Education* (Princeton: Princeton University Press, 2003).

10. For trade in human body parts for transplant purposes, see Brian Kates, "Black Market in Transplant Organs," *New York Daily News*/Knight Ridder Tribune News Service, August 28, 2003. For one instance of speculative growth on the basis of genetic and human cell research see Paul Jacobs, "Geron's Stock Spikes on Cell Growth News," *The Los Angeles Times*, November 7, 1998.

11. For a more detailed discussion of this dynamic of "the leveling of meaning see Philip Rossi, "The Leveling of Meaning: Religious Ethics in the Face of a Culture of Unconcern," *Ethics in the World Religions,* ed. Nancy Martin and Joseph Runzo (Oxford: Oneworld Press, 2000), 161–174.

Chapter Seven

1 An influential analysis and criticism of the understanding of human agency presupposed in this view of the scope of interest can be found in Michael Sandel, *Liberalism and the Limits of Justice* (Cambridge: Cambridge University Press, 1982). Onora O'Neill, "Kant's Conception of Public Reason," *Kant und die Berliner Aufklärung: Akten des IX. Internationalen Kant-Kongresses,* Band 1, eds. Volker Gerhardt, Rolf-Peter Horstmann, and Ralph Schumacher (Berlin: Walter de Gruyter, 2001), 35–47, suggests some important ways in which Kant's own notion of autonomy needs to be differentiated from the uses to which this notion has been put in subsequent liberal political discourse; she notes that "Kant never equates autonomy with independence; unlike most recent 'Kantian' writers he views *autonomy* or *self-legislation* not as emphasizing some (quite amazing) self that 'legislates' but rather 'legislation' that is not derived from other sources, that is not derivative" (44).

2. Or, in a different but quite relevant terminology, a "common good."

3. "Kant's Conception of Public Reason," 45–46.

4. Flikschuh, *Kant and Modern Political Philosophy,* 179, makes a provocative observation about how "Kant's image of the earth's spherical surface [functions] as that unavoidable constraint of nature within the limits of which finite rational beings must resolve conflicts of external freedom and justice." (This image is found in *MdS*, 6: 311/455). See also Sankar Muthu, "Justice and Foreigners: Kant's Cosmopolitan Right," *Constellations* 7: 1 (2000), 34: "the very idea of a 'globe' entails that individuals and societies *cannot* avoid interacting with one another."

5. For a more extensive discussion of the problems involved in making these distinctions parallel, see Philip Rossi, "Critical Persuasion: Argument

and Coercion in Kant's Account of Politics," in *Recht, Staat und Völkerrecht bei Immanuel Kant,* ed. Dieter Hüning and Burkhard Tuschling (Berlin: Duncker and Humblot, 1998), 13–33.

6. For a discussion that suggests that there is a wide range of social practice that can be appropriately informed by attention to the mutual moral recognition articulated in Kant's universal principle of right, see Sarah Holtman, "Civility and Hospitality: Justice and Social Grace in Trying Times," *Kantian Review* 6 (2002), 85–108.

7. Pauline Kleingeld, "Nature or Providence? On the Theoretical and Moral Importance of Kant's Philosophy of History," *American Catholic Philosophical Quarterly* 70 (2001), 201–219 offers a useful analysis of the different emphases in Kant's use of each term.

8. This is consistent with his view that political reform is properly and effectively instituted "from above" (*SF,* 7: 92/167) and accords with the stringent limits he placed upon "active citizenship," which restricted effective political voice and power to male-property holders (*TP,* 8: 294–297/294–296; *MdS,* 6: 314–315/458–459). See, however, Patrick Riley, *Kant's Political Philosophy* (Towtowa, NJ: Rowman and Littlefield, 1993), 111–113 for an interpretation that eventually allows a notion of citizenship comprehending all adults. Kant does nonetheless remark, with some irony, that rulers still need sage counsel from philosophers to recognize clearly the moral demand for perpetual peace and its bearing upon the decisions these rulers then make (*EF,* 8: 368–369/337–338).

9. An instructive—though still evolving instance—seems to be the peace process in Northern Ireland. Though it has had only a lurching and slow movement forward, it does seem to have a dynamic in which a slowly emerging "on the ground" consensus against violence among the populace has probably been more effective than the public posturing of politicians in staying the hand of militant factions as well as in making possible forms of previously "unthinkable" forms of cooperation and even reconciliation.

10. One could quite legitimately argue that a certain form of moral irresponsibility was shown in media coverage of the Kosovo conflict—before, during, and after—that reenforced the idea that "It is [will be] impossible for Serbs and Albanians ever to live together."

11. Adam Clymer, "Voter Bill Passes in G. O. P. Defeat," *The New York Times,* 11 May 1993. Another report unsurprisingly suggests that this dynamic is not peculiar to politics in the United States: " 'It all comes down to this,' an editorial in the *Jerusalem Post* said Wednesday [with reference to

forming a coalition government after the 1999 election]. 'When there are spoils to be divided, the good of the country as a whole comes second.' " ("Barak Creates Wide Coalition With 7 Parties," Deborah Sontag. *The New York Times,* July 1, 1999).

Index

agency. *See* moral agency
Anderson-Gold, Sharon, 178n6, 181n15
*Anthropology from a Pragmatic Point
of View*: and cosmopolitan perspective, 184n11
Appleby, Julie, 186n8
Arendt, Hannah, 181n14
argument: and critique, 141, 143–144;
and ethical commonwealth, 169; and
freedom, 14, 15–16, 166–167, 169;
and hope, 169; and interest of
reason, 141, 151, 167–169; and
interests, 166–168; and public use of
reason, 118, 167–170; and self-
governance of reason, 76; and social
authority of reason, 10–11, 76, 111,
166, 168; and social respect, 166–
167, 169; and unsociable sociability,
169. *See also* public use of reason
atheism: Kant's influence on, 180n4
Augustine, St., 76, 180n8
autonomy: as choice, 31–32; and
critique, 47, 114, 176n5; as freedom,
22, 29–32, 33, 41, 43, 47, 114, 140,
148, 151, 167, 169; and highest
good, 100, 140; and hope, 60; as
intelligible causality, 37; and interest
of reason, 151; introduction of, 22;
individualistic interpretation, 31, 43–
44, 47, 48, 176n6, 178n2; and
kingdom of ends, 31–32, 44, 45,

140, 167; and law, 31, 140; and
liberalism, 114, 140, 146, 185n3,
187n1; and moral agency, 30–32,
43–44, 47, 140, 153, 167; as
practical (moral) reason, 29–30, 32,
37, 41–42, 50, 146, 151, 153; and
public use of reason, 167, 169; as
relational, 43–46, 128; and respect,
37–38; as self-governance of
freedom, 29–30, 31–32, 43; as self-
governance of reason, 29–30, 32, 42–
43, 45, 47, 57, 60; and sensible/
intelligible distinction, 32–33, 57; as
social, 45, 47, 48, 50, 140, 148, 151,
169; and social authority of reason,
146, 148, 151–153; and social
relationships, 31, 43–44, 148; and
social respect, 153–154, 169; and
spontaneity, 29–30, 32, 41; and unity
of reason, 45. *See also* freedom,
heteronomy, moral agency, nature
and freedom, self-governance of
reason
Axinn, Sidney, 173n2

Baumgartner, Michael, 184n8
Beck, Lewis White, 176n2, 177n7
Behrens, C. B. A., 185n1
Beiner, Ronald, 181n14, 183n5, 185n3
Beiser, Frederick, C., 173n1
Bernstein, Richard, 174n3

Bok, Derek, 186n9
Booth, William James, 183n5, 185n3
Buckley, Michael, 174n3

Cassirer, Ernst, 174n5, 179n1
church. *See* ethical commonwealth
Collins, James, 181n10
commodification: and critical project,
171; and education, 131; and
globalization, 129–131; and human
connectedness, 130; and medical
practice, 130–132; and public use of
reason, 170; and social authority of
reason, 129–130, 138, 168
Conflict of the Faculties, 51, 84, 175n8;
and perpetual peace, 92; and war,
182n3
cosmopolitan perspective: and critical
project, 149; and ethical commonwealth, 108–109, 111, 118; and
globalization, 120–123, 130; and
highest good, 108; and history, 108–
111, 184n11; and hope, 107–108,
116, 118; and human connectedness,
130; and human destiny, 8, 108–111,
184n11; and human differences, 130;
and interest of reason, 149, 172; and
international law, 184n11; and moral
progress, 184n11; and nature and
freedom, 108–111; and perpetual
peace, 116, 118; and practical use of
reason, 110–111; and social authority
of reason, 91, 99, 105, 107–111,
116–119; and social union, 9, 99,
105, 107, 111; and unsociable
sociability, 138
Clymer, Adam, 188n11
critical project: and commodification,
171; contemporary significance of, 1;
and cosmopolitanism, 149; development of, 21–22, 25, 44–47, 54–56,
114–116, 143; and the Enlightenment, 70; and ethical commonwealth,
57, 77, 149; and freedom, 3, 25–26,
36, 41, 89–90, 114, 172; and highest
good, 48–50; and history, 181n14;
and immediacy, 171; and interests,

172; and moral agency, 44, 108–109,
114–115; moral trajectory of, 6–7,
19–20; nature and freedom as
central, 6, 20–23, 27–28, 33, 41, 49–
50, 75, 109, 114–115; origin in inner
conflict of reason, 80; and radical
evil, 2–5; reassessment of, 1; role in
human destiny, 19–20, 89; and
perpetual peace, 90, 149; and public
use of reason, 149; and sensible/
intelligible distinction, 6–7, 32–39,
41; social dimensions of, 3–5, 65,
67, 85, 88, 108, 149; unfinished
tasks of, 9–10, 89–90, 171; and unity
of reason, 108–109; and unsociable
sociability, 78–80, 172. *See also*
critique, reason
critique: and anthropology, 182n15; and
argument, 141, 143–144; and
autonomy, 47, 114, 176n5; and
culture, 42, 182n15; ethical commonwealth as social embodiment of, 3–4,
106; and freedom, 3, 41, 47, 106,
114, 142, 149–150, 158; and history,
84–85, 182n15; and hope, 5; and
human connectedness, 136–137; and
human destiny, 6–7, 19–20, 22, 89,
141–142, 148; and human differences, 136–137; and interest of
reason, 150, 158; and kingdom of
ends, 158; and moral agency, 4–5,
32, 140–141, 178n4; and public use
of reason, 106, 178n4; and radical
evil, 2, 19, 85; and recognition of
the other, 142–143; as reflective
procedure, 21; as self-discipline of
reason, 4–6, 19, 22, 28–30, 41, 52,
133, 142–143, 153; as self-governance of reason, 22, 30, 45–47; and
social union, 140–142; and society,
42, 178n4; society as image of, 46;
transformative function of, 6–7, 83;
and unsociable sociability, 141–142.
See also critical project, reason
Critique of Practical Reason: antinomy
of reason, 94, 96; and *Critique of
Pure Reason*, 24; fundamental law of